BlackBerry
vodafone
09:27
WED, SEP 29
vodafone
GPRS
Messages
live!
vodafone

THE WORLD IN 2005

EDITOR:
Daniel Franklin
MANAGING EDITOR:
Harriet Ziegler
DEPUTY EDITOR:
Steve King
EDITORIAL ASSISTANT:
Hannah Marshall
COUNTRIES EDITOR:
Leo Abruzzese
INDUSTRIES EDITOR:
Carla Rapoport
DESIGN:
Bailey and Kenny
DESIGN ASSISTANT:
Anita Wright
CHARTS:
Phil Kenny, Michael Robinson, Peter Winfield
ILLUSTRATIONS:
Steve Carroll, Derek Cousins, Polly Moore, James Sillavan
PICTURE RESEARCH:
Juliet Brightmore
RESEARCH:
Alex Fak, Roxanne Khamsi, Paul Pedley
EDITORIAL ASSISTANCE:
Ingrid Esling, Sheila Allen
ADVERTISING DIRECTOR:
John Dunn
CIRCULATION DIRECTOR:
Alastair Cotton
PRODUCTION:
Andrew Rollings, Sophie Hawe, Lydia Dye-Stonebridge
FOREIGN RIGHTS:
Hutton-Williams Agency
ASSOCIATE PUBLISHER:
David Gill
PUBLISHER:
David Hanger
ENTERPRISES DIRECTOR:
Martin Giles

Published by The Economist Newspaper Limited.

ISBN 0 86218 197 6

The Economist

25 St James's Street, London SW1A 1HG
Telephone: 020 7830 7084
E-mail: worldineditor@economist.com
Internet: www.theworldin.com

Leaders

Britain

Europe

United States

The Americas

Asia

They're back

After a hard-fought campaign, George Bush is back in the White House for another four years: what to expect of Bush 2, *pages 13* and *55*. Out west, **Arnold Schwarzenegger** predicts a California Comeback, *page 62*. Will foreign students keep coming to America? asks **Robert Gates**, *page 60*.

In Britain, Tony Blair will win a third term, *page 27*. But is Britain's economic Golden Age, which has its roots in the reforms of the Thatcher era, coming to an end? *page 28*. It will still be Europe's best country for entrepreneurs, expects **Stelios Haji-Ioannou**, *page 38*.

War and peace

Despite relentlessly gloomy headlines, peace is breaking out around the world, especially in Africa, *page 86*. The challenge will be keeping the peace, *page 91*. International collaboration will help, predicts Europe's **Javier Solana**, *page 93*; so must strong states, argues Canada's **Paul Martin**, *page 70*. A critical year ahead for both Iraq, *page 84*, and Israel-Palestine, *page 83*.

As the al-Qaeda franchise spreads, its weakness will become clear, *page 89*. But a strong transatlantic relationship will be needed to defend freedom, insists **José María Aznar**, *page 54*.

Asia rising

Adjusting to the rise of China and India will be one of the world's great challenges. Countries that prepare nimbly for the strategic shifts will make the most of the opportunities, forecasts Singapore's **Lee Hsien Loong**, *page 82*. The Chindia story, *page 77*. Japan, land of the rising sum, *page 73*.

After much election-year controversy over jobs migration in America, the world will learn to love outsourcing, *page 20*; and to love the Global Dream, says the Shell/Economist prizewinning essay, *page 64*. **Narayana Murthy**, of India's Infosys Technologies, describes the emerging global-talent-tapping corporation, *page 114*. China learns the trade rules, *page 117*.

JOHNNIE WALKER
Blue Label

Middle East and Africa

International

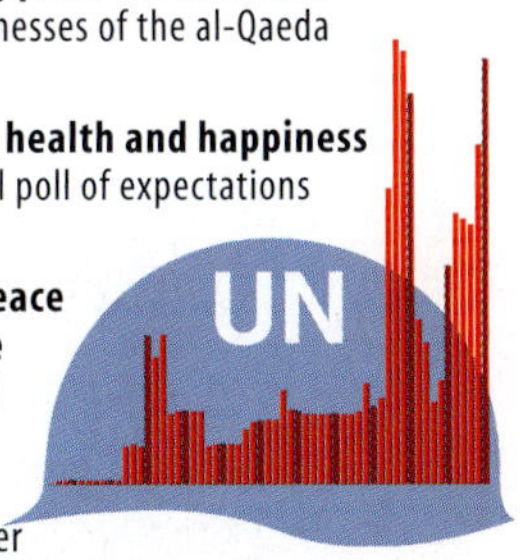

The world in figures

Business

Finance

Science and technology

Crisis, anyone?

OPEC will keep only a precarious grip on oil prices as it faces threats from free-riding Russia and unpredictable Iraq, *page 134*. The IMF's **Rodrigo Rato** explains how crises can be avoided, *page 140*. A fairly benign cocktail for world markets, *page 131*—though not for house prices, *page 133*.

To tackle the HIV/AIDS pandemic, the World Health Organisation has set the target of providing treatment for 3m AIDS sufferers in poor countries by the end of 2005, *page 144*. The rich world must act now if it is to live up to its promises to halve global poverty by 2015, urges **Jeffrey Sachs**, *page 96*.

Digitally does it

You ain't seen nothing yet in the digital revolution, predicts Hewlett-Packard's **Carly Fiorina**, *page 128*. Hollywood goes digital, *page 58*. So do cameras, but will camera-phones beat all the rest? *page 118*.

It will be a new world for brands, expects Burberry's **Rose Marie Bravo**, as they compete ever more creatively to attract the customer's attention, *page 121*. Private firms will become more attractive, *page 113*; as will cars, *page 122*. If companies are sensible, they will make the workplace more appealing too: prepare for corporate democracy, says **Charles Handy**, *page 124*.

Relative values

Hats off (and T-shirts on) for Albert Einstein: 100 years on, the relative is still everywhere, *page 22*. Scientists will continue to cross new frontiers: they may create life, *page 145*; and more robots will replace humans, *page 141*. Architects can help save the planet, according to **Norman Foster**, *page 146*.

The year ahead will be a relatively good one, in the view of our annual opinion survey, *page 90*. For culture, it will be a relatively rich and varied one, *page 95*. And for the lucky Irish, it will be absolutely splendid: Ireland comes top of our 2005 quality-of-life league, ahead of 110 other countries, *page 94*.

PHOTOGRAPHIC SOURCES:
Action Images: Brandon Malone Livepic. Alamy Images: Ace Stock Ltd, Fotosonline, I Dream Stock, Rob James, Jeremy Nicholl, Ian Shaw, Joseph Sohm. AP/Wide World Photos: Claude Paris. Bettmann/Corbis. Corbis: France Keyser/In Visu, Liba Taylor, Frank Trapper, David Turnley. Digital Vision. Getty Images: Thomas J Abercrombie/National Geographic, Arif Ali/AFP, Adek Berry/AFP, Grant Faint, Luke Frazza/AFP, Mike Fuentes, Chris Hondros, Hulton Archive, Sajjad Hussain/AFP, Chris Livingstone, Norbert Millauer/AFP, Kazuhiro Nogi/AFP, Joseph Van Os, Mustafa Ozer/AFP, Uriel Sinai, Prakash Singh/AFP, Howard Sochurek/Time Life Pictures, Mark Wilson. Niall McDiarmid. The Picture Desk: The Kobal Collection/MGM. Reuters: Karen Ballard, Will Burgess, China Photos, Jeff Christensen, Dan Chung, Claro Cortes IV, Nir Elias, John Gress, Faleh Kheiber, Daniel Leclair, Paul McErlane, Win McNamee, Toby Melville, Jeff Mitchell, Guang Niu, Raj Patidar, Sergio Perez, Oleg Popov, Jim Ruymen, Fatih Saribas, Mike Segar, Brian Snyder, Susana Vera, Alexandra Winkler.

Printed by Cooper Clegg Limited, Tewkwsbury, England

Reprographics by Mullis Morgan Group Ltd

Printed on UPM-Kymmene Star 80gsm

THE WORLD IN 2005

> Despite relentless headlines about bombs and bloodshed, there will be fewer deaths through conflict around the world than at almost any time since the 1920s as wars wind down, especially in Africa

The world in 2005 will in many ways be a tale of two countries. Post-election America and still-booming China will be the places to watch, whether for their impact on the global economy or their influence on global security. And the spectacle should be mildly reassuring.

True, the world economy will slow, after growing in 2004 at its fastest pace for more than 20 years, as interest rates rise in America and as China applies the brakes. There is a chance that the slowdown will be nasty, brutal and bumpy. More likely, it will be boringly benign—leaving worriers to focus on the world's other potential sources of instability. They will watch particularly closely China's uneasy relations with independent-minded Taiwan, which will nevertheless fail to come to a crisis. And they will watch America's efforts to change the political landscape in Iraq and the wider Middle East, where 2005 will be a momentous year. Depending on the success or otherwise of the planned elections in Iraq and Ariel Sharon's proposed withdrawal from occupied Gaza, the Middle East will end the year looking either much better or far worse.

After a record year for voters in 2004, there will be relatively few elections in 2005. But in Europe, the voters will be having their say. In Britain, they will give Tony Blair a third term, just as the country's economic "Golden Age" is in danger of drawing to an end. Elsewhere in the European Union, the people will start to pass judgment on their politicians' handiwork, with a series of referendums on a new EU constitution. If the Poles say *Nie* or, in particular, if the French say *Non*, Europe will plunge into crisis. All this will be a big distraction from the liberalising economic agenda and the ambitious targets of what is known in Euro-speak as the Lisbon strategy.

Targets will be much talked about in relation to the world's poor. Five years on from noble pledges made at the UN Millennium Assembly to cut extreme poverty by half by 2015, it will be time to take stock of how much remains to be done. Meanwhile, a lot will be done in the year ahead in an effort to meet another mind-concentrating target: to get 3m AIDS sufferers in the developing world on anti-retroviral drugs by the end of 2005. A surprising success, if not the reaching of the goal, is possible. So is a continuation of another surprising trend: despite relentless headlines about bombs and bloodshed, there will be fewer deaths through conflict around the world than at almost any time since the 1920s as wars wind down, especially in Africa.

In many places, of course, the peace is fragile. From Congo to Kashmir, conflict could all too easily erupt. Add that danger to a long list of other risks hanging over the world—higher oil prices, a property bust, a dollar crisis, a showdown with Iran or North Korea over nuclear weapons, not to mention the possibility of another terrorist mega-strike—and it would be easy to get gloomy about the year ahead.

Yet there are also many reasons to be cheerful, as the respondents to *The World in 2005*'s opinion survey broadly are: optimists on 2005 outnumber pessimists by nearly two to one. Also among the optimists, unsurprisingly, is Arnold Schwarzenegger, who in these pages confidently predicts the California Comeback. The worldwide internet population will be heading above 1 billion. In the Middle East, despite its troubles, the world's tallest building (Burj Dubai) will ostentatiously be going up. France will complete the world's highest bridge. Japan will at long last emerge from deflation. And Irish eyes will have a special reason to be smiling: Ireland comes top of the global quality-of-life index published here. With its mix of modernity and tradition, Ireland gets the combination right.

So, I hope, does this publication. It is, as ever, packed with predictions. The year ahead, say our contributors, will be a great one for outsourcing, for private firms and for robots; it will be less good for hedge funds, film-based cameras and al-Qaeda. Some of these predictions may actually prove to be right. Right or wrong, they should be thought-provoking. Relatively speaking—which is the way one should speak in 2005, it being the centenary of Einstein's famous theory—it promises to be a fascinating year.

Daniel Franklin
editor, *The World in 2005*

When it comes to the most effective approach to operating an oil field, traditional 3-D seismic imaging only paints part of the picture. That's why at ChevronTexaco we use a space-based technology called hyperspectral imaging to allow us to see what the human eye cannot. Combining this with

www.chevrontexaco.com/technologyintegration

A kinder, gentler Bush?

John Micklethwait forecasts that the second Bush term will prove a more conciliatory one—but only if Europe is prepared to deal with the "toxic Texan"

Second terms always pose a problem. With nothing left to run for, the president feels the power slip away from him the moment the applause dies down at his second inauguration. George Bush has an advantage, because he has been here before. In 2000 it was generally assumed that a man elected with such a weak mandate would be a lame-duck president. But Mr Bush drove his presidency in a determinedly conservative direction.

What does Mr Bush want to do? Turning back to the campaign for clues has two problems. First, Mr Bush did not propose that much—he focused on attacking John Kerry. And second, if his first term is any guide, he may not govern as he campaigned. In 2001 the "compassionate conservative" who promised to bring a new style of politics to Washington and to usher in a humble but strong foreign policy soon morphed into one of the most divisive presidents yet seen, both at home and abroad.

With those two caveats, Mr Bush's basic course would seem to come down to four words: more of the same. At home, he wants to make his tax cuts permanent, to push through some form of partial privatisation of the big entitlement programmes and to keep on driving the judiciary in a conservative direction (though probably not to the extent that would see abortion banned). Abroad, Mr Bush's priority remains the war on terrorism: seeing through Iraq and continuing his battle to spread democracy in the Middle East. He wants his time in office to be seen as a transformative presidency—one that ushered in a period of Republican hegemony at home and that reasserted American power abroad.

Given the radicalism of his first four years, it would be foolish to discount the president. But this time there appear to be even clearer limits between what he wants and what he can do; and it seems even clearer that he can only get what he wants with some co-operation from the Democrats and Europeans who so despise him.

At home, these limits should be a good thing. Mr Bush's room for manoeuvre is restricted by the rotten state of the government's finances. The budget deficit for the next decade is now estimated to be $2.3 trillion; and that figure more than doubles if you add in the cost of making his first-term tax cuts permanent (which Mr Bush has promised to do) and adjusting the alternative minimum tax (AMT, a complicated levy designed to tax just the rich, but which will now affect millions of middle-class Americans). And then there is the colossal challenge posed by the entitlement programmes for health and pensions: Medicare and Social Security will face severe fiscal problems as the huge baby-boom generation starts to retire at the end of this decade.

Mr Bush showed no fiscal discipline in his first term. Spending on his watch rose quicker than it had done under Bill Clinton, even if you exclude the costs of homeland security and the war on terrorism.

With luck, the fiscal bind Mr Bush will be confronted with in 2005 will both make him more frugal and push him towards ▶

John Micklethwait: United States editor of *The Economist* and co-author of "The Right Nation" (Penguin) structural change. For instance, fixing the AMT should give him a chance to reform America's extremely complicated tax code. During the campaign Mr Bush talked a little vaguely about creating an ownership society giving people more control over their pensions (through partially privatising Social Security) and setting up private health accounts. Here the aims of reform and political strategy go together: wean voters off the state and they are more likely to vote Republican. The problem for Mr Bush is that the "transition" costs of such reforms are enormous. So he may have to compromise—which will mean striking some form of deal with the Democrats.

Overseas, the limits on Mr Bush's range of movement will be more depressing. Having ousted Saddam Hussein easily, Mr Bush has discovered that rebuilding countries is much harder. America does not have enough troops on the ground in Iraq; nor, alas, does it have enough allies helping it there. Even if the election in January 2005 brings to power a credible government, to make Iraq into any kind of exemplar of a free, prosperous Arab society Mr Bush desperately needs more help from allies.

Does he deserve that support? Mr Bush's critics abroad rubbish his "neo-conservative" dream of bringing democracy to the Middle East. Europeans point out that the White House was naive about the chances of democratising Iraq, that it put too little thought into reconstruction, that it has shown contempt for multilateral organisations and that it has neglected the biggest source of Arab tension, the Israel-Palestine problem. All these criticisms ring true, but it is not in Europe's long-term interests to see America fail in Iraq.

The correct response should be a weary Gallic shrug of the shoulders, followed by a round of old-style horse-trading

Most European governments would have preferred John Kerry to have won; but it has not happened. The correct response should be a weary Gallic shrug of the shoulders, followed by a round of old-style horse-trading. For instance, if the Europeans really care so much about the Palestinians, why not make American pressure on Israel to stop building settlements on the West Bank the price of their participating in Iraq? Strangely enough, such an approach might go down quite well in Washington. Ever since Iraq turned sour Mr Bush has actually taken a much more conciliatory approach to his allies.

Europeans must now realise the Bush presidency is not an aberration. The "toxic Texan" represents many quintessentially American traits, from religiosity to patriotism. It may not be the America that Europe warms to, but it is one it has to deal with. In 2005 we will discover how pragmatic both sides can be. □

Next year's news
GDP growth
% change on year earlier

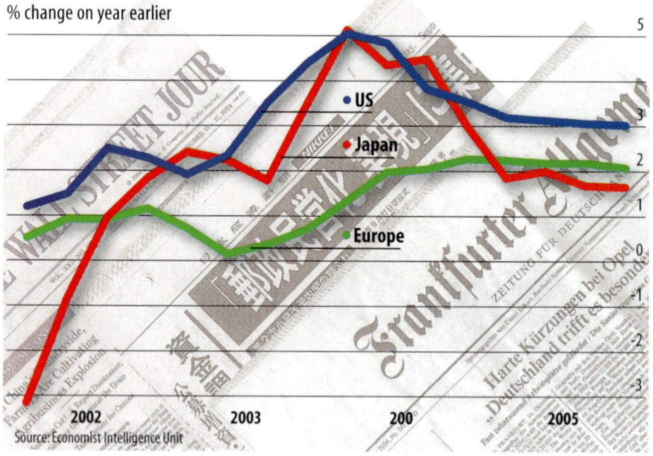

Living with the slowdown

The party's over, says **Robin Bew**

It may not feel like it to most people, but the world economy has been having a ball. Since the dark days of 2001, when much of the world was in the doldrums, the economic situation has steadily improved. By 2004 global GDP was growing at about 5%, its fastest pace for over 20 years. Businesses have started to relax and get into the swing of things, casting off thoughts of recession—cost-cutting is down (if not out), sales growth is back—and doing swashbuckling deals in places like Vietnam and Romania.

The fun won't last. In all probability, 2004 will prove to have been the high-water mark of the current global expansion. In 2005 global growth—though still over 4%, perfectly reasonable by historical standards—will be markedly lower. In the coming months, therefore, boardroom conversations will gradually change: from heady optimism to worries about the lack of momentum and nervousness about the gathering risks. Eventually, a grudging acceptance will set in of the need to adjust to the slowdown.

On the face of it, the recovery of the past few years has been remarkably broad-based. Yet scratch the surface and it becomes apparent that there have really been just three key factors influencing global growth: the strength of American demand, the Chinese economic boom and cheap money. All three are starting to change.

Robin Bew: chief economist, Economist Intelligence Unit

> Only in western Europe and the Middle East are growth prospects for 2005 on a par with those of 2004

First, America. Strong demand there has lifted growth across the world in recent years. This has owed much to the aggressive loosening of fiscal and monetary policies by, respectively, George Bush and Alan Greenspan. But no such help will be available in 2005. America's swelling budget deficit virtually rules out further tax cuts or another jump in spending. And the Fed is determined to bring interest rates back to a more normal level. So businesses and consumers will have to put more aside every month to service their debts—debts that, for households, are at record levels.

This will inevitably eat into spending in America. But on top of that, there is the impact of higher interest rates on the housing market. In recent years consumers have fuelled their spending spree by extracting equity from the bloated value of their property. At the very least, this will end as interest rates rise and house prices stall. And if house prices drop back—which seems likely in some cities—the economic fallout could be more serious, as consumers come to view their debts in a new, more worrying light. Cracks in the American economy that have been papered over for some time by the Bush/Greenspan expansion—high debts, overvalued property, an unwillingness to save—will become all too visible in 2005.

The unwinding of America's astonishingly lax monetary policy will have implications far beyond America itself. It will also affect international liquidity. When American rates are low, money tends to flood from the developed world in search of higher returns in emerging markets. But as American interest rates rise, this flow will be reversed—in 2005 emerging markets will lose out as investors are tempted by the rising yields on dollar assets.

In China, a slowdown from the rampant growth of recent years is also in prospect. The government has become increasingly concerned about an investment-led boom that, if not carefully managed, could turn to bust. In many sectors—including those that some western companies regard as "hot"—there is evidence of over-capacity and falling margins. China's dodgy banking system does not seem capable of assessing credit risk properly. Chinese provinces, which still place great store in having their own car factory or steel mill, continue to subsidise investment without worrying too much about its profitability. Government policy is clear: provinces are being told to hold off on investment approvals, banks are being asked to restrain lending. Even if, as seems likely, the much feared "hard landing" is avoided, the government's efforts to rein in investment will inevitably hurt the rest of China's economy.

The repercussions of policy tightening and slowing of these economic giants will be felt around the globe. Japan, still the world's second-largest economy, has performed spectacularly over the past year. But its growth is highly dependent on exports to China and America. Emerging Asian economies, which traditionally thrive when world trade is rising rapidly, will have to get used to slower demand in their key markets. Latin America, reliant on foreign capital in order to roll over substantial debts, will face rising borrowing costs. Only in western Europe and the Middle East are growth prospects for 2005 on a par with those of 2004. In the case of the Middle East, this is because oil revenues will boost government coffers and allow increased investment. But in western Europe the lack of a slowdown in 2005 merely serves to highlight the paucity, relative to other regions, of the upturn in 2004.

It is important to keep this in context. A slowdown is in prospect. A collapse is not—at least, not unless some really nasty shock causes it (oil at $70 a barrel, say, or a sudden collapse of the dollar). Indeed, 2005 should be a reasonable year for world growth, in comparison with much of the past ten years. But it will be considerably weaker than 2004, and the momentum will be in the wrong direction. In such circumstances, the unwary can suffer disappointment, or worse. But for those who refused to get carried away as the good times started to roll again, there may still be room for some swashbuckling in 2005. □

No middle way in the Middle East

In 2005 the region will become either dramatically better or dramatically worse, predicts **Peter David**

Last year in this space I argued that 2004 would be an eventful but not decisive year in the Middle East. By contrast, 2005 is likely to be both eventful and decisive: not only in Iraq but also in the conflict between Israel and the Palestinians and in the showdown between the West and Iran over the Islamic republic's apparent quest to acquire nuclear weapons.

In the case of Iraq, 2004 could not be decisive because of America's presidential election. George Bush could hardly tell the American people that invading Iraq had been a triumph at the same time as he made visible preparations to scurry for the exit. So it was obvious that he would vow to "stay the course". ▶

Peter David: foreign editor, *The Economist*

And it could get worse

But in 2005, with America's own election out of the way, an early exit will become all too possible, depending on how things look on the ground. Moreover, it should be possible quite early in the year for President Bush to tell whether it is wiser to persevere or to quit.

A strong indication will come from the fate of Iraq's own general election, which is pencilled in for January. Given the ferocity of the insurgency, it would be no surprise if the timetable slipped. But it would be dangerous to postpone it for long. So far, the interim UN-appointed government of Iyad Allawi has not shown itself to be either effective or legitimate in the eyes of a majority of Iraqis. Only an election stands a chance of endowing Iraq with a government that has the moral authority to oversee the necessary crackdown on the extremists.

If it proves impossible even to hold an election, America and Britain will at some point conclude that their military presence has become part of the problem rather than part of the solution. They will then need a plan B that enables them to pull out without abandoning Iraq to chaos. That, of course, is easier said than done. When America pulled out of South Vietnam in 1973, the north swiftly won. When Britain walked away from the Palestine mandate in 1948, the Israelis and Arabs simply fought it out. Iraq might benefit from the fact that none of its neighbours wants to see chaos in America's wake. But Saudis, Iranians, Syrians and Turks will find it mightily hard to agree about what sort of Iraq they want to help.

Plainly, it will be better if an election can be held. And this is by no means impossible: for all the violence, most Iraqis still seem eager to cast a vote. In the best of outcomes, this will produce a government broadly representative of Shias, Sunnis and Kurds, and of religious as well as secular Iraqis. Such a government, with a multinational force to back it, would stand a fair chance of fighting the remaining insurgents while bargaining internally on how to share power and drafting a constitution. The danger will come if whole groups, such as the Sunni minority in central Iraq, cannot or will not vote in the election and so feel no loyalty to a central government dominated by Shias. At the very worst, such an outcome might lead to the civil war that has so often been predicted for Iraq.

In Israel-Palestine 2005 will be decisive in another way, as Ariel Sharon tries to push through his plan to evacuate Jewish settlements from the Gaza strip in the teeth of fierce and possibly violent opposition from Israel's settler movement and its supporters inside the prime minister's own party. The outside world will support him in this, while also making it plain that although leaving Gaza is a good start, it is not enough for Israel to earn peace with the Palestinians. Mr Bush, still concentrating on Iraq, was soft on Mr Sharon in 2004. In 2005 America will feel a greater need to step up the pressure for a West Bank withdrawal too. That will be especially true if failure in Iraq makes it even more necessary for America to restore its credibility in the Arab and wider Muslim world.

> In 2005 America will feel a greater need to step up the pressure for a West Bank withdrawal too

As for a nuclear Iran, the Europeans (led by Britain, France and Germany) spent 2004 quarrelling with the Americans about whether it was better to engage the Iranians constructively or use the UN Security Council to punish them for their nuclear skulduggery. If within the first few months of 2005 the Iranians have still not decided or been pressured to give up their nuclear ambitions, even the Europeans will have to admit that their constructive engagement has failed. But what then?

Europe will not want to deepen the breach with Iran while Iraq is still in trouble. And a pre-emptive strike by Israel or America will not necessarily succeed in destroying Iran's hidden and dispersed nuclear facilities. The mullahs who run Iran are a cautious and patient lot: they might not announce in 2005 that Iran intends to, or has, become a nuclear-armed power. But 2005 might very well be the year in which the divided response of the world convinces them that they can do so and get away with it—thus sparking a nuclear-arms race to add to the conventional one in the Middle East. □

Learning to love outsourcing

The West will start to see it as part of the solution to its labour problems, predicts **Ben Edwards**

Faced with the spectacle of multinational firms shedding workers in the rich West and hiring cheaper replacements in India, China and elsewhere, the chattering classes in America and Europe have been arguing among themselves about whether this type of "outsourcing" is a good thing. Their worries are misplaced. And 2005 will be the year in which their confusion is, thankfully and happily, put straight.

The sudden creation of large numbers of IT jobs in India coincided with a sharp fall in demand for IT among companies in America and Europe. From a peak in 2001, employment in the IT industry contracted sharply in rich countries, as firms adjusted to the new, lower level of demand. Politicians, IT workers and commentators then linked these two events: companies were firing workers in the West so that they could hire cheaper ones in the East. Then new sorts of "outsourced" jobs began appearing in India: staffing call centres, processing health-insurance claims, writing stockmarket research, handling credit-card applications. Suddenly all sorts of categories of employment supposedly faced the same fate that had befallen IT workers in America and Europe.

This hysterical analysis was wrong on several counts. For a start, the link between the firing in America and Europe and the hiring in India has not endured. Indian IT firms such as Wipro, Infosys and Cognizant are hiring more furiously than ever. But IT firms in America, Europe and Japan are hiring again too. McKinsey, a consultancy, forecasts that worldwide jobs in the IT services industry will grow from 6.7m in 2004 to 10.6m by 2008. Some employers in America and Europe already report difficulties in hiring IT staff for certain jobs, like systems architects. Because so few students in rich countries study engineering, these labour shortages are certain to grow.

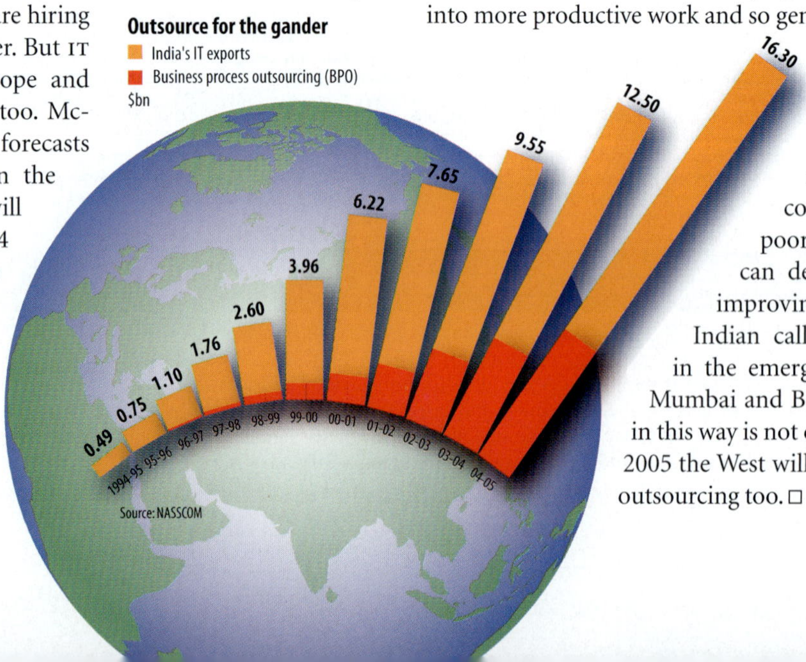

Ben Edwards: American business editor, *The Economist*

The same is true for workers in the call-centre industry. Call-centre companies in India are growing as fast as they can teach their employees how to aspirate their "P"s the American way. At the same time, call-centre firms are also trying to expand employment—albeit more modestly—in America too, and are finding the going tough. One gauge of that: staff turnover in the industry is 80% in America.

As America and parts of Europe push closer to full employment, a big change in the politics of outsourcing will take place. In 2005 the rise of India will come to be seen not as a problem for the West, but as a potential solution.

One of the biggest problems that rich countries must tackle over the next few decades is the ageing of their populations. This will raise the cost of health-care systems, place a greater financial burden on the working population and create labour shortages in Europe and Japan as working populations shrink. Outsourcing can help with all three problems.

Rich economies can redeploy their shrinking workforces into more productive work

The cost of America's health-care system is rising at 12% a year; sourcing large chunks of labour-intensive administration could help to bring costs under control. Britain's National Health Service manages rising costs and demand by rationing the supply of health care. Expanding its brave decision to outsource some of its IT work to an Indian firm, Tata Consultancy Services, would help more Britons get more timely access to health-care services. By sourcing lower-value jobs from abroad, rich economies can redeploy their shrinking workforces into more productive work and so generate the wealth required to help support larger numbers of retirees.

Anti-globalisers claim that firms which source work from low-cost countries exploit the poor in "sweat shops". Yet who can deny that globalisation is improving the livelihoods of the Indian call-centre and IT workers in the emerging affluent suburbs of Mumbai and Bangalore? Sourcing work in this way is not only good for the West: in 2005 the West will learn to feel good about outsourcing too. □

Relatively speaking

Excuse us, blame Einstein, says **John Grimond**

Next year may not be quite what it seems. Although every care has been taken in the preparation of *The World in 2005*, it has been pointed out that certain difficulties attach to the concept of time, and thus to the concept of "next year", adding a certain *je ne sais quoi* to our thoughts about the future. These difficulties were first elaborated by Albert Einstein in 1905—100 years ago.

Suppose, for a moment, that you are alighting from a spaceship. Suppose, too, that you are a twin travelling on your own, and that you whizzed away from Earth for ten years at 0.9 times the speed of light before turning round and whizzing back. Einstein's "Special Theory of Relativity" has some implications for you.

One is that you think you have been away for 20 years and are therefore 20 years older than when you left—making you 45 years old if, say, you were 25 when you set off. But your confused twin thinks you have been away for 46 years, making him 71. This, the "twin paradox", is all a consequence of various inadequacies in Sir Isaac Newton's belief that space and time were absolute concepts that existed independently of the Universe. Einstein was the first to jot down what now seems so obvious—that the Universe should be considered as a continuum with both spatial and temporal dimensions.

> The relative is everywhere—and that is not a reference to your great-aunt

All this adds up to the awkward fact—awkward for prognosticators, anyway—that the time that elapses between two events will depend on the motion of the observer. If, therefore, an event predicted in this publication strangely does not come to pass in 2005, the explanation is almost sure to be that the observer of the non-event is not at rest but travelling. And the closer his speed is to the speed of light, the greater the likelihood of his stumbling on some seeming inexactitude.

Happily, most people try to keep travel at the speed of light to an absolute minimum. For them the good news is that large particles travelling at speeds much less than that abide by the laws set by Sir Isaac, and the same goes for travellers. For all practical purposes, they can carry on regardless.

Where does that leave Einstein's special theory? Well, with quite a bit to say about other things, notably the relationship between matter and energy. That is because particles accelerated to something close to the speed of light gain in mass, and are unable to go any faster than that speed. This implies not just a relationship between matter and energy but an equivalence, summed up in the formula $E=mc^2$, where E is energy, "m" is mass and "c" is the unsurpassable speed of light.

Once again, the implications seem to be greatest for particles rather than human beings going about their daily business. But humans are affected. First, philosophers, who have much to explain; second, T-shirt designers, who can emblazon their wares with the familiar formula and a picture of the most photogenic nutty professor ever; and third, everyone, since the mass-energy equivalence makes nuclear weapons possible.

In fact, the relative is everywhere—and that is not a reference to your great-aunt. There is, of course, moral relativism, much frowned upon these days by those who deplore the associated belief that moral standards vary according to circumstance and from person to person. And there is the widespread reckoning in mundane affairs not just of absolutes but of rates of change. Thus economists are more concerned about inflation rates than actual prices. Carmakers sell their products less by their top speeds than their ability to get away from the lights. And, at least in rich countries, it is not absolute indigence that raises questions about social justice so much as the relative poverty of those who cannot keep up with the Joneses.

If such reflections owe more to Archimedes and the other Greeks who cottoned on to the differential calculus than they do to Einstein, that should not detract from his genius in drawing attention to the curious nature of relativity. In 2005 the least he deserves is a centennial T-shirt. □

John Grimond: writer at large, *The Economist*

WE LEAD.
WE LEARN.
UPM
Our objective is a clean run.
Sustainable development is at the heart of UPM's operations. We take responsibility for what we do and constantly strive to improve our processes. We ensure our environmental performance is available for all to see – you can find details on our website.
www.upm-kymmene.com

DIARY FOR 2005

Our selection of events around the world

JANUARY

Luxembourg takes over the presidency of the European Union from the Netherlands.

America's president, George Bush, is sworn in.

The World Economic Forum meets in Davos, Switzerland.

Elections are planned in Iraq by the end of the month, security permitting.

Hundreds of camels, splendidly attired in Rajasthani textiles, are led to Bikaner in northern India for the annual celebration of the camel.

FEBRUARY

America's president sends his budget to Congress.

The EU decides whether or not to extend sanctions against Zimbabwe.

Chinese celebrate the Year of the Rooster, which begins on the 9th. Those born this year may make excellent restaurateurs or world travellers.

The 25th annual Golden Raspberry Awards, honouring the year's most dreadful films, are presented in Los Angeles, to be followed by the more po-faced Academy Awards.

MARCH

Deadline for a report, commissioned by George Bush, on American intelligence and weapons of mass destruction.

Tony Blair's Commission for Africa delivers its report and recommendations on G8 policy towards the continent.

Parliamentary elections are due in Zimbabwe around now.

More than 700,000 revellers attend the Sydney Mardi Gras, a highlight of the world's gay calendar.

Some 170m French speakers around the world celebrate International Francophone Day.

APRIL

Parliamentary elections are due in Chechnya around now.

A value-added tax is introduced in India, going some way to reducing the country's budget deficit of around 10% of GDP.

Story-lovers around the world mark the 200th anniversary of the birth of Hans Christian Andersen, the Danish author of "The Emperor's New Clothes" and many other tales.

More than 200,000 music enthusiasts attend the New Orleans Jazz and Heritage Festival.

MAY

Britons go to the polls around now for a general election.

UN officials meet in New York for the five-yearly review of the Nuclear Weapons Non-Proliferation Treaty.

The third summit of the Council of Europe is held in Warsaw. The first took place in Vienna in 1993, following the fall of communism. The second, in Strasbourg in 1997, gave new impetus to human-rights protection.

World Turtle Day focuses attention on the plight of the planet's dwindling turtle populations.

JUNE

Post-conflict elections in the Democratic Republic of Congo; a presidential election in Iran.

Defence ministers from the Asia-Pacific region meet in Singapore to discuss security issues.

Deadline for renewal of America's Trade Promotion Authority, which used to be known as "fast track" and allows the president to negotiate trade agreements without his hands being tied by Congress.

Events across the globe mark the UN's World Environment Day.

JULY

Britain takes over the presidency of the EU.

G8 leaders gather in Gleneagles, Scotland, for their annual summit.

The International Olympic Committee decides the venue for the 2012 Olympics.

Excitable boys of all ages run with bulls through the streets of Pamplona in Spain.

AUGUST

Heads of southern African states gather at the Summit of the Southern African Development Community in Gaborone, Botswana; heads of Pacific island states meet in Port Moresby, Papua New Guinea.

North and South Koreans celebrate the 60th anniversary of the end of Japanese colonial rule.

The European Congress on Biotechnology is held in Copenhagen.

Health permitting, Pope John Paul II hosts World Youth Day in Cologne, the 20th international gathering of young Catholics.

SEPTEMBER

The 60th session of the UN General Assembly gets under way in New York.

The World Bank and the IMF gather in Washington, DC.

Munich reverberates to the sound of drinking songs and beer burps during the fortnight-long Oktoberfest, the largest festival in the world.

Culture vultures descend on Venice for the city's biennial art fair.

OCTOBER

The defence case for Slobodan Milosevic is due to conclude around now at the International Criminal Court in The Hague.

Presidential and parliamentary elections in Côte d'Ivoire, Liberia and Tanzania.

Bookworms squirm with delight at the Frankfurt Book Fair.

Britons celebrate the 200th anniversary of Lord Nelson's victory at the Battle of Trafalgar.

NOVEMBER

The Fourth Summit of the Americas, bringing together the leaders of 34 member-states, meets in Buenos Aires, Argentina.

21 heads of state meet at the Asia-Pacific Economic Co-operation summit in Busan, South Korea.

The Commonwealth Heads of Government meeting is held in Valletta, Malta.

The fourth pan-African conference on malaria—the largest gathering of its kind—is held in Yaoundé, Cameroon.

The European Space Agency launches a Russian Soyuz-Fregat rocket from Kazakhstan to put a satellite into orbit around Venus.

DECEMBER

The sixth WTO ministerial conference is held in Hong Kong.

Presidential elections in Sudan and Sri Lanka.

Experts frighten one another at the UN's Biological Weapons Convention in Geneva.

Deadline for the WHO's plan to treat 3m people living with AIDS in poor countries.

The fifth Francophone Games, with participants from 56 French-speaking countries, are held in Niger.

With the help of contributions from foresightnews www.foresightnews.co.uk

Britain

Judgment day

Emma Duncan

Tony Blair will win a third term but few friends

It will be a year of reckoning for Tony Blair. The last general election took place in June 2001. The next one is therefore due by June 2006. To avoid getting trapped into holding elections at bad times (as James Callaghan was by the 1978 winter of discontent), prime ministers tend to call them after four years, and pundits who pore over the political calendar have pencilled in May 5th 2005 as the likeliest date. Mr Blair will hold off until 2006 only if things are going particularly badly for him; so not having an election in 2005 will be as much a judgment on his performance as having one.

Which groups of people will be for Mr Blair in 2005 and which groups against him? The latter are easier to identify than the former.

The left will be against Mr Blair. When he first came to power, some of them were inclined to give him the benefit of the doubt. Now it is hard to find any who are. Iraq and his close relationship with George Bush have been the biggest factors in turning them against him, but there are plenty of other reasons too. The left hates the market-oriented reforms he has introduced in the public sector; his hostility towards the unions, most sharply illustrated by his battle with the Fire Brigades Union; his failure to roll back the Tory privatisation of the railways. The left regards him as Thatcherlite.

The countryside will be against him. Rural folk have long been aware that the soul of New Labour is deeply metropolitan: its luminaries regard the countryside as an alien land populated by strange, backward, cruel people. But the countryside's hostility turned to violence over Mr Blair's determination to ban foxhunting (because it seemed a cheap bone to throw to the Labour left); and more civil disobedience is promised.

Anti-Europeans will be against him. Mr Blair once saw it as his destiny to take Britain into the euro. That hope faded, largely because Britain's economy performed so much better than those in the euro zone. But Mr Blair has promised a referendum on the European constitution and the prospect of that vote (expected in 2006) will galvanise anti-Europeans once more. Now that the United Kingdom Independence Party has successes in local and European elections behind it, there is a plausible focus for anti-European feeling.

The poor will be for Mr Blair. Thanks to the tax credits that have boosted the incomes of low earners, the poor have done well out of this government's quietly redistributionist policies. They never voted Tory much anyway; and over the past two elections the Tories' vote in the poor bits of cities has disappeared.

2005

A new licensing act, which will allow pubs to remain open around the clock, is likely to take effect in Britain towards the end of the year. And a new gambling bill may lift restrictions on gaming hours and herald the spread of big casinos.

Emma Duncan: Britain editor, *The Economist*

For me or against me?

But nobody is fighting over these groups. Their allegiances are already largely determined. The election will be won or lost in the towns and suburbs where the great mass of middle England lives. The factors that determine which way it goes will be partly emotional and partly material.

Iraq will have most bearing on how people feel about Mr Blair. It's not so much that Britons are moved by the Iraqis' plight. Indeed, once Iraqis took over running the ▸

government, the country slipped off the front pages; it takes the deaths of foreigners, or of several dozen Iraqis, to get it back on again. What's more important for British politics is how the Iraq war eroded faith in Mr Blair. Some people no longer trust him because they think he lied, and some people because he got the assessment of the danger from Iraq disastrously wrong. Whether they think he is guilty of dishonesty or incompetence, Iraq has changed perceptions of Mr Blair.

Money will have most bearing on how people think about Mr Blair. The most remarkable feature of Labour's time in power has been the economy's performance. Growth has remained high and stable, unemployment low. That will persist going into the election. The house-price boom will be going into reverse, but not fast enough to undermine the government's reputation for sound economic management.

Taxes have increased, and people have noticed. The middle classes are aware that they have done worse than the poor and are grumpy about it. But the crucial question in the election will be whether people feel that the improvements in the public services (health in particular) that their taxes have paid for have been sufficient. Those improvements are beginning to come through, but it is not clear that they are coming through fast enough to impress the people paying for them.

But even if the public services don't come through for Mr Blair in 2005, one factor is fairly certain to: the Conservative Party. It will go into the next election in almost as much despair as it went into the last.

Changing leaders twice has done the Tories no good. The current one, Michael Howard, has failed to revive their fortunes, partly because Mr Blair has deftly occupied many of the policy areas—tough immigration and law-and-order policies, market-oriented public-service reforms—that are naturally the Tories', and partly because he supported the war against Iraq and has therefore been ill-placed to criticise Mr Blair's foreign policy. Charles Kennedy, the leader of the Liberal Democrats, took a strong stance against the war, and has thus benefited from the fallout. But the Lib Dems are the perennial losers in British politics, and even they do not believe that their post-war bounce will propel them into government. Apathy looks like a more serious enemy for Labour than either the Tories or the Lib Dems: many disaffected Labour voters will simply stay at home.

A credible opposition is a necessary if not a sufficient condition for defeating an incumbent government. Expect Labour to enter its third term in government with a much-reduced majority and a discredited leader. And expect the Tories, shortly thereafter, to get themselves a new leader and a new lease of life. On all sides, change will be in the air. Mr Blair has already announced that, if elected, his third term in Number Ten will be his last. In 2005 preparations for post-Blair politics in Britain will begin in earnest. □

The crucial question in the election will be whether people feel that the improvements in the public services (health in particular) that their taxes have paid for have been sufficient

End of the Golden Age?

Anatole Kaletsky

Britain's economy risks losing its competitive edge

Since the mid-1990s Britain has enjoyed an economic Golden Age, coming from far behind to achieve the lowest unemployment, the steadiest growth and the securest price stability among the G7 countries, as well as the highest per capita income after America and Canada. But is this Golden Age coming to an end, just when Britain has finally been recognised around the world as an economic role model?

Until recently, many viewed the spectacular improvement in Britain's economy with incredulity. Most Britons still suspect that the country's new-found prosperity is "done with mirrors", a cheap trick conjured up by Tony Blair and Gordon Brown. But these suspicions have been misplaced—at least until now. This publication has argued throughout the past decade that Britain's apparently inexplicable prosperity was actually built on quite solid foundations. The worry for 2005 is that these may start to erode, especially after the general election expected in May. Consumer confidence and economic growth are always strong just before elections, but a hangover is likely by the end of 2005.

Anatole Kaletsky: columnist, *The Times*, and director of GaveKal Research

The shoch-aye of the noo

Beware of a looming fashion disaster

"What Not To Wear", a television series in which two Sloaney harridans humiliate frumpy women whose figures and dress sense are only fractionally worse than their own, has been a surprise hit in Britain. But for a real masterclass in fashion faux pas in 2005, forget Trinny and Susannah. Look instead to July's G8 summit at Gleneagles, a Scottish luxury hotel and golfing resort with a fine pedigree.

Seeing a statesman wearing anything other than a suit and tie is a bit like seeing one's parents naked. Rationally, one accepts this is bound to happen sometimes. Nevertheless, one wishes it did not. At G8 summits, where leaders are supposed to look relaxed in the local surroundings, the risk of a sartorial fiasco is high.

What makes the prospect of Gleneagles so scary is the Scottish theme-park element. Remember the time this past August when Silvio Berlusconi, Italy's prime minister, stepped out in the sunny streets of Porto Cervo in Sardinia wearing white loafers, linen pantaloons, a shirt unbuttoned to the navel and a bandana? Now factor in tasselled brogues, some tartan socks, plus-fours and the obligatory flat cap. Be afraid. Be very afraid. □

To understand what could go wrong, we have to recall why things have gone so right since the mid-1990s. Britain's economic success was built on three pillars. The first was the trade-union reform, deregulation and privatisation of the Thatcher era. Thatcherism created a truly competitive market economy in Britain for the first time in the 20th century, at a time when most continental nations embarked on exactly the opposite course. This gave Britain a big advantage over its European neighbours, but Thatcherism on its own was not enough to assure either growth or stability, as became apparent in the boom and bust of 1988-92.

The second reason for Britain's revival was the macroeconomic revolution triggered, ironically, by the very event that discredited Tory economic management. The ejection of the pound from the European exchange-rate mechanism on Black Wednesday (September 16th 1992) freed Britain from a century of servitude to quasi-religious obsession with "defending" or "stabilising" sterling, an obsession which replaced the management of demand as the top priority of the Treasury and the Bank of England. Only when all efforts to defend the pound were finally abandoned could Britain move towards a rational policy for managing growth—and it did not take long for the Treasury to devise a sensible demand-management policy, which was skilfully codified and entrenched by Gordon Brown when he transferred control of interest rates to the Bank.

Completing the explanation of Britain's prosperity was a third long-term trend: the way that globalisation and technological change have played to Britain's comparative advantage in knowledge-based services. As a result of technological progress and Asian competition, the goods which Britain has never been very good at making and has had to buy from the rest of the world—mainly mass-produced manufactures—have got dramatically cheaper. Meanwhile, the items Britain has always sold successfully—financial services, scientific research, education, entertainment—have risen in price. Because of this shift in relative prices, Britons have in effect enjoyed a large pay increase.

But all three pillars of Britain's Golden Age are now starting to erode. Some of the benefits of Thatcherite deregulation could be undone by a swing to the left in the Labour Party after next year's election, triggered by a split between Messrs Blair and Brown. The Bank of England's monetary management will certainly be complicated if the debt-financed property boom collapses. And the rise in oil and commodity prices will reverse some of the gains in Britain's terms of trade.

The threat that draws most attention is a bust in the property market, but this is actually the least troubling of the three problems. The scale of the price correction could be quite modest and it will certainly not produce the devastating economic effects of the 1989-92 slump. Mortgage borrowing has not been nearly as important as generally believed in financing consumption. In fact, Britain's savings rate has held steady throughout the housing bubble. Instead of bingeing on the high streets, British home-owners have reinvested essentially all the money they took out of the housing market—and mostly in safe liquid assets such as bank deposits. It is quite plausible, therefore, that a fall in house prices will have little or no effect on consumption growth.

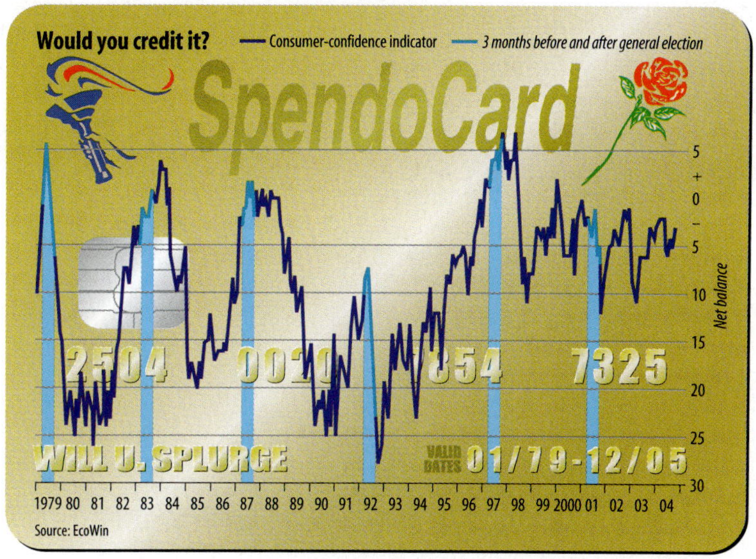

A more serious threat to the British economy is the deteriorating terms of trade. This will definitely hit living standards and economic growth in 2005. Judging by recent national-accounts revisions, the shift in relative prices of British exports and imports and the strength of sterling have added as much as 5% annually to Britain's GDP since 1995—more than the peak value of North Sea oil. Part of this gain will now be reversed through higher energy and commodity prices, and possibly a weaker pound. The impact will be quite painful, and could become very serious if British workers try to recoup their losses through inflationary pay demands in a labour market which is getting increasingly tight.

This leads to the third and most serious threat to the British economy: the relentless rise in public spending and government employment, which could start contributing to inflationary pressures in the year ahead,

> Little by little, the spirit of enterprise created by the Thatcher revolution is being weakened by all these regulations and the ever-rising public spending

especially when combined with the deluge of new regulations, both from Brussels and Whitehall, which add to labour costs and stifle market competition. Government has accounted for all the growth of employment in Britain since the end of 2001 and the burden of this huge expansion is becoming hard to bear for the private sector. Worse, on top of that come the proliferating regulations, from new restrictions on working hours to the restrictions on animal experiments which are forcing the export of pharmaceutical research.

Little by little, the spirit of enterprise created by the Thatcher revolution is being weakened by all these regulations and the ever-rising public spending. Given the chances of a war of succession within the Labour Party after the election—with the trade unions and the left-wing activists as the chief kingmakers—the obstacles to enterprise in Britain are likely to grow in the year ahead. The atavistic longing in sections of the Labour Party for a regulated, high-tax, state-run economy is now the greatest threat to Britain's Golden Age. □

2005

British households earning under £58,000 ($105,000) will be able to claim up to £140 a week in tax breaks to pay for at-home nannies, as well as for their kids' after-school activities.

The English patient

Paul Wallace

Introducing the new-model National Health Service

Health care will be uppermost among voters' concerns in the British general election expected in 2005. But the future of the National Health Service, financed through tax and free at the point of use, is of international interest. The Labour government is striving to transform the NHS from a restrictive service plagued by long waiting times for treatment into one offering swift access and patient choice. If it succeeds, this could create an appealing model for other countries. If it fails, the harsh verdict will be that the NHS is beyond repair and must be replaced by a new system.

Labour's crusade to modernise the NHS, which the party founded in 1948, will pass some crucial milestones in 2005. The big surge in spending, which started in 1999 and is due to end in 2007, will enter its final phase. In 1998 Britain spent less than 7% of GDP on health care. In 2005 this share will rise to 8.6%; and by 2007 it will exceed 9%. Britain will no longer be one of the low spenders on health care among developed countries.

> The nightmare scenario is that the NHS will lose its one big advantage of relative cheapness but will still perform poorly

The shift of resources into the NHS is the result of continuing yearly increases in its cash budget of 10%, equivalent to over 7% after inflation. The election campaign will bring to the fore worries about whether the health service is delivering value for money. Much of the cash has leaked into higher pay or has been absorbed in bloated regulatory and administrative costs. As a result, the actual output of the health service rose at an annual rate of less than 4% in the first five years of the spending splurge. The nightmare scenario is that the NHS will lose its one big advantage of relative cheapness but will still perform poorly.

One undeniable improvement is that fewer people are having to wait excessively long times for operations. In 2005 the maximum waiting time for hospital treatment is scheduled to fall to six months. The government will hail this as a major achievement, but it will still fall short of the prompt access to medical care that is taken for granted in many countries.

Successful modernisation of the NHS requires structural reform as well as extra money. Belatedly, the Labour government has set about creating an internal market in which health care is bought and sold within the NHS. In the past, hospital budgets have been only loosely linked to the amount of work that each hospital does.

Paul Wallace: economy and finance correspondent, *The Economist*

Cash injection

Total health spending in Britain as % of GDP

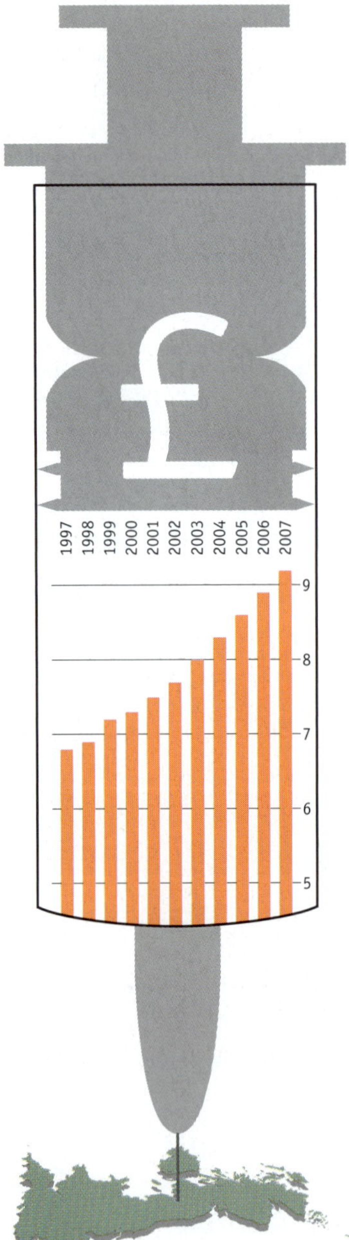

Figures from 2003 are for fiscal years starting in April
Sources: OECD, HM Treasury

In 2005 this will change so that payment by results becomes the general rule. The more a hospital does, the more it will get paid.

The new payments system will give financial teeth to Labour's policy of patient choice. By the end of 2005 anyone requiring an elective operation, like a hip or knee replacement, will be able to choose among four or five hospitals. Since money will follow the patients, hospitals will have an incentive to win their custom and to carry out treatments more efficiently.

That incentive will be enhanced as more hospitals win greater independence within the NHS. These "foundation" hospitals will get more freedom to run their affairs without constant meddling by ministers and government bureaucrats. Crucially, they will be able to retain some of their surpluses, so that they gain financially when they become more productive. They can then plough this money back into better facilities and services.

A spur to all state-run hospitals will come from private-sector competition. The government is opening the NHS market to private providers. By the end of 2005 they will be carrying out around 5% of publicly funded elective treatments. The government wants this share to rise rapidly, to 15% by 2008.

In the past, Britain's independent medical-care sector has catered for the niche private-insurance market. It is gearing up for a high-volume future in which it will compete for a substantial chunk of NHS work. Britain is moving towards the mixed economy of providers that is common in many other countries where public money also finances most health care.

In short, the new-model NHS takes to the road in 2005. If all goes well, the health service will make much more productive use of its cash bonanza. As hospitals become busier, the waiting list will shorten. This will add credibility to Labour's election pledge to cut the maximum waiting time for an elective operation to 18 weeks by 2008.

However, there are risks that the new-model NHS will not prove roadworthy. First, some hospitals with higher costs will be hard pressed to compete under the new payments system. The government will face pressure to bail them out. But if it does so, the internal market will lose credibility. Second, empowering patients may lead to an explosion of demand. This could destabilise the finances of the health service, despite the public largesse being lavished on it.

In 2005 it will still be too early to reach a final judgment on whether the government's reforms will succeed. If the combination of a massive cash injection and major structural changes fails to cure the English patient, voters will eventually lose patience. But the British have an almost totemic commitment to the National Health Service. In the 2005 general election they will give it the benefit of the doubt. □

2005

From April new rules in Britain will lift anonymity from sperm, egg and embryo donors and allow donor-conceived children to learn the identity of their parents after they turn 18.

Minority report

Trevor Phillips

Integration has a long way to go

When the 17-year-old British boxer Amir Khan won a silver medal at the Athens Olympics, the celebrations went far into the night in two places. In the Pakistani village where his bride-to-be currently lives, his in-laws could boast that they had made a great deal. But the celebration in the sub-continent was a tea party by comparison with the media circus in Britain. The fuss had less to do with Mr Khan's boxing than with his father's dress sense—in particular his Union flag waistcoat. The message was that the Khans were winning it for Britain. Yet the family was still hedging its bets. Alongside Mr Khan, Amir's uncle sported a T-shirt carrying the national flag of Pakistan.

The Khans' uneasiness symbolises a dilemma faced across Europe. Can migrant families assume that even if they want to be British (or French or Spanish) they will be accepted as such? How to reconcile the economic integration of people bringing new skills and labour with the social integration that makes societies work.

The 4.5m migrants who came to Britain since 1945 will be surpassed by the numbers who arrive in the next quarter century to do hard-to-fill jobs (and pay our pensions)

In the past, most migration into Britain was post-colonial—the descendants of African slaves from the Caribbean, textile workers and farmers from the Indian sub-continent. Today the flows are from states around the edges of Europe's rich heartland: Turkey, Iraq, Somalia and of course eastern Europe. Yesterday's West Indian nurses and Sikh bus drivers are being followed by today's Czech carpenters and Polish nannies.

The 4.5m migrants who came to Britain since 1945 will be surpassed by the numbers who arrive in the next quarter century to do hard-to-fill jobs (and pay our pensions). These migrants will be lighter-skinned, which may make them stand out less. But they won't speak English and they are more likely to be Muslims than Christians.

The lessons of the past aren't encouraging for their integration. It is only three years since Britain's northern towns were rocked by riots between young Asians and the police. The summer of 2004 narrowly escaped similar clashes, this time with new migrants cooped up in small, suspicious provincial towns. Britain's much-maligned Home Office, working with the grass-roots network of the Commission for Racial Equality, can claim some credit for anticipating trouble and stepping in before it took off.

But the summer of 2005 may not be so quiet. It only takes a spark—a turf war between Somali and Caribbean gangs, or a row between an Iraqi Kurd and a young white over who has looked too long at whose girlfriend's legs—to touch off a conflagration.

Integration has been patchy at best. Though students of Chinese and Indian origin are outperforming the national average by the time they leave school—by 50% and 25% respectively—black, Pakistani and gypsy children fall far below. The police remains a largely white force patrolling increasingly diverse communities. According to a YouGov poll, more than half of white Britons do not have a single non-white person in their circle of friends. Even more astonishing, young people from ethnic minorities are twice as likely as their parents to have a circle of friends which includes no whites.

Today immigration regularly turns up in the top five concerns for British voters. The Tory leader, Michael Howard (the son of a Jewish immigrant from Romania), has cleverly positioned his party to take advantage of public anxiety without opening himself to charges of "playing the race card", proposing a sensible Australian-style points system to regulate the flow of migrants.

Expect the home secretary, David Blunkett, to come forward with not-too-different proposals shortly before the election. Labour's support among ethnic minorities has dwindled to less than half what it was 20 years ago—about 35%. Mr Blunkett plans to launch a strategy for "race equality and community cohesion" by early 2005. This will involve more citizenship teaching, more support for summer camps to bring young people together, more insistence on everybody speaking English.

Above all, the government will need to send some signals to the Khans—both at home and abroad—that Britain respects Muslims. One way would be a law to protect Muslims from discrimination based on religion. Today it remains perfectly legal to post a "No Muslims Allowed" sign outside a hotel, restaurant or pub; British laws prohibit this kind of discrimination on the ground of race but not of religion. For Muslim extremists this is manna from heaven.

When Britain takes over the EU presidency in mid-2005 Tony Blair will want to be able to show the rest of Europe—way behind on these issues—how to avoid the dreadful traps that have produced revivals of far-right politics and Muslim extremism in France, Germany, Belgium and the Netherlands. Fulfilling his promise to make Muslims equal should be his first step. □

Trevor Phillips: chair, Commission for Racial Equality

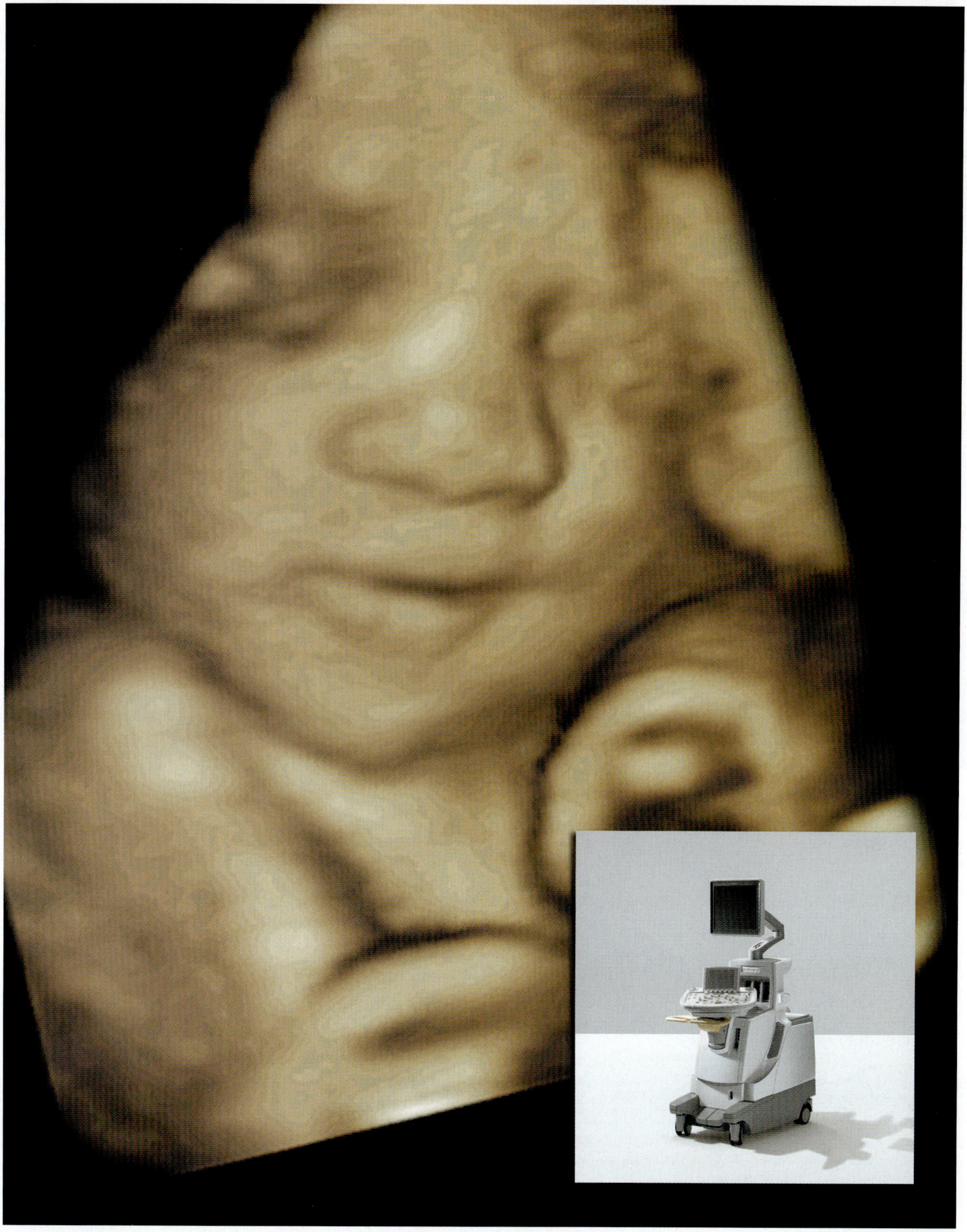

Risky business

Stelios Haji-Ioannou, serial entrepreneur, explains why the unpronounceable will achieve the improbable in Britain

Since the collapse of communism no politician in the western world can do anything other than support free enterprise. That's why I won't lose any sleep over who wins the next general election in Britain. Having created a dozen companies in 12 years in industries that trade in as many countries, I am sure that Britain will remain the best place to do business in Europe in 2005.

But Britain's entrepreneurs will be changing. Immigrants tend to be dynamic people, willing to take the risk of leaving their homeland for a better future. In 2005, thanks partly to the enlargement of the European Union, more and more successful entrepreneurs in Britain will not have been born there. And more people will start real businesses in less than glamorous sectors (as opposed to ventures comprising little more than a dotcom after a trendy name). As a judge in an entrepreneurial competition organised by Ernst & Young in late 2004, I saw only a couple of dotcoms after the names of 40 finalists.

But will this be enough? Britain needs many more smaller entrepreneurs since they, in large numbers, can change the dynamics of the whole economy. It also needs high-profile role models, like Richard Branson, who inspire youngsters (including myself in the early 1990s) to start their own business.

What's in a word

The politicians will talk a lot about "entrepreneurs" and "enterprise culture", but few will really understand what true entrepreneurship means. The dictionary defines an entrepreneur as "a person who organises, operates and assumes the risk for a business venture", so the term should not be used for people who take risks with other people's money. "Entrepreneurial CEO", a phrase sometimes applied to corporate high-fliers, is a contradiction in terms. They should be called managers and, unless laws are broken, they walk away from failed ventures wealthier than when they started by at least the amount of their salary. The only true entrepreneurs are the ones who embark on a business venture knowing that they may end up poorer than when they started.

> I have no doubt that in 2005 the French and the Germans will continue to be less receptive to foreign entrepreneurs than the British

The French invented the term entrepreneur but their economy, with a nanny state and heavy social and legal penalties for failure, has created a nation of risk-averse people whose dream as youngsters is more often to work for the government than to start a business. In countries with a strong socialist background, like my own birthplace, Greece, one sees a preponderance of another type of entrepreneur: the type that excels at servicing one customer only, the government. The problem with these people, in the eyes of the public at least, is that they profit at the expense of the taxpayer, thanks to unscrupulous politicians; rightly or wrongly, they tend to be seen as the bad guys, exploiting the system. The real problem for the economy is that fewer young people have the desire to risk any of their own money to become true entrepreneurs.

That is why I chose Britain ten years ago to launch my first "easy"-branded venture, easyJet, a low-cost airline. I chose Britain, not Greece, for the launch and my father, also a Greek who lent me the money, agreed. I believed then and am even more convinced now that Britain has the best legal system in Europe, one that you can trust to sue the so-called flag-carrier airline and still get a fair hearing. I do not think this would have been the case in Greece, or even France or Germany.

I am an economic immigrant myself, albeit one who is a graduate of the London School of Economics and who has a rich father. I found British society much more open than even some Brits would admit, accepting someone with an unpronounceable surname and a Greek accent to launch an airline which they are happy to trust with their lives. More than 70m passengers later, easyJet, now a PLC run by professional management, is still struggling to be perceived as a local airline (as opposed to a British one) in both France and Germany, despite significant investment in those markets. I have no doubt that in 2005 the French and the Germans will continue to be less receptive to foreign entrepreneurs than the British.

But any British complacency would be misguided. The country still lags far behind America in entrepreneurial spirit. The main reason: attitudes to risk.

If you are not failing occasionally, you are not taking enough risk and there is no reward without risk. In America a past business failure is almost a badge of honour (Donald Trump's status as a star of reality TV's "The Apprentice" soars even as one of his listed companies announces impending bankruptcy). In Britain it is a lasting handicap. Gordon Brown, the chancellor, has said he might change the law to destigmatise non-fraudulent business failure, and I applaud that. But it will take more than that to alter the nation's attitude to business failure. The problem lies deep in the British psyche: what will always stand in the way of entrepreneurship is that Brits all love the underdog until he or she succeeds and then they love to shoot them down. This will not change in 2005.

What other predictions? Of the 54 low-cost airlines that started in Europe in the past couple of years, the majority will go bust in 2005. The valuations of easyJet and Ryanair have come down recently, so will capital availability for the sector, and fewer entrepreneurs will dig into their back pockets for a second round of funding for a loss-making start-up airline. Last but not least, I predict that in 2005 Britons will see another half a dozen new "easy"-branded services and products, from cruises to men's toiletries, courtesy of a serial entrepreneur called Stelios. In 2005 entrepreneurship will continue to be addictive, as once you start it's difficult to stop. □

AEROFLOT – MARCHING TOWARDS THE WORLD AVIATION ELITE

Aeroflot – Russian Airlines is a leading air carrier in Russian Federation and all post-Soviet airspace as well as one of the most dynamic airlines in Europe. We fly passengers and cargo to 88 destinations in 42 countries around the world. Aeroflot, with its history dating back to the dawn of civil aviation in the Soviet Union in 1923, is one of the world's longest-established carriers. But nevertheless, despite of its venerable age, the company shows strong results. Quickly shedding the image of cold soviet-style airline, within the last five years Aeroflot boosted its annual after-tax profits by more than 21 times – from $6.1 million in 1999 up to $128.3 million in 2003. By 2003 its results put Aeroflot among the 15 top world airlines by net profit. Under the new market oriented management, the company capitalization doubled last year.

Today the Russian domestic air transportation market is developing very dynamically, growing by 10-11% annually within the last three years alone. Therefore Aeroflot's intermediate term plans are based on boosting its activities in the Russian home market. By 2010 the company intends to increase its share in this market to above 20%.

In addition to Russia and the CIS – the main "battlefield" for Aeroflot is still the international market where its prime targets are Western Europe, South East Asia, the Far East and North America. During the last three years Aeroflot was busy reforming its network, including cutting unprofitable routes. As a result the geography of the flights became more compact, but the network is better controlled and much more efficient.

IMPROVING THE IMAGE
The airline has also boosted its image with radical improvements in quality and redesigning of the whole look of the company.

A brand new concept of premium-class in-flight service was introduced on flights to New York, LA, Tokyo, Vienna, Zurich, Munich, Brussels, Geneva, Helsinki, and Hong Kong. By the end of 2005 it will cover all routes. This project is accompanied by an intensive cabin crew retraining programme.

JOINING THE ALLIANCE
In May 2004 Aeroflot and Air France signed an MoU to pave the way for the Russian flag-carrier to join the SkyTeam alliance. Aeroflot will become a full member most probably in 2005, the first Russian airline to enter a global alliance.

Invitation from the SkyTeam is a recognition of the Russian flag carrier's high standards, graphic evidence of its success.

HUB IN MOSCOW
Aeroflot believes its further and successful development depends on having a modern hub linking Europe and Asia.

The airline believes its future is in transit traffic and convenient connections, considering Moscow as strategically promising hub for the markets of Russia, the CIS, Europe and America as well as Far East and Southeast Asia.

The airline has plans to participate in the reconstruction and expansion of Sheremetyevo airport – still its main operational base.
Aeroflot's strategic goal is to construct the new terminal and increase its business activity at Sheremetyevo.

AEROFLOT
Russian Airlines

After Aeroflot becomes a full member of SkyTeam, the volume of traffic at Sheremetyevo can be increased dramatically, to up to 22 million passengers a year. Aeroflot is planning on Terminal 3 commencing operations in 2007

CARGO
Aeroflot has four DC-10-40F freighters. These aircraft make scheduled flights between Oslo, Hahn, Tokyo, Seoul, Beijing, Shanghai, Hong Kong and Helsinki. Aeroflot's favourable position between the Far East and Western Europe helps to reduce costs and offer competitive prices. The carrier also has a time advantage on the Europe/Asia route, as most carriers fly around Russia to avoid overflight fees. Last year the airline carried 114,000 tons of cargo, up 4% on 2002. Within the first six months of 2004, freight flown by Aeroflot increased by 30,3 % in comparison to the previous year.
The carrier expects to double cargo revenues within the three years. There are plans to upgrade its freighter fleet with MD-lls increasing the number of freighters to 6.

AIR FLEET
The company's air fleet consists of 92 aircraft (owned and leased), including the latest models of Airbus and Boeing jets.

As a result of a two-year-long air fleet restructuring, by the end of 2004 Aeroflot's foreign fleet will include two Boeing 777-200ERs, seven 767-300ERs and eighteen Airbus A319/320/321s that replace less effective A310-300s.

Aeroflot still uses over 20 home-built Tu-154Ms that were re-engineered in order to meet all international standards on noise and emission. In January 2004 Aeroflot signed a leasing contract for six more Il-96 airliners to add to the existing six.

By 2007 Aeroflot needs to acquire up to 29 additional modern medium-haul airliners. Shortly, Aeroflot intends to open a tender for acquisition of 50 short-range aircraft.

	2003	2002	2001	2000	1999
Financial ($ million)					
Total revenue	1,716	1,563	1,558	1,406.9	1,166.2
Net profit/loss	128.3	91.3	21.8	10.9	6.1
Operating					
Passengers (000s)	5,844	5,489	5,830	5,101	4,609
RPKs (million)	18,203	17,647	18,943	17,434	16,409
Cargo (tons)	114,200	109,500	101,600	107,400	89,500

Source: Aeroflot

Europe

Yes or No?

Gideon Rachman *BRUSSELS*

The people vote on Europe's new constitution

The European Union has been built by elites. But 2005 will be Europe's year of the people. A new constitution for the Union, drafted over two painful years by political leaders, will be put to a referendum in several EU countries. The collision between an elite project and public opinion could be bruising—and potentially dangerous for the European Union.

The 25 national governments of the EU have given themselves two years to ratify the constitution, after its signing in October 2004. Some of the governments that are most nervous about their electorates' reaction—in particular Britain and Denmark—will probably delay their referendums until 2006, hoping that a series of approvals elsewhere in Europe will create momentum for a positive result. Other countries will choose to ratify by parliamentary vote alone; Finland, Sweden and probably Germany fall into this category. But a sizeable group of countries will hold referendums in 2005.

Spain, which will vote first in February, should be unproblematic for the pro-constitution camp. It is a country that has done well out of the EU and which seems to be in a mood to re-assert its European credentials, after the withdrawal of Spanish troops from Iraq. The Netherlands is likely to be next to vote in the spring. As founder members of the EU and archetypal "good Europeans", the Dutch would also normally be regarded as a safe bet. But a new strain of populism entered Dutch politics with the emergence of Pim Fortuyn, a flamboyant anti-immigration campaigner who was assassinated in 2002. The Dutch also dislike the fact that they pay more into the EU than anyone else. If, as seems likely, the EU starts entry negotiations with Turkey in 2005, that could also damage the Union's image in the Netherlands, where Muslim immigration is a very sensitive issue. All the ingredients for an upset seem to be there. But the country's entire establishment is pushing for approval of the constitution and that—allied with traditional Dutch pro-European sentiment—should still be enough to secure a Yes.

> A No in a big country like Britain or, particularly, France, which has been so central to the European project, might doom the constitution

The real shocks could come in France and Poland. The Poles lose voting power in the proposed constitution and the Catholic Church—a powerful force in Poland—has expressed unhappiness with the text's failure to refer to Europe's Christian heritage. But the mood could change. Polish farmers will begin to receive generous payments from Brussels at the beginning of 2005, which could turn opinion around in a section of the population that has traditionally been most hostile to the EU. By contrast, the French seem to be increasingly disillusioned with the Union. The enlargement of the EU ▶

2005

The European Carbon Market is scheduled to open in January, allowing for the trade of carbon-dioxide emissions credits.

Gideon Rachman: Brussels correspondent, *The Economist*

Exclusive! The British press is different

Charles Grant

A preview of the referendum coverage

Many countries will vote on Europe's new constitution. To judge from the opinion polls, only in Britain does a No seem nigh certain. Could that have something to do with the peculiarities of the British press?

In most EU countries the mainstream newspapers tend to be pro-European or without strong views on the EU. In the Netherlands, for example (no longer quite the Europhile country it once was), leading papers such as *VolksKrant* and *NRC Handelsblad* will back the treaty. The *Telegraaf*, more populist and right-leaning, may be more critical. In France the hard left opposes the treaty on the ground that it enshrines "liberal" economic values, and the far right because it supposedly weakens national sovereignty. But the mainstream papers (*Libération*, *Le Monde* and *Le Figaro*) will support the constitution.

If Italy holds a popular vote, all the papers are likely to back the treaty, bar *La Padania* (run by the populist Northern League) and *Liberazione* (run by hardline communists). Germany's right-leaning broadsheets, such as *Süddeutsche Zeitung*, and its left-leaning ones, such as *Frankfurter Allgemeine Zeitung*, would back the constitution. So would *Bild*, the only German tabloid.

In Poland there may be less of a media consensus in favour of a Yes. Traditionally, Polish newspapers do not urge their readers to vote a particular way, but the tone of their commentary on the treaty is likely to be unenthusiastic and sometimes negative. That more critical tone, however, will have little in common with the feisty, fantastical coverage of the treaty in the British press.

Of the 30m Britons who read a daily, about a quarter read papers which, though broadly pro-European, print much that criticises the EU. The remaining three-quarters read papers that are unremittingly hostile to France, Germany and "Brussels". This camp includes broadsheets as well as tabloids: *The Times* and the *Daily Telegraph* virtually never print an opinion piece that presents the EU in a favourable light.

A flavour of the *Sun*'s likely style during the referendum campaign can be gleaned from its already published "Guide to the EU constitution": "Our army will have to follow EU orders"; "We will be ordered what to say at the UN: the new EU foreign minister will speak for Britain at the Security Council"; "We will lose control of our borders and have no say in who enters the country." There is no truth in any of those statements: all armies will remain under national control; the EU foreign minister will not be able to speak for Britain unless every country (including Britain) first signs up to a common policy; and Britain has an opt-out from EU policies on borders.

British journalists get away with such factual inaccuracies because editors and proprietors encourage them, and because they face no sanction. Whatever the rights and wrongs of the constitutional treaty (*The Economist* has argued that it belongs in the dustbin), no fair-minded person can claim that the British press will cover the referendum in an even-handed way. Eurosceptics can justly argue that in other EU countries the media will lean towards the treaty. But the bias of the continental papers will lack the strident, visceral and mendacious style of the British press. □

Charles Grant: director, Centre for European Reform

to 25 countries in 2004 has made it harder for France to assert its leadership role in Europe. The French are morose about the decline of their influence in Brussels and the rise of English as the EU's working language.

In France—as in the Netherlands and Poland—the odds still probably narrowly favour a Yes vote. But if something went wrong in any of those countries (or in the referendum expected in 2006 in Britain, where the odds are strongly on a No), the EU would face a crisis. Legally, the constitution cannot come into force unless all 25 countries ratify it. A small country could probably be forced to vote again. But a No in a big country like Britain or, particularly, France, which has been so central to the European project, might doom the constitution. Technically, that would simply mean that the EU would be run according to the existing rule book. But politically it would be a grievous blow.

The steady stream of referendums will make 2005 a nervous year for the EU. But other business will go on. The new European Commission, led by José Manuel Barroso, a former Portuguese prime minister, will be settling in after its baptism of fire at the hands of the European Parliament. Mr Barroso will try to restore confidence and morale in an institution that has suffered from two successive weak presidencies.

A big test for Mr Barroso may come in March, when he will have to preside over an EU summit charged with the mid-term review of the EU's Lisbon agenda—a piece of jargon that refers to the Union's efforts to drive through economic reform and raise growth rates. In 2000 EU leaders meeting in Lisbon promised to make Europe "the world's most competitive knowledge-based economy by 2010". That pledge has looked increasingly ludicrous with the passing years, as European economic growth has consistently lagged behind that of America and emerging Asia. Those leaders, like Germany's Gerhard Schröder, who have attempted to push through difficult economic reforms have suffered near-calamitous political consequences.

Mr Barroso must find ways of reinvigorating the economic-reform process, while retaining the confidence of big member-states like France and Germany that already suspect him of being a doctrinaire liberal. By taking personal charge of the Lisbon process, Mr Barroso has shown that he intends to step up to the challenge. A reinvigorated drive for economic reform and a series of successful referendums would mark out 2005 as a very good year for the European Union. □

NO
KRUG
NO
THANKS
KRUG CHAMPAGNE, REIMS, FRANCE

Jacques v Nicolas

Sophie Pedder *PARIS*

France decides, Europe watches

Two choices loom in France in 2005 and the outcomes will resonate across the continent. One is a referendum on the European Union's constitution. The other is broader: an intensified power struggle on the political right between President Jacques Chirac and Nicolas Sarkozy, his ruling party's new head. A rejection of the constitution by France, a founding member and architect of the EU, would be dramatic for all of Europe. And France's battle of ideas about its future, embodied by the Chirac-Sarkozy tussle, reflects a wider European debate between leaders whose instincts lie in the tradition of Franco-German tutelage and the continental social model, and an economically liberal, more Atlantic-leaning generation.

Sophie Pedder: France correspondent, *The Economist*

France plans to hold its referendum in the autumn, though it could be brought forward. Mr Chirac will push hard for approval and should have Mr Sarkozy's support. But in 1992 the French said Yes to the Maastricht treaty by a wafer-thin 51%. Low morale and disillusionment with the centre-right government will confuse the vote. So will widespread French unease prompted by the EU's enlargement: over the drift of industrial jobs to lower-cost new members, the possibility of Turkish entry and the waning of French influence.

Furthermore, the opposition Socialist Party, which leads in the polls and is traditionally Europhile, is sharply divided on the issue. The referendum has opened up a parallel power struggle on the left. This pits François Hollande, the party's boss (in favour), against Laurent Fabius, his number two (against). The vote will probably determine whether either of these two emerges as a favourite for the 2007 presidential election. In short, the campaign will be hard and the outcome close.

France's less explicit choice in 2005 is between two competing visions on the political right, embodied by the 73-year-old Mr Chirac and his chief rival, Mr Sarkozy, who turns 50 in January. The year ahead will bring an uncomfortable form of cohabitation between the head of state and the head of his ruling party. Whether Mr Sarkozy can sustain his popularity in his new job will be an early guide to whether Mr Chirac will stand for a third presidential term.

Mr Chirac's idea of France is rooted in Gaullism, republicanism and tradition. He advocates a Europe that counterbalances American power in a "multi-polar" world and in which the Franco-German axis maintains French influence. A politician of the right, he nonetheless favours France's "social model", with both its high costs and high protections. He defends the French tradition of integration, based on republican principles of equal treatment and *laïcité* (secularism).

Mr Sarkozy, by contrast, presents himself as a ▶

Spantastic

Good news if you want to zoom through south-west France

The first people to walk across Norman Foster's Millennium Bridge in London complained of seasickness. The bridge looked great but it swayed like a tipsy teenager in stilettos. No matter. The French government soon commissioned Lord Foster to design the highest bridge in the world: the Millau Viaduct, which is due to open in January 2005.

The bridge crosses the Tarn river near Millau, cutting 100km (60 miles) off the trip between Paris and Barcelona. Its long, curvy swish disguises its vertical scale. Its tallest column rises nearly 340 metres above the gorge. Locals hope it will become a tourist attraction like the Eiffel Tower (a mere 300 metres high) or the Pont du Gard (49 metres). □

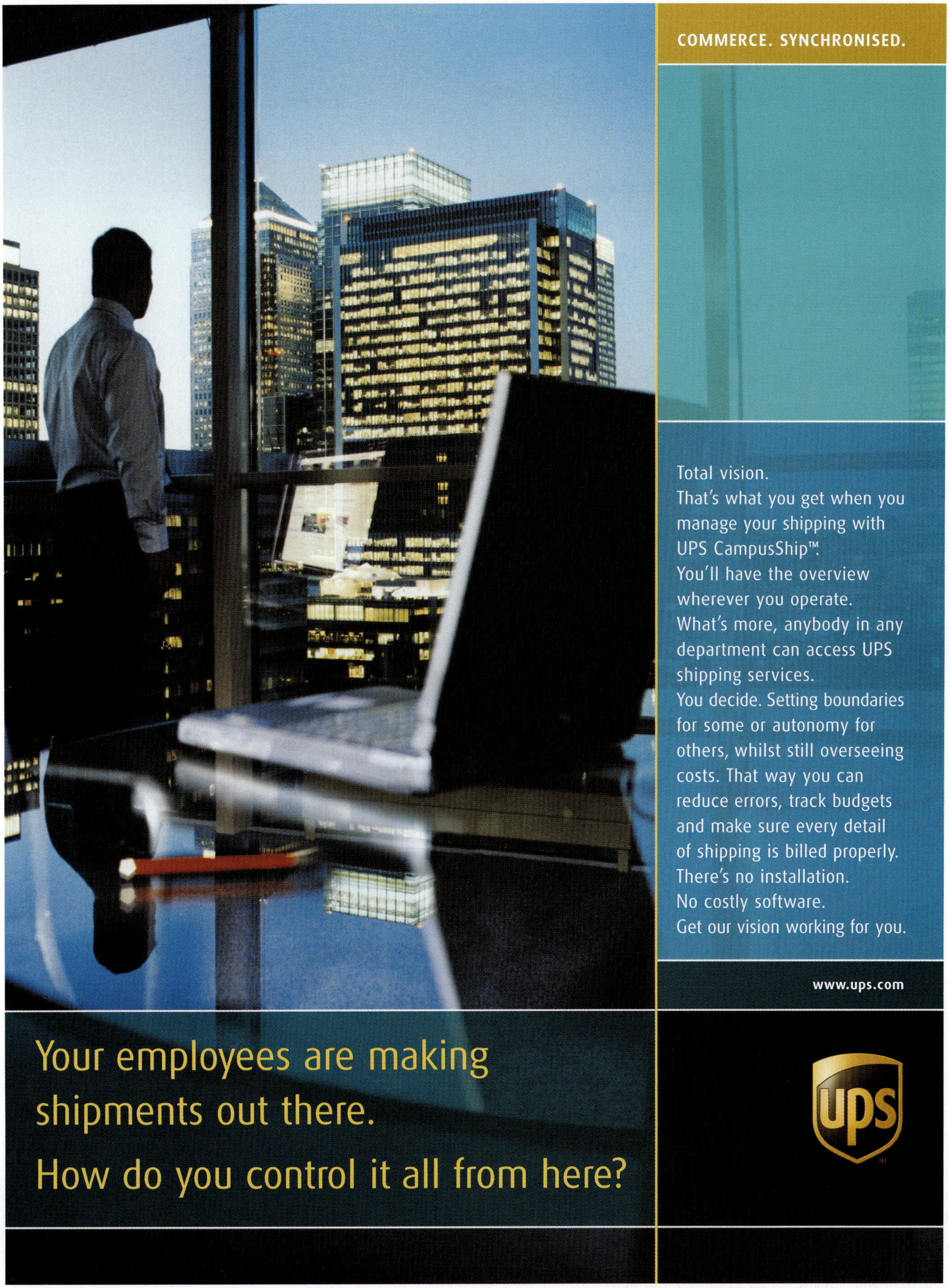
COMMERCE. SYNCHRONISED.
Total vision.
That's what you get when you manage your shipping with UPS CampusShip™.
You'll have the overview wherever you operate.
What's more, anybody in any department can access UPS shipping services.
You decide. Setting boundaries for some or autonomy for others, whilst still overseeing costs. That way you can reduce errors, track budgets and make sure every detail of shipping is billed properly.
There's no installation.
No costly software.
Get our vision working for you.
www.ups.com
Your employees are making shipments out there.
How do you control it all from here?
ups

moderniser. To refresh the ruling party, the Union for a Popular Movement, he will draw inspiration for both ideas and style from Tony Blair's New Labour in Britain and Spain's People's Party. He is less attached to the Franco-German relationship, keener on a Group of Five that embraces Britain, Italy and Spain, as well as on a less confrontational approach to America. He will advocate reforms to promote entrepreneurship, job creation and American-style social mobility. He will be careful, however, to temper his calls for economic liberalism—fewer taxes, more deregulation—with more populist proposals, to protect his broader electoral chances.

Mr Sarkozy uncannily resembles Mr Chirac in his early, energetic days, but his appeal relies on differentiating himself from the president. This will bring awkward clashes with the government and will marginalise the already weak prime minister, Jean-Pierre Raffarin. Mr Chirac may well try to restore authority by replacing him. The most likely successor is Dominique de Villepin, the interior minister and former foreign minister.

Given this awkward power struggle, policymaking will be uncertain and reform may well stall. An economic upturn will relieve the pressure on belt-tightening in government. GDP growth could reach 2.5%—though unemployment will remain above 9%. The government has pledged to bring its budget deficit down to 2.9%, just below the EU's 3% limit. But the consensus-seeking Mr Chirac is likely to press for more spending, not less. After partial reforms of state pensions (in 2003) and of health insurance (in 2004), school reform is promised in 2005, to modernise the curriculum and improve standards. There will be an effort to guarantee minimum public services during strikes. The 35-hour-week rules may be relaxed a bit. Electricité de France will be partly floated.

> Never underestimate Mr Chirac, France's great political survivor

France's relations with the Muslim world will preoccupy minds, both at home and abroad. Mr Chirac is unlikely to soften his refusal to send troops to Iraq, preferring to limit assistance to debt relief and military training outside the country. He will lean on a Russian-German-Spanish anti-war alliance, stressing solidarity in the face of new Islamic terror threats. At home, there will be tense elections in April to the French Council of the Muslim Faith, an official body. Dalil Boubakeur, its moderate leader, was nominated and—under current rules—would probably lose to one of the harder-talking Islamists. Indeed, Mr Boubakeur may decide not to stand. Controversy about religious expression in schools and public institutions will remain fierce.

In a year of such uncertainty, there is always a possibility that Mr Chirac might spring a surprise. If another European country rejects the constitution first, will he use this pretext to cancel France's referendum? If he holds it and France votes No, will he dissolve parliament? Mr Chirac unexpectedly did just that in 1997, ushering in—to his dismay—a Socialist government. But disaffection with its rule led ultimately to his re-election as president. Never underestimate Mr Chirac, France's great political survivor. □

Germany on the mend

Ludwig Siegele *BERLIN*

At last, it gets serious about taking the tablets

Is Germany going the way of Japan, which spent a decade in the doldrums, or even Argentina, which was once the world's fifth-largest economy? A distant observer might get that impression, given all the bad news coming from Europe's biggest economy recently: slow growth, high unemployment, record budget deficits, mass protest rallies. Unemployment is hovering around 4.5m, the pace of reform is still too slow and, particularly in the country's eastern part, reform's losers are taking to the streets.

Yet in 2005 the sick man of Europe, as Germany is now regularly called, will at last begin its recovery. The package of liberalising reforms called Agenda 2010 appears to be working and there are increasing signs of a return to growth. Even so, it is unlikely that this will be enough to revive Gerhard Schröder's chancellorship.

2005

The Frauenkirche, a church largely destroyed in the bombing of Dresden during the second world war, will be re-consecrated in October.

Although Agenda 2010 is not quite the "biggest package of changes in post-war German history", as Mr Schröder claims, it is a respectable start. First on the list of reforms was health care, where costs were spiralling out of control. Although Germans were up in arms to begin with, the treatment has worked surprisingly well: Germany's statutory health-insurance firms are again profitable. Health care will again be on the political agenda in 2005, with a heated debate about how to reform the antiquated funding system of statutory health insurers, which has become a crippling tax on labour. The debate is unlikely to yield any tangible results before the next general election in 2006.

But an equally important overhaul will come into effect in January 2005: the controversial labour-market reform, called Hartz IV. The long-term unemployed will now receive a flat-rate benefit, means-tested and paid only to those who seek work seriously. The idea is to penalise the unemployed if they are not really look-

Ludwig Siegele: Germany correspondent, *The Economist*

Hurry up before someone else takes it

ing for a new job, but also to support them to find one. The threat is already having an impact. Even before the measures come into effect, employers report a sharp increase in applications for vacant jobs.

What is more, companies are deregulating the labour market from the bottom up. First Siemens, then DaimlerChrysler used the threat of relocating production to cheaper places, such as eastern Europe, to get trade unions to agree to longer working hours and cuts in fringe benefits. Smaller companies will follow suit in 2005.

Germany is proving that it is reformable—and could once again become formidable

None of this will help much to reduce unemployment if growth doesn't return. Fortunately, forecasters now expect the economy to expand by about 2% in 2005, albeit driven mostly by exports. This will also help Germany's government to stop the deterioration of its finances, although not enough to get below the 3% deficit limit of the EU's stability and growth pact.

Despite the good news (and some better-than-expected election results), Mr Schröder will have to fight for survival in 2005, which is why he won't tackle further reforms in the coming year. A crucial date will be May 22nd, when elections will be held in North Rhine-Westphalia, Germany's most populous state and the Social Democrats' main power base. A victory for the Christian Democrats would turn Mr Schröder into a lame duck.

Yet not all is well for the conservatives: many voters no longer see them as a better alternative. The opposition still has to come up with a candidate for chancellor and a coherent programme. Angela Merkel, the chairwoman of the Christian Democrats, has not been successful in getting her colleagues, especially those from the Bavarian Christian Social Union, to sign up to her radical reform proposals, which have earned her the nickname "Maggie" (as in Thatcher).

Still, a compromise programme, which the conservatives will settle on by the end of 2005, will be more far-reaching than Mr Schröder's Agenda 2010. And it would be easier for a Chancellor Merkel to push through because her party holds a majority in the upper house. Albeit belatedly, Germany is proving that it is reformable—and could once again become formidable. □

The Turks are coming

John Peet

A big Muslim country knocks at the EU's door

Here is an oddity. The most important country for the European Union in 2005 will be one that is not even in the club. The country is Turkey. In 2005 the EU is set to open negotiations on Turkish membership.

Since its origins in the 1950s, when the European project embraced just six countries (France, West Germany, Italy and the Benelux trio), it has expanded on five separate occasions, to reach today's membership of 25. The most dramatic and biggest enlargement came in 2004, when the EU took in eight ex-communist countries, plus Cyprus and Malta. Yet the membership talks with Turkey will be the most momentous of them all.

That is partly because Turkey is so big. Already it has over 70m people, and its population is growing: soon after 2015 it will overtake Germany, so it could become the most populous country in the Union. Turkey is poor, with a GDP per person less than a third of the average for the EU 25. That will feed fears of large-scale

John Peet: Europe editor, *The Economist*

THE NORDIC COUNTRIES *FORECAST*

If you thought the four Nordic countries—Denmark, Norway, Finland and Sweden—were boringly similar, think again. Yes, all are prosperous places that favour sensible, consensus politics (albeit with hard-fought elections in Denmark and Norway in 2005). But connoisseurs will delight in the differences between them.

Take cars. The thrill-seeking Danes have enjoyed driving at 130kph (80mph) on motorways since April 2004, and will be importing SUVs and other gas-guzzling vehicles in 2005 in large numbers. The environmentally conscious Swedes, despite pleas from their domestic producer, Volvo, are expected to levy a tax on drivers of SUVs, which could add SKr6,500 ($8,100) to the price of an XC90, the country's biggest single export.

Or take alcohol. With alcohol available only in state-controlled outlets in Norway and Sweden, Denmark's liberal licensing laws have always acted as a magnet for Norwegians and Swedes. In 2005 the Swedes will see taxes on distilled spirits reduced by up to 40%, in response to pressure from the state alcohol monopoly, Systembolaget, which complained that domestic alcohol sales plummeted following tax reductions in Denmark in 2003 and Finland in 2004. In Norway, however, the teetotal prime minister, Kjell Magne Bondevik, has flatly refused to negotiate any cuts in liquor taxes, despite the fact that the border trade with both Sweden (where prices are still lower than in Norway) and Finland will be a drain in 2005.

Norway, thanks to its oil riches, can afford to remain aloof from the other Nordics. Having twice rejected EU membership, the Norwegians will be watching in wonder as the Danes narrowly reject the European Union's new constitution in a referendum in 2005, while the Swedish government, prudently, will have the constitution passed by parliament. The Finns, ever the good pupils in Europe, will also opt for ratification by parliament.

GDP GROWTH (%)	2003	2004	2005
Denmark	0.5	2.6	2.5
Norway	0.3	3.1	3.0
Sweden	1.7	3.3	2.7
Finland	2.1	3.1	3.0
Iceland	4.3	4.8	5.0

Economist Intelligence Unit

2005

Paris is favourite to win the race to host the 2012 Olympics. But London, Madrid and New York are also in the running. The International Olympic Committee will announce the winner in July.

migration into western Europe. Turkey is also heavily agricultural, so it could easily become a ruinous drain on Europe's lavish common agricultural policy, as well as on regional aid.

Yet it is not matters of money that most concern Europe's citizens and governments. After all, it will take at least ten years, after membership talks have begun, before Turkey can actually join the EU. The bigger worry now is that Turkey has a long history of instability, plus a dreadful record of human-rights abuses; and, even more important, that it is a Muslim country.

The government of Recep Tayyip Erdogan's Justice and Development (AK) party has gone a long way to putting right the first set of objections. The economy has been growing strongly, and the AK's big parliamentary majority has produced political stability. Since the government now has its sights set firmly on EU membership, it has also been pushing through a sweeping series of reforms. Although there may be more hiccups over such matters as a new penal code, women's rights and the position of the Kurds, these changes ought to give the membership talks a fair wind.

But they do not deal with the second big concern, which is Islam. Most Europeans are determinedly secular nowadays, and they are also aware that as many as 12m Muslims are already citizens of EU member-countries, including at least 3m Turks. There is less talk than there once was of Europe being a Christian club.

Even so, the idea of the biggest EU member being a Muslim country that borders Iraq, Iran and Syria makes many Europeans queasy. As membership talks get under way, more people will raise their voices against the whole notion of letting Turkey in. Some will follow the French in proposing to hold national referendums to approve Turkish entry, as a way of keeping the country out.

Yet the arguments voiced in favour of Turkish membership will also be strong. Many will be heard from far beyond Europe. America is keenly interested in Turkey's prospective EU membership. This partly reflects the country's strategic position as a member of NATO, located in the eastern Mediterranean and bordering the Black Sea. America is also eager to foster the idea that Muslim countries can be liberal democracies.

More pointedly, the Americans—and many Europeans, notably the British—fear that if the Union were to say no to Turkey on the ground that it is Muslim, the rest of the Islamic world would see this as a slap in the face for all of Islam. It would be seized on by those who believe that a clash of civilisations is inevitable after

> America would see a rejection of Turkey as a big setback in the war on terrorism

September 11th 2001. America would see a rejection of Turkey as a big setback in the war on terrorism.

In fact, other Muslim countries, especially in the Middle East, do not see Turkey as a model. It is non-Arab, it is pro-Israel and, to many, it represents the remnants of the colonial Ottoman empire. Yet they would still see any outright rejection of Turkey as an insult. And that is why the Europeans will have no alternative but to begin membership talks—and why they will also eventually have to let Turkey in to their club. □

Spain's new transition

Guillermo de la Dehesa

The going will get tougher for the government

After his surprise election victory in March 2004, Spain's Socialist prime minister, José Luis Rodríguez Zapatero, quickly set about introducing a sharp and popular change of direction. In foreign policy, he organised a quick exit from the war in Iraq (while strongly affirming Spain's determination to fight terrorism), cosied back up to France and Germany and, as a "good European", helped to unblock the European Union's new constitution. At home he promised to work towards equality between the sexes, starting with the appointment of the same number of men and women to his cabinet. New laws addressed punishing domestic violence against women and allowing homosexuals to marry and adopt children. Mr Zapatero also scrapped

Zapatero speaks European

an extravagant river-diversion plan, increased the minimum wage and urged employers and unions to work together to create jobs. His popularity soared.

But in 2005 the going will get tougher for Mr Zapatero. From its economy to its politics, Spain faces a period of transition, for which it is not yet fully prepared. And it could be a bumpy ride.

First, there is the challenge of moving upmarket. For years Spain was able to attract huge flows of foreign investment thanks to its excellent mix of low labour costs and decent productivity. Not any more. That investment is flooding instead to central and eastern Europe and Asia, while Spain is starting to experience an exodus of its manufacturing and services through outsourcing and offshoring. In future the country must compete through the quality of its human capital, its innovation and its research and development. Spain also used to be the preferred destination of European tourists looking for sun and cheap hotels, booze and tobacco; now it needs to upgrade its infrastructure to cater for richer, fussier folk.

Second, Spain's Euro-bonanza is over. Spain was

Guillermo de la Dehesa: chairman, Centre for Economic Policy Research

> Spain will have to learn to compete on its own, without help from Brussels

able to grow faster than the European average mainly because it benefited from large capital inflows in the 1980s through joining the EU, and from a large drop in interest rates in the 1990s through joining the euro. Moreover, it has received more than €100 billion ($125 billion) in EU transfers since its accession in 1986. The Union's new enlargement to the east will present a market opportunity but also a competitive threat: the much poorer new members offer high-skilled and low-cost labour, and they will draw aid money that previously went to Spain, which will become a net contributor to the EU's coffers. So Spain will have to learn to compete on its own, without help from Brussels.

Then there is the matter of immigration. Spain, until recently a net exporter of people, has become a large net importer. Spaniards are living longer and having fewer babies (the birth rate is among the lowest in Europe), and the population is ageing fast. The nation needs to find a reasonable way to accommodate and assimilate hundreds of thousands of immigrants arriving every year from Africa, Latin America and eastern Europe (now 5% of the total population)—particularly demanding for a country that is not used to immigrants and where employment levels are still low.

In domestic politics, the perennial challenge of balancing central and regional government is, if anything, becoming harder. How to accommodate the increasingly strong demands of Basque and Catalan nationalists for more self-government without creating new privileges for them at the cost of the rest of the regions? Not least, Mr Zapatero faces the problem of adapting his generous election pledges (made in a bid to win against all the odds) to the new reality of power. The promised resources for social services, education, housing, health, infrastructure and R&D—among other things—may not be compatible with the government's target of a zero budget deficit.

Still, the economy will grow at a slightly faster pace in 2005 (despite the country's vulnerability to higher oil prices), as demand for Spanish goods picks up elsewhere in Europe. If Mr Zapatero spends his political capital wisely, he can rise to the challenge of Spain's new transition. But his honeymoon may soon be over. □

Enjoy Italy while it lasts

Beppe Severgnini

The country is set to shrink

Italy is getting older, but not wiser. Individuals know, as always, how to tackle the future; the country as a whole doesn't. This will be the issue in 2005. Everything else—Silvio Berlusconi's ego-government, the forthcoming regional elections, the planned (and worrying) overhaul of the constitution, the likely economic doldrums—will pale compared with the difficulty of planning ahead. Population, immigration, innovation, transportation, higher education: wherever the country's future is concerned, Italy seems at a loss.

Take demography. Today the populations in Italy and Britain are similar in size, but the dynamics are different. Italy's population will soon start to shrink. By 2050, according to the UN's "medium" projections, there will be 21m more people in Britain than in Italy. Italy's population loss between 2005 and 2050 will be by far the steepest among big EU countries, according to the UN: 22% against 9% for Spain and 4% for Germany

Beppe Severgnini: columnist, *Corriere della Sera*

BENELUX *FORECAST*

In a European Union still struggling to find a sense of direction with its enlarged membership, the Benelux countries—three of the original six members—have a chance in 2005 to help set a course. The Belgian government of Guy Verhofstadt is probably itself too weak to make much of an impact (under constant threat of being torn apart by a crisis between the Flemish- and French-speaking communities, the latter pressing for almost complete autonomy). But the Netherlands and Luxembourg could play their part, helped by the fact that the Netherlands hands over the agenda-setting EU presidency to Luxembourg for the first half of 2005.

The Netherlands has good relations with Europe-wary Britain (and America) but is also a committed euro member, determined that the euro area's fiscal rules be better observed. It has taken stringent measures of its own to ensure that it is in a position to encourage others to do the same. The Dutch could be among the first to hold a referendum on the EU constitution, probably in March 2005. Despite growing Euro-scepticism in the country and a critical view of how EU institutions are run, the three major Dutch parties favour the constitution and (though not to be taken as given) the Dutch could give it a good start on its uphill trek to ratification by 25 member-states.

The best opportunity for influence, however, will lie with the small Duchy of Luxembourg. Its prime minister, Jean-Claude Juncker, turned down an offer to be president of the European Commission—an offer which showed a recognition of his diplomatic skills—but has been elected as two-year chairman of the euro area finance ministers from January 1st 2005. During Luxembourg's six-month EU presidency, he will have a chance both to forge agreement on a revised euro-area fiscal policy and to narrow the foreign-policy differences in the wider EU.

GDP GROWTH (%)	2003	2004	2005
Belgium	1.1	2.5	2.5
The Netherlands	-0.9	1.4	2.0
Luxembourg	2.1	2.9	3.4

Economist Intelligence Unit

Dear, dazzling Dublin

Getting less gummed-up

Nobody was more intimately acquainted with or eloquently responsive to the grubbiness of Dublin than James Joyce. "Dear, dirty Dublin," he called it. But the great novelist would barely recognise the place if he saw it today. It's not just the turbo-charged economy, the sky-high property market and all the other trappings of rude good health that, in *The World in 2005*'s ranking, make Ireland such a terrific place to live. It is also setting the pace in cleaning up the urban environment.

In 2004 it banned smoking in pubs and outlawed drinking in the street. In 2005 it may well become the first country in the world to introduce a tax on chewing gum.

The government has announced plans for a levy of 10% on every one of the 80m or so packets of chewing gum sold annually in Ireland. The €4m ($5m) this would raise would be used to help fund the cost of cleaning the republic's gum-encrusted streets.

A tax on plastic shopping bags has already been a great success in Ireland. Similar plans are afoot to reduce fast-food packaging and ATM receipts. "Dear, dirty Dublin" may soon be a place you can only read about in books. □

▸ (France and Britain will grow in the same period by 6% and 11% respectively).

These figures are hardly debated in Italy. And even if they were, it is unlikely that Italians would start to make babies because of statistics. The solution could be immigration, but it is a difficult one. History didn't hand Italy a recent imperial past such as Britain's or France's, and its foreign-born population is therefore smaller than in those countries; but geographically Italy is right next door to Africa, the Balkans and the Near East—the poor world's exit routes. Despite a stricter law on immigration, boatloads of desperate people kept coming to southern Italy in 2004—and will do so again in 2005.

Demography is not the only question mark that hangs over life in one of the most pleasant countries in the world. According to the World Economic Forum, Italy has plunged to 47th place in the global-competitiveness league. Spending on research and development is low (1% of GNP compared with an EU average of 1.9%). Few Italians choose scientific careers (5.7 out of every 1,000 people; the EU average is 11.9). More young scientists will leave the country. There are many reasons for this, from academic nepotism to entry salaries that are lower than they were ten years ago.

2005

Work begins on a €5 billion ($6 billion) suspension bridge to join Sicily and mainland Italy.

Uncertainty, and fear of the future, convinced some of the best Italian capitalists to put their money into banks, property, telephones, motorways, airports—which are largely shielded from international competition. Most of them have found ways of living with the prime minister's conflict of interest. In 2005 there won't be much debate about it, but every player will know that the referee can play too, if he so wishes. Over the coming year, public television (Rai) will be partly privatised; terrestrial digital television will start to air *Serie A* soccer games; Rupert Murdoch's satellite operation (Sky Italia) will enter a make-or-break year. The prime minister has a finger—often more than one—in each of these pies.

Even small and medium-sized companies, Italy's economic backbone, seem to be getting worried about the future. For decades, low labour costs, great inventiveness and periodical devaluations of the lira helped to sell the country's products all over the world. "Made in Italy" still sounds nice—but here, too, things are changing. The key word is now *delocalizzazione*: move production abroad. In the past ten years 345,000 jobs left the country, 100,000 from the Veneto region alone. Today more than a third of all Italian companies produce their goods abroad: textiles and shoes in Romania and India, kitchen appliances in Slovakia and Ukraine, air-conditioners in China. Expect this to intensify.

Expect also politicians' calls to locate production

> Expect to meet fewer people in restaurants and on holiday; and to see cautious consumers, at long last

in southern Italy, where unemployment is higher than in the north. This will not happen. It's not only a matter of labour costs or legislation; there is also lack of infrastructure—the *autostrada* between Naples and Reggio Calabria offers the challenge of a post-modern rally—as well as red tape and greedy local authorities. Many educated young southerners are not ready to put up with it, and will do what their uneducated parents and grandparents did: they will leave, seeking jobs in Milan, northern Europe and America.

Italian lifestyle—rightly considered a form of art—will be affected by all these changes. Italy has a new class of *quasi poveri* (nearly poor): people whose salaries are not enough to make ends meet. According to Istat, the official statistical body, 10% of Italians live in poverty (only 4% in Veneto, but 25% in Sicily). Another 8% nationwide are just above that level. So expect to meet fewer people in restaurants and on holiday; and to see cautious consumers, at long last. The only savings in sight are linked to the proposed liberalisation of some professions (accountants, notaries, chemists).

This won't be enough, of course, to cheer up an exhausted nation, which will find consolation in gadgetry (more and better mobile phones), advertising, soccer and television. "Carpe diem," said Horace—who lived in Rome, after all. □

Central Europe's choice

Robert Cottrell *WARSAW*

Mainstream or extreme?

Poland, the biggest country in central Europe, enters 2005 with a general election ahead which could decide its prosperity and stability for the rest of the decade. The ruling socialist government will be coming to the end of its term weak, divided and barely hanging on to power. At the election, pencilled in for May, voters will have to make a big, stark choice about what comes next. They can put their faith in the centre-right and vote for Poland's two conservative parties, Civic Platform and Law and Justice, inviting them to form a coalition which would have all the qualities for ruling well. Or they can throw common sense to the wind and vote for the country's two big populist and Eurosceptical parties—Samoobrona (Self-defence) on the left and the League of Polish Families (LPF) on the right—ensuring that one or the other of them forces its way into the next coalition.

If Samoobrona has a strong position in the next government, it will urge disastrous policies for the economy—cheap loans to farmers, and social welfare schemes even more wasteful than Poland's present ones, paid for by raiding the central bank's reserves. The League of Polish Families stands for Catholicism, nationalism and a hostility to the European Union, which it regards as a vehicle for the German domination of Europe.

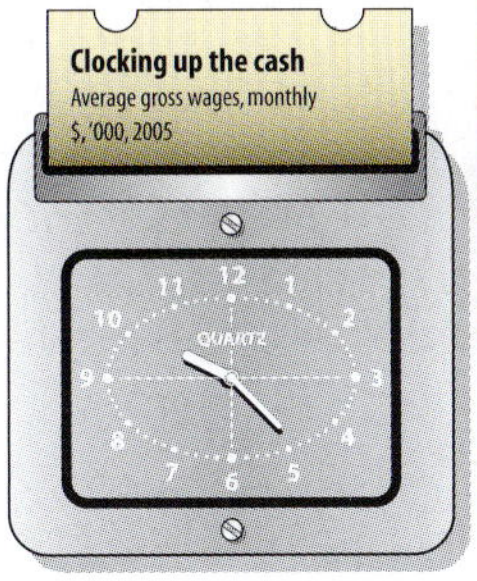

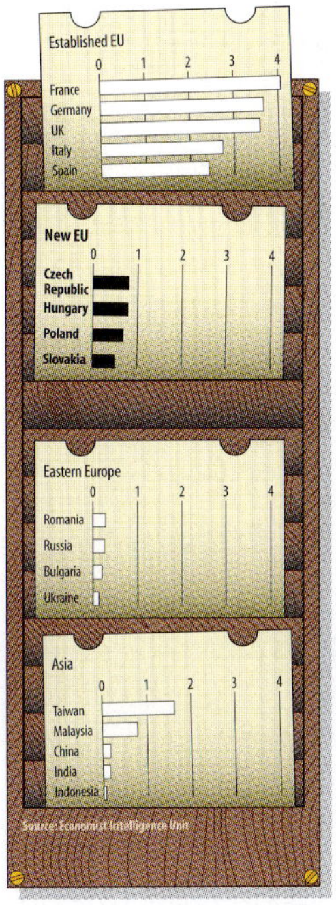

The good news is that the prospect of an election victory for the populists is receding, while the chances of a strong centre-right government are growing. The appeal of Samoobrona and the LPF may have peaked in the spring of 2004, when they were preaching doom and gloom ahead of Poland's EU entry. But entry has proved to be good for Poland in general, and in particular for its farmers, the bedrock of Samoobrona's support. Now Polish farmers are delightedly selling meat and vegetables to Germany and Scandinavia at fancy prices. They are getting subsidy cheques from Brussels. By the time the 2005 election comes round, they will be asking themselves what on earth they were so worried about.

If Poland does get the centre-right government it needs, it will be setting the trend for the region. The Czech Republic's shaky centre-left coalition will have trouble surviving 2005 with its one-seat majority in parliament, and when it falls, the right-wing Civic Democrats look set to replace it. Hungary's struggling Socialist government is more likely to survive the year, but will probably still be the underdog when it confronts the conservative opposition party, Fidesz, in 2006.

Roughly speaking, conservative and populist parties have been gaining ground again in central Europe because the left-wing parties in government have failed to do what they promised. They told voters they could temper the economic reforms required for EU entry while promoting growth and employment, but all they produced was slower growth and budget deficits.

The winners of the region's next round of elections will inherit much better economic conditions. The benefits of EU membership will be feeding through, including access to EU development funds for depressed regions. Foreign inward investment will remain strong, because firms are still discovering that high productivity and low transport costs make central Europe a cheaper manufacturing base even than China for many goods going to EU markets. This should help bring down high unemployment rates among the region's lower-skilled workers, all the more so if governments act to ease rigid labour laws.

The changing national mood means that Poland will be much less likely to reject the EU's proposed constitution in a referendum set for autumn—coinciding ▶

2005

Both football's Champions League and the Eurovision Song Contest will be won for the 50th time. Back in 1956, Real Madrid won the first European Cup (as it was then called) and Lys Assia won the first Eurovision contest for Switzerland, with a song called "Refrain".

Robert Cottrell: central Europe correspondent, *The Economist*

ROMANIA *FORECAST*

Romania faces a watershed year. It will either sign an accession treaty to join the European Union in 2007, or else see its hopes of quick integration into the EU dashed.

Dismissed as a no-hoper in 2000, when it was censured by the European Commission in its annual report on would-be members, Romania is now a contender to join the EU after four years of stability, reform and growth. Yet Romania is still keeping us guessing. Will the former communists, who presided over this turnaround in fortunes, still be in power after the end-2004 elections? And, crucially, with elections distracting the politicians, will the country finish negotiations in time to sign the accession treaty, along with Bulgaria, in 2005?

The new government will have its work cut out to convince Brussels that Romania is ready to join the club. Now that they have seen in a first batch of new joiners from eastern Europe, the EU is wary. It is expected to include a "safeguard clause" in the accession treaty, allowing for delayed entry if membership conditions are not fulfilled.

Bucharest's crane-filled skyline and mushrooming shopping malls reflect heady economic times. GDP will expand by more than 5% in 2005, after 6% growth in 2004. The country is benefiting from the foreign-investment bandwagon rolling across the Balkans, with likely inflows to Romania of more than $2 billion to $3 billion a year.

Booming Romania may be, but that may not be enough. It is still dirt poor, with GDP per head of about $3,700, less than a third of Hungary's level. Romania is also big, with a population of 22m, and not as easy for the EU to absorb as an Estonia or even a Bulgaria. The onus is on Romania to silence the doubters. The main risk is that policy implementation may fall short, especially if there is a fractious coalition government.

KEY INDICATORS	2003	2004	2005
GDP growth (%)	4.9	6.0	5.2
Budget balance (% GDP)	-2.3	-1.6	-2.3
Unemployment (%)	7.2	6.3	6.6
Inflation (%, ave)	15.3	11.8	8.4

Economist Intelligence Unit

2005

EU accession negotiations with Croatia will begin.

with elections for the Polish presidency at which Marek Belka, the country's socialist prime minister from May 2004, may emerge as the favoured candidate to succeed the retiring Alexander Kwasniewski. The EU's other new members also look likely to accept the constitution.

But acceptance of the EU constitution does not mean that the central Europeans will necessarily become even more deferential members of the club. If anything, expect the reverse. As their experience grows, so will their self-confidence. They will become more vocal and argumentative, especially when questions of special interest to them are on the table, such as tax harmonisation, aid budgets, farm subsidies and policy towards Russia and Ukraine. They will become, in other words, even more like the EU's other countries—which will make 2005 a very satisfactory year for them indeed. □

A state of weakness

Dmitri Trenin *MOSCOW*

Russia will be a country under siege

How much is freedom?

The terrorist atrocity at Beslan in September 2004 marked a watershed in Russia, much as September 2001 did in America. There is a perception of the country being under attack and poorly equipped to protect itself. The enemy has been designated as "international terrorism", with a Chechen arch-terrorist, Shamil Basayev, cast in the role of Osama bin Laden. The Russian government proceeded to strengthen homeland security. Abroad, Russia sought recognition of its efforts as part of the global war on terrorism.

Russia's predicament is more difficult than America's. The state is often incompetent, vastly inefficient and hollowed out by corruption. The political system is failing. Its only functioning independent institution is the presidency, which essentially means one-man rule.

The war on terrorism has dramatically exacerbated these deficiencies. Popularly elected regional governors have been turned into presidential appointees. The parliament, which no longer admits independent members, has become a rubber-stamp legislature. The courts' independence has been greatly damaged in the Yukos affair. President Vladimir Putin's first-term "managed democracy" has become unabashed personal rule in the second term: It's the war, stupid!

To defend their specific interests, people will start organising themselves at the grass-roots

Rather than rallying around the flag, Russians feel alienated. Mr Putin's popularity is slipping: he has failed to keep his central promise, to make the country safe.

Geopolitically, Russia is increasingly vulnerable. From the Caspian to the Black Sea, the north Caucasus is boiling. Mr Putin's attempts to stabilise it run up against the usual enemies: rampant corruption, incompetence and crime that lives off the war. In fact, to deal effectively with the challenge of terrorism, the Russian president needs to take on the state apparatus and start reforming it in earnest. He cannot hope to perform this feat without allies and greater reliance on independent institutions. So far his policies have been going in precisely the opposite direction, towards more centralisation and stricter control.

The seemingly all-powerful state remains extremely weak at the level of ordinary citizens. This is exactly where the terrorists strike, exposing the government's impotence. Few Russians doubt that new terrorist attacks will follow.

So, despite continuing economic growth, helped by high oil prices, Mr Putin's vaunted stability is coming to an end. Again, the country faces a fork in the road. It might stumble along a path of xenophobic dictatorship, which will put an end to yet another attempt at modernisation and integration with the advanced world. Or it might develop energies, and leaders, pushing towards more transparency, efficiency and accountability.

The chances of such an outcome are surprisingly good. A significant number of Russians are benefiting from the economic boom. Salaries are rising fast. Property rights are becoming more firmly entrenched. A consumer society is emerging, at least among some Russians. People have become accustomed to choosing among the vast number of products and services now available to them on the market. The country is not democratic, but its people are basically free. And freedom cannot indefinitely be restricted to the economic, cultural and recreational spheres.

Indeed, over-centralisation and lack of accountability at all levels of government are likely to provoke political action of a kind that has so far been absent in Russia. To defend their specific interests, people will start organising themselves at the grass-roots.

Russia in 2005 will be a country under siege. The 60th anniversary of victory in the second world war, known in Russia as the Great Patriotic War, will be used to extol patriotism. Yet the new war which has been imposed on the country demands a much bolder approach. Russia will not be able to fight terrorism effectively—let alone defeat it—unless it remakes the Russian state. □

Dmitri Trenin: senior associate and director of studies, Carnegie Moscow Centre

Wanted: freedom fighters

José María Aznar, former prime minister of Spain, outlines an agenda for Europe's leaders

It is the job of political leaders to try to ensure that the future for the people they represent is safer and better than the present. I would like to share a few thoughts, in the light of my experience in government, on what might be a suitable agenda for European leaders in 2005.

We can be reasonably sure that during the year ahead the main threats to freedom that we have witnessed for some years now will persist. These threats place our security, our economic growth and the prospects for development in large areas of the planet at risk. What can Europe do?

The alliance between the United States and Europe will continue to be fundamental. We must not forget the lessons of Normandy or the fall of the Berlin Wall. In my view, the Atlantic link must be strengthened. And we will need a greater sense of determination than those who wish to eradicate our freedoms.

As it happens, 2005 will be a year of great opportunity when it comes to re-establishing a positive agenda in the Atlantic relationship. In post-election Washington, DC, it will be a time for political renewal. And in Brussels a new European Commission will have begun its work, headed by a fine politician and a firm believer in the Atlantic relationship, José Manuel Durão Barroso.

This offers Europeans and Americans the chance to create a fresh impetus in our fight against terror. Terrorists have demonstrated their willingness to destroy the way of life of free and open societies. And they do so by using all the opportunities that our democratic system concedes to those who wish to blast it away.

> We in Europe should not mistake our enemy. Europe must assume its responsibilities and accept its status as a target for terrorism

Regrettably, among us there are also those who try to justify terror by invoking injustices and humiliations. We must be clear about this, because confused ideas sometimes encourage terrorism. There are no excuses for terrorism. Terrorism simply loathes freedom.

In order to defeat it we must continue to defend our rights with determination, strength and persistence. We must update our laws, strengthen international co-operation and enhance collaboration among our intelligence services. We must not allow any safe havens for terrorists. The elaboration of a universal list of terrorist organisations and the effective pursuit of these groups' sources of finance are tools that we need to develop.

In the fight against terrorism, Iraq and Afghanistan will be the main arenas. It is essential that the United States and its allies should be successful in both these ventures. We in Europe should not mistake our enemy. Europe must assume its responsibilities and accept its status as a target for terrorism. Nobody will win if Iraq and Afghanistan are lost, if it proves impossible to stabilise and democratise these countries. However, Europeans are among those who are liable to lose the most. The United Nations must lend its support in order to ensure that these experiments in freedom and democracy prosper. Iraq and Afghanistan must be a success and serve as an example for other countries in the region.

Terrorists will continue to fight in order to undermine these two exercises in freedom. These groups will seek to influence electoral processes, as we saw in Spain with the atrocities of March 11th 2004, while also attempting to split the international coalition aligned against them. In order to prevent this, the Atlantic community must show determination and a sense of responsibility. Terrorists would like nothing more than to destroy this link. It would be irresponsible to let them do so.

Open for business

Beyond terrorism, Europe faces a second big challenge: increasing its lacklustre economic growth. The European economy is an engine that does not work as it should. Europe has only recently reunified, with ten countries joining the EU in 2004, yet scepticism about greater economic openness is rife. This is happening because political leaders are drawing precisely the wrong conclusions and are failing to introduce the reforms that Europe needs.

Europe needs more dynamic growth. In order to achieve this, we must enhance the region's economic freedom and open up to the outside world. However, powerful forces view these reforms and economic freedom with suspicion. The new European Commission must, as a priority, promote the liberalising Lisbon agenda, to make the European economy more flexible and provide a definitive impetus for the reforms needed to create a genuine single market.

Europe should also look beyond its borders and promote global economic liberalisation. It could play a more active role within the framework of the WTO. It must work alongside the United States in an Atlantic economic region that goes beyond mere trade, one based on liberalisation and openness. This project should also welcome the involvement of other nations.

The opportunities and benefits for all would be only too evident. The coming year would be an ideal moment for the two main economic blocks in the world to boost global economic freedom. Europe and America, both intent on ensuring freedom and economic openness, could be an irresistible force for promoting progress in other regions, especially Latin America and the countries in the southern Mediterranean basin and the Middle East.

In these two tasks—fighting terror and fostering economic freedom—collaboration between the United States and Europe could be decisive. It can help ensure the freedom, security and economic progress of millions of people. □

United States

2005

The 52-storey 7 World Trade Centre is the first new building to be completed on the site of Ground Zero.

When Bush comes to shove

Anne Applebaum *WASHINGTON, DC*

A man with a mandate—and a divided nation

In recent American history, it has been a rare president whose second term in office resembled his first four years. George Bush, who won his second term after a hard-fought and bitter election, is unlikely to break that rule. Historically, many presidents have lost their way in the second term, grown tired and started to drift. But after the anger of the campaign, and the criticism heaped upon Mr Bush from Americans and foreigners alike, something like the opposite may well occur. Mr Bush and his administration are in fact much more likely to interpret the result as a mandate for their policies, and to begin prosecuting their ideas with even greater vigour now that re-election is not something they have to worry about any more. Yet to govern effectively, whether at home or abroad, Mr Bush will need to reach out across divides that have become all too deep.

> Central to Mr Bush's second term will be an overhaul of the intelligence services and the armed forces, with the aim of better preparing the country to fight the war on terrorism

Will he? There is certainly a danger of over-confidence. The return of a Republican Congress with enlarged majorities in both the House and the Senate will reinforce the self-belief of the White House. If anything, having Republicans in control of both the executive office and the legislature will contribute to the Bush administration's penchant for the expansion of government, since neither is particularly inclined to restrain the spending ambitions of the other. Expect this big spending, and the ballooning deficit, to lead to much louder criticism from some rebellious Republicans in Congress and from conservative think-tanks.

Central to Mr Bush's second term will be an overhaul of the intelligence services and the armed forces, with the aim of better preparing the country to fight the war on terrorism. Some idea of what is to come for the armed forces has already been announced: the shrinking of bases in western Europe and South Korea; the opening of newer, smaller bases containing more flexible forces elsewhere; the creation of more mobile "special forces" better able to combat failed states, rogue states and terrorists; the elimination of some of the infantry who were prepared to fight a European tank battle against the Soviet Union.

One of the results of this downscaling of operations, which is likely to accelerate in 2005, may be a further cooling of relations between America and traditional allies like Germany and South Korea, as the sense of ▸

Anne Applebaum: columnist, *Washington Post*

mutual dependence that bound these nations together grows dimmer. Administration officials spoke privately, in the weeks before the election, of launching a campaign to renew alliances, particularly in Europe, in the election's aftermath. But this is not an administration with much intuitive sympathy for the needs and views of foreigners—even Britons or Poles. The best that can be hoped for is a wary pragmatism on all sides.

While there will be changes among the top cabinet officers, some of the deep divides that have hampered foreign policy over the past four years—between the Pentagon, the State Department and the White House—will remain. The internal argument between pragmatists and those who advocate various forms of "regime change" will make it difficult for the president to carve out a clear policy on Iran or North Korea, whose nuclear plans will be a focus of renewed attention in 2005. The overhaul of the intelligence bureaucracy, mandated by Congress, could also prove a distraction.

Domestically, the president will push for entitlement reforms. In 2005, as in every previous year of his presidency, some of his administration will try hard to put Social Security reform on the agenda, in particular the creation of individual retirement accounts. It's a debate that could easily get bogged down in congressional wrangling, and will not be resolved quickly. But it is something the president has intended to do since he was first elected and he may feel, given his new mandate, that this is the time to throw his full weight behind it.

Simultaneously, there will be efforts to press forward on tax reform and on measures to control the costs of health care. The administration will push its health savings accounts, a financial change which could in the long term have a big impact on how both companies and consumers pay for health care. The debate on the importing of prescription drugs from Canada will continue and is likely to result in the legalisation of the practice: political opposition is melting in the face of overwhelming popular support. Paradoxically, the new Medicare drug benefit, scheduled to begin in 2005, will intensify debate about the cost of drugs, as seniors struggle to understand the complex entitlement.

In the wider culture, the re-election of Mr Bush could have a profound effect on his many opponents. Expect a backlash against his social agenda: a further, louder push for the right to gay marriage, protests over judicial appointments, protests from civil-liberties activists. Arguments will rage within the Democratic Party over its future direction, and the battle to be the party's presidential candidate in 2008 will already be on (with Hillary Clinton an early favourite). The re-election of Mr Bush will confirm many Americans' perception that they live in a divided country.

The divide could grow into a chasm if there is a major increase in the number of American deaths in Iraq. As long as the insurgents there attack mainly Iraqi targets, popular opposition to the war will remain muted. But large numbers of American deaths could help anti-war sentiment spread out of big cities and campuses into the rest of the country. A major national debate on America's presence in Iraq could consume enormous amounts of political energy, curtailing Mr Bush's ability to push his domestic agenda. It hasn't happened yet but it cannot be ruled out. □

Patchy progress

Zanny Minton-Beddoes *WASHINGTON, DC*

America's economy will feel sluggish, but will be heading in the right direction

Economists will begin 2005 worrying about how long America's latest soft patch will last. The combination of higher oil prices and still-sluggish labour markets will constrain consumers' capacity to spend. If the housing market wobbles or the dollar suddenly weakens, that soft patch could become a more serious slowdown.

America's consumers—whose spending accounts for almost 70% of GDP—have repeatedly confounded pessimists. During the past three years their spending has been bolstered by lower interest rates and rising house prices, as well as tax cuts. As a result, the household saving rate is at a record low and debt-service ratios are near record highs.

No one doubts that over the medium-term saving rates need to rise substantially. One estimate from economists at Goldman Sachs suggests that household saving rates need to go from 1% of disposable income to 10%. That kind of adjustment will not occur overnight, but it will at least begin in 2005 as a weaker housing market, in particular, removes consumers' painless substitute for saving. Even a modest shift by Americans towards higher saving will have a big impact on consumer spending.

At the same time, consumers will feel a hit from higher oil prices, at least in the early part of 2005. The $50-plus per barrel in late 2004 will translate into more expensive heating oil and higher prices at the petrol pumps over subsequent months. Both will curb consumers' ability to spend elsewhere.

Nor will income from wages and salaries be strong enough to make up for the oil-price shock. That is because the jobs market will remain unusually slack in 2005. Throughout this recovery, America's labour market has perplexed economists: job losses continued for almost two years after the recession officially ended

2005

Retailers in America and Canada will have to join their European counterparts and introduce a 13-digit bar code, replacing the 12-digit Universal Product Code (UPC) that has been used since the 1970s.

Zanny Minton-Beddoes: Washington correspondent, *The Economist*

Flagging up trouble

Personal saving rate

% of personal disposable income

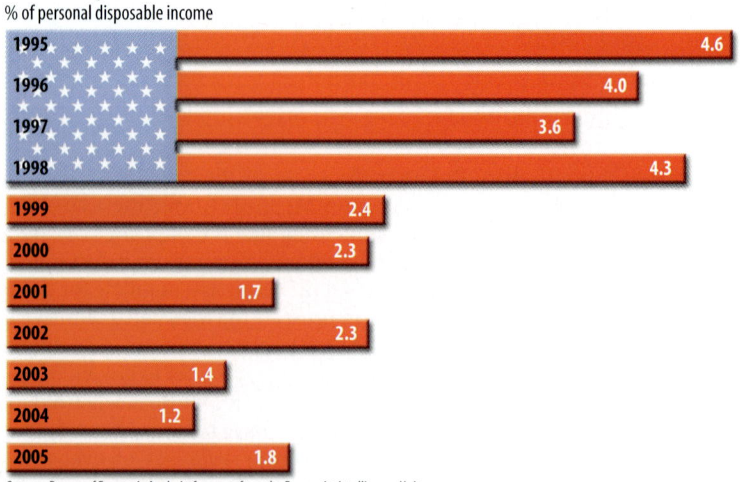

Sources: Bureau of Economic Analysis; forecasts from the Economist Intelligence Unit

Dinosaurs in the Ozarks

Suzi Parker *EUREKA SPRINGS*

Courtesy of the Museum of Earth History

Were dinosaurs in the Bible or not? The Museum of Earth History, which opens in April 2005 in the quirky hamlet of Eureka Springs, Arkansas, will attempt to address this question. The museum will be the only one in the United States where the Earth's history is presented in a literal biblical way.

Funded in part by Oklahoma's Creation Truth Foundation, the museum will display nine full-sized dinosaur-skeleton replicas and propose the creationist theory that a pair of dinosaurs was on Noah's ark. Most scientists contend that dinosaurs became extinct millions of years before man existed. Not the museum's founders. They insist that the confusion lies in the translation of the Hebrew word meaning "great lizard". That word is found throughout the Old Testament.

If a museum of this sort is to open, no better place for it exists. Before Mel Gibson's "The Passion of the Christ" became a blockbuster film, the annual Great Passion Play in this tiny Ozark hamlet, known for its new-age healing waters and arty citizenry, attracted thousands of people from around the world. The two-hour outdoor drama, launched in 1968 to tell the story of Christ from crucifixion to ascension, is overlooked by a 67-foot ghostly white Christ of the Ozarks statue atop a mountain.

For the past few years, the Elna M. Smith Foundation has created a virtual-reality Christian park, complete with a tram tour of the 50-acre (20-hectare) New Holy Land, a 6,000-volume Bible museum, a sacred-arts centre with ninth-century art and, oddly, a large section of the Berlin Wall. The new museum will draw an eager audience hungry for another slant on the bestselling book of all time. □

Suzi Parker: journalist and author of "Sex in the South" (Justin, Charles)

in November 2001. And although the economy began adding new jobs from September 2003, the pace has barely been fast enough to keep up with new entrants to the labour force. High productivity growth enabled firms to produce more without adding new workers. In addition, the weakness of the labour market kept wage growth sluggish.

That picture will change somewhat in 2005 as productivity growth disappoints. Even in 2004 the acceleration in output per worker slowed as firms reached the limit of their post-bubble cost-cutting. Although America's trend rate of productivity growth remains well above historical norms, productivity in 2005 will grow much more slowly than it has been doing of late. Lower productivity growth means that even modest increases in output will translate into more jobs. The unemployment rate is likely to hold steady at around 5.4% for much of the year. But at the same time slower productivity growth will make it harder for firms to absorb wage costs—and keep the pressure on the Federal Reserve to tighten monetary policy.

Steering monetary policy will be tricky in 2005. The Fed will start the year with short-term rates at or just above 2%: still extremely low by historical standards. The Fed's goal will be to continue raising short-term rates towards a more neutral level in a series of small increments.

That strategy will come under pressure from several sides. With output growth slacking and consumers wobbly, there will be a case for slowing the pace of monetary tightening. But slower productivity growth will raise the risk that overly loose monetary policy translates into higher inflation. Given that core-inflation levels are still at 2%, the Fed has some wiggle room. But if higher oil prices feed through into bigger jumps in core consumer prices, the pressure to raise rates more quickly will increase.

The central bankers' task will be made even tougher by the behaviour of the dollar—probably the biggest wild card for the economy in 2005. With America's current-account deficit close to 6% of GDP and rising, downward pressure on the dollar will mount. The greenback will end 2005 significantly weaker than it began it.

> The Fed's goal will be to continue raising short-term rates to a more neutral level in a series of small increments

Despite the enormity of its external imbalance, the odds are that America will still pull off an orderly, gradual dollar correction. Provided that growth in the rest of the world is not knocked too hard by higher oil prices, America could begin to unwind its enormous imbalances without too much pain during 2005. Higher exports could help make up for slower consumer spending. With GDP growing at just over 3%, the economy will certainly feel sluggish. But at least it will be heading in the right direction. □

Hollywood's digital moment

John Andrews *LOS ANGELES*

A welcome revolution

2005

Baseball, a national pastime, returns to Washington, DC, after a 33-year absence. The Expos, a failed Montreal club, will relocate (under a new name) in time for the start of the season in the spring.

Ignore the paparazzi-thronged Academy Awards on February 27th. Of course Nicole Kidman's latest Oscars dress will grab the headlines. But behind the headlines the important story for the movie-industry in 2005 will be the long-awaited switch from delicate, perishable 35mm film to the computerised world of digital bits and bytes. "Switch" is actually the wrong word. It costs more than $100,000 to convert a cinema to digital projection—which means the world's movie-houses are not all about to install digital projectors overnight. But with cinemas around the world, from Britain to China, making the change, digital advocates can talk legitimately of 2005 as a tipping point in the evolution of film-making. There are presently around 300 digital screens worldwide; by the end of 2005 there will be around 2,000.

Three factors are driving the process. One is the enthusiasm of some of Hollywood's leading film-makers. George Lucas, of "Star Wars" fame, has been preaching the digital message for years. His 2002 movie, "Star Wars: Episode II—Attack of the Clones", was the first to be shot entirely on digital video—even if it then had to be transferred onto 35mm film for most cinemas to show it. Michael Mann used digital cameras to shoot the Oscar-competitive "Collateral", starring Tom Cruise. Andrew Adamson had a huge, digitally made hit for the Dreamworks studio in 2004 with "Shrek 2".

Success will breed success: among the digital releases for 2005 will be "Star Wars: Episode III—Revenge of the Sith"; Warner Brothers will have released "Phantom of the Opera" in time for the new year cinema screens; and in May Dreamworks will release "Madagascar", an animated film in the style of "Shrek 2" (a "Shrek 3" will also be in the works, for release in 2006).

The second factor is money. Making a movie with film can be hundreds of times more expensive than with digital videotape. Shooting multiple takes gobbles up film, and the film has to be processed before it can be viewed. By contrast, digital tape can be edited on the spot and used again and again. The producers of "Attack of the Clones" reckon they spent $16,000 on 220 hours of digital tape; if they had used the same amount of film, it would have cost them $1.8m. Moreover, in the traditional world of film there are other costs to add to the bill: each print of a film costs $1,500—and it deteriorates with scratches and dirt every time it is run through a cinema's projector. With the average movie now costing over $90m to make and market, it is little wonder that the Hollywood studios are so often risk-averse, preferring sequels and copycat films to anything truly original.

Digital advocates can talk legitimately of 2005 as a tipping point in the evolution of film-making

Whether the lower costs of digital film-making will encourage more creativity from the big studios is an open question (after all, they belong to industrial conglomerates where the bottom line counts for more than the artistic élan). What is certain is that the world's independent film-makers will have a better chance to blossom. As Mike Figgis, an Oscar-nominee in 1995 for "Leaving Las Vegas", said at the 2004 Venice International Film Festival: "The future's digital, without a doubt. I f***ing well hope so, because if the economics of production are not in the hands of the artist, I'm not interested in cinema any more."

And the third factor? Quite simply, film is the odd-man-out in the digital world of the media conglomerates that dominate the movie business. It makes sense to hedge the corporate bet on a film by releasing it not just for the cinema screen but also for the DVD player, the TV screen and the video-game—and, in some not too distant future, the hand-held cell-phone or personal organiser. All that can happen more easily if the movie starts off in a digital format.

But while digital cinema will come of age in 2005, it will still have its problems. One, shades of the VHS and Betamax conflict a generation ago, will be a battle between Texas Instruments (the market leader) and Sony over digital-projection technology. In addition, some purists reckon that digital tape will fail to match the nuanced texture of film. ▸

It takes three to tangle

John Andrews: West Coast editor, *The Economist*

The next blockbuster

Nora Rawlinson

2005's bestselling books

What is a publishing "blockbuster"? Whereas perennial brand-name bestsellers hit the lists immediately on release and typically sell 2m copies in nearly no time, true blockbusters are a different matter. They are from previously unknown authors, but once they make the list they hang on for months, eventually selling 9m copies or more. These are the titles that publishers mourn the lack of in subsequent earnings reports.

The greatest example is J.K. Rowling, who put the lie to deeply held publishing beliefs—English children's books do not cross over to America; adults will not read children's books; books that appeal to boys have a small audience. "Harry Potter and the Sorcerer's Stone", re-titled and released in America in 1998 with a brave first printing of 50,000 copies, went on to sell 1.4m in its first year. Sales grew with each subsequent title. Harry Potter V, "Harry Potter and the Order of the Phoenix", sold 12.5m in 2003. Major bookshop chains noted that their sales in 2004 were affected by the lack of a new Potter title.

It is no wonder, then, that the business has all its fingers crossed that the muse is not eluding Ms Rowling. There is a chance of Potter VI arriving in 2005. Ms Rowling has given her fans hope by announcing its title on her website: "Harry Potter and the Half Blood Prince". A fourth Potter movie is more certain. Scheduled for November 2005, it will add to Potter mania.

The other gift booksellers have wished for to make 2005 bright is a new title by Dan Brown. "The Da Vinci Code" was released in March 2003 and has been on the bestseller lists ever since, for much of that time in the number-one spot. Even John Grisham, used to being the top-selling fiction author, had to step down. Mr Brown's next book will be a continuation of the story. The timing of its publication has been carefully managed in order to maintain a thriving franchise. The publisher, Doubleday, waited until it saw sales of "The Da Vinci Code" start to slide before swiftly announcing, in October 2004, that the next title would be published in the autumn of 2005.

Television has long been recognised as both a competitor and a powerful promotional tool for books. But an even stronger venue has grown up in the past few years—church pulpits and religious retreats. Rick Warren's "The Purpose-Driven Life", published by Zondervan (now a division of HarperCollins) in 2002 has sold almost 20m books and ancillary products. It has even beaten out the previous pulpit/retreat favourite, "The Prayer of Jabez", which sold a mere 9m copies. HarperCollins regretfully says that there will not be a new Rick Warren title in 2005. Will another pulpit favourite emerge in 2005? Let's just say you may find lots of publishers in pews these days.

Americans continue to add pounds and to buy books about how to take them off. Low-carb diets have become such an obsession that Krispy Kreme has a low-carb doughnut in the works. All of this can be attributed to a renewed interest in the Atkins diet brought about by "The South Beach Diet". Published in 2003 by Rodale, the book dominated bestseller lists in 2004 and may continue to be a blockbuster in 2005. Atkins's original publisher, St Martin's, has announced that "The Atkins Advantage", by Stuart L. Trager, will appear in March.

And what about the well-known perennial bestselling authors? Yes, there will be a new John Grisham suspense novel in January, but this time the profession seems to have changed. After a string of titles such as "The Last Juror", "The Street Lawyer" and "The Firm", suspense has a new arena in "The Broker". A Tom Clancy novel, "Net Force #9: Springboard", with a stunning author advance of $22m, is scheduled for January 2005. Nicholas Sparks, whose soggy romances include "Message in a Bottle" and "The Notebook", is set to release a novel, "True Believer", in April to the tune of 1.5m copies. Americans who have not yet been sated by the many bestselling bios of the Founding Fathers can look forward to David McCullough's "1776", set for May and a 1m-copy first printing.

But if the past is truly a prologue, an unknown author with a small advance and a modest first printing will emerge and blow every one of the above out of the water. □

Nora Rawlinson: editor, *Publishers Weekly*

The biggest problem, however, will be the risk of piracy in a digital world where every copy is perfect. Even with celluloid, the American film industry loses $5 billion a year through illegal, but far from perfect, copying. The urgent task in 2005 for Dan Glickman, the new boss of the Motion Picture Association of America, will be to ensure that in going digital the film industry avoids the losses suffered by the music industry.

In the meantime, spare a thought for the megastar. With the exception of Tom Cruise and a few others, no actor will be able to extort fees of $25m a film. Those wages could be justified for a film budgeted at $100m, since the star could attract investors by guaranteeing (in theory, if not always in practice) also to attract the audience. It was one way, albeit an expensive one, of lessening the risk of a cinematic flop. But with a cheap digital movie, any flop will be by definition less costly—and the studio will have less need for a megastar. Clearly Arnold Schwarzenegger, once the highest-paid star in Hollywood, moved into politics at the right moment. □

Land of the freeze

Robert Gates

America will hurt itself unless it resumes its warm welcome to foreign students and scholars

Each year fewer American students pursue advanced degrees in science and engineering, at a time when the economy requires a growing supply of such talent. There are far from enough Americans qualified to fill these jobs. As a result, American companies and research organisations are increasingly dependent on foreign nationals—especially those who have earned advanced degrees from American universities. Yet the visa quota established by the Department of Homeland Security is so small compared with the need for such highly qualified experts that, unless corrective action is taken, many qualified individuals will have to return home. All too often they will go to work for foreign competitors of American companies.

Making matters worse is an increasing tendency to interpret regulations so restrictively as to create potential havoc across a wide swathe of American institutions. For example, the inspector-general at the commerce department has recommended that its Bureau of Industry and Security require universities to apply for export licences for employees or visitors who have access to dual-use technology (ie, with a potential for military as well as civilian use) if they were born in a country subject to American control over transfer of that technology—regardless of their most recent citizenship or permanent-residence status. This would compel universities to apply for thousands of export licences annually, swamping administration and prompting many international scholars and students to do their work outside America. These and related regulations could require universities to track and restrict international students' participation in certain classes and research, even though they would have been granted visas and thus deemed not to be a security threat.

How to stay head and shoulders above the rest

Robert Gates: president, Texas A&M University; former director, CIA (1991-93)

Despite successful efforts by senior government officials to correct long delays in processing visas for international students, lasting damage may already have been done. The experience of the past two years may have led to long-term shifts in the number of students coming to the United States to study, prompting many to study elsewhere—especially in Britain and Australia. Top American research universities have seen applications from international students decline by between 20% and 30%.

Who cares? America should. All through the cold war, programmes bringing students from other countries to America to study were one of the most effective means of winning lifelong friends for the country. America faces a similar challenge today. Radical Islamists, in particular—not to mention much of the global media—portray America in negative terms. To win the war on terrorism, or to contain it, military and intelligence efforts need to be complemented with positive, forward-looking programmes. Welcoming students from abroad to American universities is a powerful way to win hearts and minds.

We cannot allow risk-averse bureaucracies and middle-level officials who lack a broad view of the national interest to determine our future

The secretary of state, Colin Powell, and the secretary of homeland security, Tom Ridge, have issued strong statements recognising the importance to the American economy, to science and to foreign policy of welcoming students, scholars and specialists from abroad. Yet all of these problems have a common theme: the failure of government bureaucracies three and four levels down to understand just how important is the continued flow of the best minds from around the world to these shores. The history of 20th-century science, technology and economic growth in America is one of the vital contributions by scientists, scholars and entrepreneurs from abroad. In an age when the exchange of new scientific knowledge is global, America risks doing itself grievous harm by not considering its national interest in a broader context.

As deputy director and director of central intelligence respectively under Presidents Ronald Reagan and George Bush senior, I am quite aware of the very real and ongoing security risks posed by terrorism, including the danger that terrorists will gain access to advanced technologies they can use against America. I fully support measures the American government has taken to contain those risks. But the method of implementation of some policies is, in fact, weakening the country's security. We cannot allow risk-averse bureaucracies and middle-level officials who lack a broad view of the national interest to determine our future.

The stakes are certainly high in the war on terrorism. The consequences of inadvertently allowing some methods of waging that war to bring long-term harm to America's economy and to its future scientific and technological progress also are serious. America's friends in Britain seem to have understood this and acted sensibly. Surely Americans can do so as well. □

The good celebrity-trial guide

Lucy Tallon

When O.J. Simpson was acquitted of murdering his wife in 1995 an estimated 100m television viewers sat on the edge of their seats. Since then celebrity trials have become part of American life: subscriptions to the cable channel Court TV have risen hugely in the past decade—from 15m in 1994 to nearly 83m in 2004 . A vintage year for celebrity trials is in prospect in 2005. Here is a guide to the cream of the crop, rated according to our carefully calibrated gavelometer, in which five gavels denote maximum media hysteria.

Michael Jackson

The King of Pop has pleaded not guilty to committing a lewd act upon a child, administering an intoxicating agent, conspiring to commit child abduction, false imprisonment and extortion. Despite tough restrictions on reporting, expect saturation publicity. California law was changed specifically to enable this prosecution.

Saddam Hussein

Mr Hussein will be tried in Iraq by a specially appointed Iraqi tribunal. The former president of Iraq is charged with 12 war crimes and crimes against humanity. There is no crime worse than genocide; if convicted, he faces the death penalty. The politics of both America and Britain are tied up with his fate. He will use the witness stand to condemn the Iraq war.

Jayson Williams

Mr Williams, a former basketballer player, "accidentally" shot a fan in his home. Acquitted of more serious charges, he now faces a retrial for reckless manslaughter. He says the gun misfired. His retrial promises to be almost as popular as the original was: Mr Williams has a superb courtroom presence, and is an attractive, wealthy, black athlete. His good community record—he set up sports camps for underprivileged children—could help him.

Madonna and Guy Ritchie

An actor, Vincent d'Onofrio (not to be confused with his namesake who appears in "Law and Order"), accuses the celebrity couple of stealing his idea for their dreadful 2002 movie "Swept Away". They tried to sweep the case away in 2003, but are due back in a Los Angeles courthouse in January. Mr D'Onofrio is seeking $10m in damages from the Material Girl and her film-director husband.

Dennis Kozlowski

In 2004 the corruption trial for this former chairman of Tyco International ended in farce after a juror was seen giving a thumbs-up sign, so Mr Kozlowski faces a retrial. The public was outraged by the mistrial. Members of the original jury have offered advice in media interviews on how the prosecution could secure a conviction. Finding jurors who slept through the original trial—and have not formed an opinion about it—will not be easy.

Kenneth Lay

Mr Lay is accused of fraud at Enron, a bankrupt energy company where he was chairman. The prosecution may use emotional testimony of elderly people ruined from buying Enron shares at Mr Lay's urging—excellent media material. Mr Lay is accused of having sold his own stock in Enron while telling his employees not to worry. The issues raised by the case seem to many to typify the greed of business in the 1990s.

Bernie Ebbers

The founder of WorldCom is also charged with accounting fraud. His former chief finance officer, Scott Sullivan, is co-operating with the prosecutors. Followers of WorldCom's disaster will be fascinated to see whether Mr Ebbers's lawyers can discredit Mr Sullivan or whether Mr Sullivan's assistance to the prosecution will be enough to bring down his ex-boss.

George Ryan

A former governor of Illinois (nominated for the 2003 Nobel peace prize after he commuted the death sentences of 167 convicted murderers to life), Mr Ryan has pleaded innocent to charges of conspiracy and fraud. He is no longer a politician and is not rich; that will limit the publicity value. And there will be no cameras: proceedings in federal courts cannot be broadcast. Still, it'll be big in Illinois.

Sami Al-Arian

When Congress passed the Patriot act in 2001 this university professor (who had been under surveillance by the FBI for over ten years) was arrested. Charged with 50 counts of racketeering, Mr Al-Arian is accused of raising money for the the Palestinian Islamic Jihad. He has had time to get used to the limelight since his arrest—his details were made public on a hostile television show. He has been in isolation in a maximum-security prison, denied normal access to his family and made to carry documents on his back while handcuffed.

2005

The Department of Energy will put the contract to manage the Los Alamos National Laboratory up for bid. The current agreement with the University of California expires in September.

Lucy Tallon: *The Economist*

We'll be back

Arnold Schwarzenegger, governor of California, announces the imminent return of the Californian dream

Some time in 2005 we will look back, call it the California Comeback, and acknowledge it came in all shapes and sizes.

A few months ago it was Genentech. This biotechnology company—California born, California bred—rejected the seductive advances of other states and broke ground on the world's largest biotech plant: a $600m, 650-employee manufacturing facility in Vacaville, a little more than 50 miles (80 kilometres) north-east of the company's headquarters in south San Francisco.

More recently I was pleased to hear that Candace Doi and Fred Powers had decided to move their 12-employee, $700,000 company, Lynch Signs, from Las Vegas, Nevada, to La Verne, California, 20 miles east of Pasadena. Lynch is a growth company. It recently signed contracts with some major retailers in California, and has plans to expand and add jobs. Doi and Powers found irresistible the attractions of our California Commission for Jobs and Economic Growth, which has launched a ten-state billboard campaign encouraging businesses to set up shop in California (or, as the billboards insist I say, *Kah-li-fornia*).

Many more companies will be coming because we are reforming the system, making California competitive again. In Sacramento we passed a bill that reformed workers' compensation, and as a result the insurance premiums, which had increased by double digits between 2000 and 2003, immediately started dropping by double digits. We passed a balanced budget with no tax increases and moved the state's finances towards structural balance. We reformed employer litigation, moved forwards on programmes to ensure clean and reliable power, and were pleased that the voters approved ballot measures to limit state spending and refinance California's debt burden.

> I followed my dreams to California and even the ones that seemed impossible—even those dreams—came true. Now, as governor, I still believe in the Californian dream

We're doing our part, and it is already making a difference. A year ago California was considered a bad bet by Wall Street. All three of the principal credit-rating agencies—Moody's, Fitch and Standard & Poor's—had us on credit watch. Now, not only have all three agencies removed us from credit watch, but they've also upgraded our credit rating. We're back on our feet again, heading in the right direction, humming along with "California Dreamin'" not "Brother, Can You Spare a Dime?".

And this isn't just good news for the shareholders of a multinational biotech corporation, the owners of a sign company or the other companies and entrepreneurs who will follow. This is good news for every worker in the state, because the bottom line is jobs. A year ago, when I was campaigning for governor, I reminded voters that in the two previous years California had lost 175,000 jobs. Now we have reversed that trend. We've created more than 100,000 new jobs in our state since the beginning of 2004. That means 100,000 more Californians can take pride every day in what they do, can provide better lives for their families, buy school books and computers for their children, and fully participate in the American dream.

California has always been home for those with big dreams, for daring optimists. Our original settlers continued to drive west, despite the hardships, because they knew there was something better on the other side of the treacherous mountains. Prospectors of every description, from every continent, have flocked to California for generations because they knew this was where they would hit the mother lode.

I wish they all could be California firms

Men like Louis B. Mayer and Sam Goldwyn landed in a place that came to be called Hollywood and built an empire of their own that remains a beacon of aspiration and creativity to all the world. Chuck Yeager came here from West Virginia and asked for that last stick of Beeman's before he tested the first rocket engine, broke the sound barrier and opened the heavens over the California desert. Bill Hewlett and Dave Packard built one electronics business in a northern California garage and, inspired by them, a generation later Steve Jobs and Steve Wozniak built the first Apple home computer in another northern California garage.

Cisco, eBay, Yahoo!, Google, Netflix, NVIDIA, Electronic Arts, Intel: they are all companies that could only have started in California. They are all companies that call California home. And they all will continue to grow and flourish with the California Comeback.

We speak 95 languages in California (96, I guess, if you include my version of English). We have the sixth-largest economy in the world. We have 840 miles of coastline, 15,000 miles of highways and freeways, 12 cargo airports, 11 cargo seaports, and economic sanctuary for those who dream big. Statistics show that California's economy started its recovery in 2004. Personal income is up; taxable sales are up; exports, construction activity and hiring are all up; tourism is recovering. And history says that when the national economy recovers, California recovers better and faster.

When I was a young boy growing up in Austria, California represented a dream to me, a dream in which anything and everything was possible. I followed my dreams to California and even the ones that seemed impossible—even those dreams—came true. Now, as governor, I still believe in the Californian dream. When it broke ground for that new plant in Vacaville, Genentech said it believed in the dream. With its decision to move here, Lynch Signs staked its claim to a piece of the dream. In 2005 the California Comeback will make the dream come alive for many more. □

The travelling bra salesman's lesson

The essay competition run by Shell and *The Economist* has reached its fifth year. This time the question posed was: "Import workers or export jobs?" Nearly 2,500 people, from all over the world, offered entries. The first prize of $20,000 was won by Claudia O'Keefe from Frankford, West Virginia, whose essay, printed here, answers the question with a refreshingly human touch

He sells his slips on Route 66

It's a little after 10am at a 20-vehicle flea market in rural West Virginia. I'm getting worried. I haven't sold enough merchandise to pay for my $7 space fee and I didn't have any money to bring with me, not even to make change. I reach into a carton of vintage clothing to mark down my prices. My fingers grasp something silky and slippery, a lacy slip Elizabeth Taylor could have worn in "Cat on a Hot Tin Roof". Instead of the thin, cheesy polyester and shoddy workmanship I'm used to seeing in contemporary lingerie from the same manufacturer, the older slip features quality fabric and lace that is not only sewn on straight but will survive a hundred washings and remain looking near new.

This isn't what I notice first, however. It's the original price tag from 1966. I'm amazed because 38 years later I can still decipher the sales codes, codes which were printed on thousands of tags exactly like it and part of my first paying job, given to me when I was eight years old.

The good life

My stepfather was a salesman during the 1960s, travelling California and the American southwest in his big, hulking Buick, selling bras, slips and girdles to small department stores and five-and-dimes. Whenever he returned from one of his two-week trips, he brought several lunch sacks full of torn price tags with him, evidence of product sold. My job was to sort and count the tags, at a nickel for every hundred I recorded.

We lived in a three-bedroom home in an upscale Los Angeles suburb, owned two cars and took annual vacations. My brother, sister and I never lacked any of the benefits of a middle-class upbringing—a new school wardrobe each year, copious Christmas presents, private lessons, even horses when we were older. In a medical emergency we worried about how to get to a doctor quickly rather than about paying the bill. All of this was affordable on my dad's sales job without incurring vast amounts of debt.

These days the same lingerie lines my dad marketed are now sold primarily in Wal-Mart. Instead of being crafted in the United States by American workers they are manufactured almost exclusively in China. Gone are the travelling salesmen who ferried clothing to small-town variety stores across the nation, and their buyers who used to decide which lines to stock. Most of the old independent retailers no longer exist. A handful of chains have replaced them, with buying decisions made at the corporate level. Jobs which comfortably supported a family have been eliminated in favour of new ones paying so little that employees are encouraged to apply for food stamps.

I have more in common today with the minimum-wage employees at my local supercentre, than my dad in his Buick cruising Route 66 with a trunk full of bras. Why? I'm currently stuck living in job-poor West Virginia. With the exception of the occasional social-worker position advertised at $19,000 a year, the positions listed in my local paper pay $6 or less an hour. When I held one of the area's top professional jobs, as a 70-hour-a-week PR director for an arts organisation, I earned just $1,103 each month after taxes, no health insurance, no benefits. I understand too well the desire of unemployed and low-wage workers throughout the world who will make any sacrifice necessary, even to the point of moving some place where they are resented and vilified, in order to find work. I sympathise with the talented and skilled employees in India and Russia who are currently gobbling up my country's offshored tech jobs. Given these nations' struggles with poverty or economic turmoil, I would do exactly as they are doing.

Unfortunately, few companies want to outsource quality jobs to West Virginia. Though I've spent the past two years trying to put together the $3,000 necessary to move myself and my mother, "Grapes of Wrath"-style, to another state with decent employment, I can't even manage to keep our utilities and rent current.

Feeling isolated here, I've looked outwards for answers and become a financial-news junkie. I comb each new statistic, wait just as eagerly for the American monthly payroll report as I would if I owned stock. I take it all in, the arguments for and against free trade, the fears of those who feel the exportation of jobs will lead to a "race to the bottom", where America loses superpower status and becomes a third-world nation.

I watch corporate spokespeople madly spinning their version of outsourcing's benefits, cheaper prices and increased jobs at home. I note Alan Greenspan's testimony suggesting that displaced workers must retrain themselves for the new jobs which will appear on the horizon to replace ones lost and unlikely to return. None who supports this belief, however, can offer a list of the positions for which the jobless should school themselves. I sit in front of the TV where verbal combatants are engaged in a heated exchange over immigration reform. Should we be more compassionate, open our borders wider to financially depressed people willing to fill all those jobs Americans don't want? Or do we need a 50-foot razor-wire fence to protect native-born and naturalised citizens from the ▸

downward pressure on wages caused by tides of illegal aliens crossing into America?

I suck in as much information as I can take before crying uncle—the attack-dog political ads about job creation, the surveys and polls and yelling and screaming from experts and average Americans alike.

Moving on

Geography can no longer prevent jobs in developed regions such as North America and Europe from migrating to cheaper, emerging markets. The outsourcing jet has already left the terminal, cleared international airspace and has enough fuel onboard to reach the far ends of the earth nonstop.

Meanwhile, those workers whose jobs have fled are crowding into that empty terminal, clamouring for protections against what they perceive as theft. They see a worker in China being paid pennies for a job that used to guarantee a nice middle-class life for their families and they're so frustrated they don't know which they want to do more, cry or shoot something, preferably a politician. They may cry, but thankfully they don't shoot. Instead they pour every ounce of their attention into complaining to those same politicians, charging them with an impossible task, returning things to the way they were.

I know first-hand the dangers of refusing to let go of the past. A decade ago I was a published writer with a promising career in fiction. Fiction publishing at that time was in the midst of a corporate sea change, devastating to authors of the type of books I wrote. Not only wasn't pay increasing, fewer and fewer books were being bought. Not wanting to give up a career that was my whole life, I sought to adjust to my shrinking income by progressively relocating to areas of the country with cheaper and cheaper costs of living. I moved from pricey California to a slightly less expensive northern New Mexico to Florida, rural Virginia and finally, with my money gone, any momentum I'd once had long expended and all contacts evaporated, I came to a disgruntled rest four years ago in West Virginia.

Similar to my experience with publishing, Americans who have lost their jobs since 2001 are having to adjust to the idea that the next one they find is likely to involve a pay cut. According to the labour department, 57% of those workers who found re-employment earned less than they did at their old jobs. A third took a cut of 20% or more in order to be employed.

What happens if, as several studies suggest, outsourcing continues to ramp up and those same workers are thrown out on the street once more? Will their next job pay even less? Could scores of computer programmers, financial analysts and paralegals end up like my West Virginia neighbours, huddled around a card table in a supercentre break room, using a Styrofoam cup for an ashtray while they grouse about their lives?

Back in the 1970s my stepfather saw his career as a travelling bra salesman coming to an end. Though he adored the freedom of the open road, he didn't balk. He mourned and moved on. He studied for a real-estate licence and found a new life as a highly successful broker.

A new dream

The question is not whether it is good or bad to import workers or export jobs. The problem is that society has hit an emotional roadblock. My country is one tremendously divided, with pro-business and pro-worker stubbornly pitted against each other. We're anxious. We're angry. Neither side wants to give and nothing can be solved until we acknowledge one crucial fact.

The past is dust. Those mythic decades, during which the American Dream was considered to be our natural right, are over. We need to wake from our state of denial, accept this golden era's passing and get on with life. Once we agree that the past cannot be recaptured, we will at last open ourselves to solutions we haven't yet considered, to business and immigration models which are still waiting to be invented. Working as willing participants of change, we will devise ways to keep businesses from discarding employees like so much surplus machinery, while making certain there is profit for all. Ingenuity will be given free rein and the synergies we so badly need to solve this international crisis can finally come together.

Standing in that West Virginia flea market, I look at the vintage, never-worn slip in my hands. Back in my home state of California, at the Rose Bowl Flea Market, it would fetch $35 or more. Here, I'll have to price it at $1. In fact, while I'm doing this, a woman approaches me.

"How much?" she asks.

I tell her, while pointing out that the slip is in mint condition and of a superior quality to comparable ones made today.

"Will you take a quarter?" she asks.

Hurry, I urge my country. Before it's too late. Only when we accept the future that awaits us can we embrace a more inclusive and thrilling successor to outmoded 20th-century ideals, a goal without boundaries or limits, not the American Dream, but the Global Dream. □

Face the facts

This essay, and the seven other prize-winning entries, can be found at www.shelleconomistprize.com or www.economist.com

The judging panel comprised:

Richard O'Brien, jury chairman and strategy consultant at Outsights;

Peter Warshall, biologist and anthropologist;

Christine Loh, co-founder and CEO, Civic Exchange;

Sally Feldman, head of the School of Media, Arts and Design, University of Westminster;

Adam Raphael, journalist and broadcaster;

Peter Cornelius, senior economist, Shell;

Bill Emmott, editor, *The Economist*

To win "*International Law Firm of the Year,*" rank among the best everywhere.

Asian Legal Business	Named "International Law Firm of the Year" and "North American Law Firm of the Year" (2003)
The BTI Consulting Group, Inc.	Ranked #1 for client service (2002 & 2004)
The BTI Consulting Group, Inc.	Topped survey of tech-savvy law firms (2003)
The National Law Journal	Second most cited as outside counsel in "Who Represents Corporate America" (2003)
Bloomberg	One of the top five U.S. bankruptcy law firms (2001 & 2002)
Thomson Financial & Bloomberg	Top M&A firm for number of deals worldwide (2000-Q1 2004)
Bloomberg	Ranked #1 worldwide by number of deals and #2 by deal volume in real estate M&A (2003)
Corporate Board Member	One of the top five "America's Best Corporate Lawyers" (2003)
Chambers and Partners	Named U.S. "Litigation Firm of the Year" (2003)
Chambers and Partners	Chosen as "Litigation—International Law Firm of the Year" (2002)
The American Lawyer	First "Litigation Department of the Year" award winner and 2004 finalist (2002 & 2004)
The American Lawyer	Named "Product Liability Litigation Department of the Year" (2004)

JONES DAY®

LEGAL MINDS. GLOBAL INTELLIGENCE.

2200 lawyers in 30 locations. One firm worldwide.
www.jonesday.com

The Americas

Promises, promises

Jeffrey Simpson *OTTAWA*

Canada rediscovers the joys of minority government

Paul Martin, Canada's prime minister, must hope that 2005 is better for him than 2004. Handed a solid majority government by his Liberal predecessor, Jean Chrétien, Mr Martin frittered away a slice of his party's support. In the spring election, the Liberals lost their parliamentary majority, and must spend 2005 steering the country's first minority government since 1979-80. His government can expect to last between 18 and 24 months, since none of the three opposition parties seeks an early rematch.

Mr Martin has gone from a tight-fisted and much-respected finance minister (1993-2002) to a lavish and not-much-respected prime minister. He won the election, in a manner of speaking, by promising to spend tens of billions of dollars in anticipated federal surpluses on everything from childcare to cities and health. Before that electoral bonfire of promises, he disappointed just about everyone who had expected so much better. He often seemed indecisive, unable to say no to anyone and much given to insisting that every issue was terribly, terribly important—to the point of inadvertent self-parody. He had so many urgent priorities that it was unclear if he had any.

Mr Martin will need the Canadian economy to continue its stellar performance to pay for his promises. Growth will probably remain around 3%. It has to stay there for many years, since Mr Martin has pledged so much additional spending. Any diminution in growth will tip the fiscal surplus into the red. And Canadians, apparently alone among G7 peoples, are fiscal hawks ready to punish any politician who presides over deficits. They learnt all about the perils of deficits from 1972 to 1995, when the country ran them every year and was rewarded with higher taxes, lower productivity and high real interest rates.

> Mr Martin has gone from a tight-fisted and much-respected finance minister to a lavish and not-much-respected prime minister

2005

A series of tattoo parlours staffed by inmates will open in Canadian prisons, offering a more hygienic alternative to compass points and Bic pens.

Will the Canadian economy continue to shine? Unlike most other rich countries, it will benefit from higher world oil prices. Canada is a net oil exporter, although the revenue flows disproportionately to one province, Alberta, whose growth already eclipses that of the other nine provinces.

The continuing rise of the Canadian dollar—expected to be worth about 85 American cents in 2005 compared with 62 cents two years ago—might cramp exports. Canadian companies that cried the blues about the higher dollar last year nonetheless coped exceedingly well. Business leaders have been remarkably sanguine about the minority government, reckoning that Mr Martin will be politically safe for a while. But markets could become skittish if, as is probable, analysts begin to doubt whether the government can spend all those billions of dollars and maintain a balanced budget.

Watch out for the bumps

The biggest spending will be on health care. Canadians, alone in the industrialised world, remain wedded to state-only delivery of all medically necessary services. Not for them the mixed public-private systems everywhere else. In 2005 more money will be lavished on their beloved but beleaguered system. The test for every federal and provincial leader will be to show results from all that spending. Critics believe the money is pouring into a bottomless pit. □

Jeffrey Simpson: national affairs columnist, the *Globe and Mail*

The winds of change in Latin America

Michael Reid

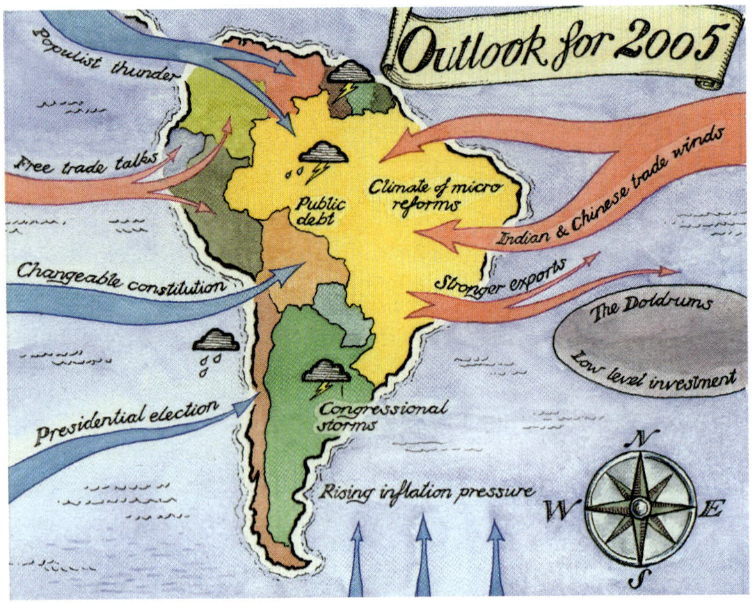

Time for democracy to deliver

The defining issue for Latin America in 2005 will be whether or not the region can sustain its strong economic recovery as conditions in the world economy turn less favourable. Closely related to this will be the emerging battle between liberal democracy and populism for the loyalties of citizens and political leaders. If all goes well, liberal democracy may start to look a bit less vulnerable. But upsets are still possible.

In 2004 Latin America posted its best economic performance since 1997: weighted by the size of economies, the region's GDP growth was close to 5%. Tighter financing conditions and still-disappointing levels of investment mean that the pace will slow a little in 2005. But barring big shocks, the region should settle into steady growth of close to 4% for the next couple of years. Two things underpin that prospect. The first is booming demand from China and India for Latin America's raw materials. The second is that the region's notoriously volatile and fragile economies are slowly acquiring better defence mechanisms. Stronger exports, floating exchange rates and, in most places, tighter fiscal policies are starting to make the region more resilient.

But that strengthening remains a work in progress. A crash in China or a sharp increase in interest rates in the United States could still cloud the region's prospects in 2005—especially if both happened simultaneously. The bigger threat would be an abrupt tightening of financial conditions for Latin America. That would raise worries about the sustainability of the public debt in Brazil, Colombia and some other countries. Absent a sudden correction, high oil prices and capacity constraints mean that Latin American central banks will still have to keep a weather eye on a recent uptick in inflation.

In other words, though the region has left behind its "lost half-decade" of 1998-2002, it still has much to do to achieve sustained growth at Asian rates. For that, governments will need to work far harder at boosting investment through micro-economic reforms, such as easing regulation and improving infrastructure. Greater political predictability would also help. Of the region's big two, Brazil looks better placed than Mexico to make progress on reforms in 2005. The government of Luiz Inácio Lula da Silva will try to push through changes to bankruptcy and labour laws, as well as a measure to attract private investment for infrastructure projects. It may also press for greater independence for the central bank. In Mexico, by contrast, Vicente Fox's government will be lucky if it gets even minor tax changes through a gridlocked Congress.

Governments throughout the region will look to economic growth to deliver extra social spending, and to boost their popularity. After the turbulence of recent years, politics should be quieter. Of the larger countries, only Chile faces a presidential election—though in several others, including Brazil and Mexico, campaigning for presidential elections in 2006 will cast a shadow over the second half of the year. In Argentina, the government of Néstor Kirchner contests an important congressional ▶

Michael Reid: Americas editor, *The Economist*

COLOMBIA *FORECAST*

Alvaro Uribe, Colombia's president, believes he is on a mission to deliver his country from 40 years of internal strife. Judging by his approval ratings (around 70% since he took office in 2002), most Colombians have faith in him. After years of recession and worsening security, Mr Uribe has given Colombians hope. The guerrillas are retreating, hounded by a strengthened army. And security has improved: murders and kidnappings, though still all too common, have fallen by over 30%. City folk can once again enjoy weekend trips out of town—unthinkable when the guerrillas roamed the highways.

Mr Uribe's handling of the economy is boosting confidence, particularly among businessmen. Private investment and exports lifted GDP by around 4% in both 2003 and 2004. Demand for posh apartments is soaring. Professionals who left in despair a few years ago are returning.

In 2005 the economy should stand up well, though growth will slow a bit and tightening international liquidity could renew concerns about Colombia's public debt—which, at over 50% of GDP, is uncomfortably high. For most Colombians, however, conditions will not improve much. Unemployment remains high. Social policy will come to the fore, as Mr Uribe shows voters his softer side.

Formidable challenges lie ahead. Improvised negotiations with paramilitary groups may backfire. A breakthrough against the FARC guerrillas appears elusive and they retain the power to strike. Squabbling congressmen and Colombia's quixotic Constitutional Court may block reforms—including one to allow Mr Uribe to stand for re-election in May 2006.

Would another term for Mr Uribe be a good idea? Colombians might do well to ponder recent experiences of leaders elsewhere in Latin America. Those of Alberto Fujimori in Peru and Carlos Menem in Argentina should give pause for thought; even Fernando Henrique Cardoso's second term in Brazil was not as successful as his first. Mr Uribe's legacy—and indeed Colombia's prospects—may best be served by pursuing his strong policies in 2005, not by prolonging his hold on power.

KEY INDICATORS	2003	2004	2005
GDP growth (%)	3.9	4.2	3.7
Budget balance (% GDP)	2.8	2.6	2.5
Unemployment (%)	14.2	13.1	11.9
Inflation (%, ave)	7.1	5.9	5.3

Economist Intelligence Unit

Out of Pinochet's shadow

Michael Reid

Chile's politics moves on

Since the end of General Augusto Pinochet's dictatorship in 1990, Chile has been governed by a centre-left coalition known as the Concertación. In that period the country has generally prospered. In the 1990s Chile was Latin America's star economy, growing at an annual average rate of 6%.

Yet not surprisingly, the Concertación has sometimes looked tired. As well as squabbles among its constituent parties, it has suffered a couple of small corruption scandals. A year ago most pundits would have bet that in the election in December 2005 the presidency would pass to Joaquín Lavín, the standard-bearer of the conservative opposition.

Now the only thing that looks certain is that the election will be very close. Following a period of stagnation induced by the troubles of Asian economies after 1998, Chile's economy is once again growing strongly, partly on the back of high copper prices. Ricardo Lagos, the outgoing president, who is a moderate Socialist, is liked and admired by many Chileans. Of all the region's current presidents, he stands out as Latin America's foremost statesman.

For its part, the opposition is riven by bitter personal feuds. However, Mr Lavín, a bland conservative who presents himself as a practical problem-solver, has no real rival for his coalition's presidential candidacy. The election could turn on who the Concertación picks to oppose him. José Miguel Insulza, the interior minister, might have the best chance of beating Mr Lavín. But he is from Mr Lagos's Socialist Party. Its main partner, the Christian Democrats, will push the claims of Eduardo Frei, a safe but unexciting former president. Another Socialist, Michelle Bachelet, Chile's first female defence minister, will also stake a claim.

No turning back

The Concertación will run on its record and its desire to levy higher taxes on mining. If Mr Lavín wins, interest will focus on whether Chile's right has shaken off its authoritarian past as effectively as Spain's People's Party did under José María Aznar, and on whether its close ties to private business will lead to an unhealthy concentration of power. Either way, the election will be the first to be held free from the shadow of General Pinochet, now a lonely figure who no longer commands public support or respect. □

election in October: this is likely to show that his position within the ruling Peronist movement is less than all-conquering. Even if his government succeeds in its go-it-alone attempt to restructure its debts, Mr Kirchner is unlikely to abandon his populist penchant for picking fights with the likes of the International Monetary Fund and foreign investors.

Given Latin America's extreme income inequalities, growth at around 4% will bring only a gradual reduction in poverty. Some governments will try to speed that up with targeted social programmes. Even so, widespread poverty will provide grist for populists—would-be saviours who offer unsustainable redistribution rather than the slow slog of strengthening institutions and creating the conditions for rising investment.

> The most aggressive face of Latin American populism in 2005 will once again be that of Venezuela's Hugo Chávez

The most aggressive face of Latin American populism in 2005 will once again be that of Venezuela's Hugo Chávez. Fortified by his victory in a recall referendum in 2004 and by high oil prices, Mr Chávez will increase the role of the state in the economy at home, while also trying to rally the region behind his "Bolivarian revolution". His example will have some appeal in another oil-rich country, Mexico. There the political theme of the year will be whether anyone can overtake Andrés Manuel López Obrador, the populist mayor of Mexico City, in the race for the presidency in 2006.

Argentina and Mexico apart, the other main battle between liberal democrats and populists will be over the Andean countries. Bolivia will be a particular worry. The president, Carlos Mesa, has promised to organise a constituent assembly in 2005 to write a new constitution. The assembly is likely to dramatise Bolivia's political fragmentation rather than help to bind it together. It could even provoke a serious attempt at secession from the country's less-poor eastern half. In both Ecuador and Peru, however, economic growth should help unpopular presidents to cling to office.

Governments in five small Central American countries will hope that the United States Congress ratifies the Central American Free-Trade Agreement in 2005. But it will be a tough fight. The United States will conclude negotiations on a similar free-trade accord with Colombia and other Andean countries. But talks on a hemisphere-wide trade pact, in which Brazil is the key counterpart, will continue to languish. In November the hemisphere's leaders are due to gather in Buenos Aires for the fourth Summit of the Americas (not counting the "Special Summit" in 2004). They may not strike any new agreements on trade or other substantive issues. But as they survey the region, at least the outlook for democracy and development will be sunnier than in the recent past. □

2005

One of the biggest infrastructure projects in Latin America will get under way if voters in Panama approve plans to upgrade the Panama Canal to take larger ships. A referendum is expected early in the year.

Lessons from the Americas

Paul Martin, prime minister of Canada, argues that effective international co-operation needs stronger states, not weaker ones

A busy year for summitry lies ahead in 2005. But all summits really come down to two issues: what are a state's responsibilities to its own people, and what are its responsibilities towards others. Everything else is detail.

We will see this clearly in the next Summit of the Americas, to be held in Argentina in 2005. Latin America has long been known for its cycles—from boom to bust, with the busts usually accompanied by political crises and autarkic economic policies. No more. In the recent downturn, the region absorbed some terrible shocks: Argentina comes to mind, and also Venezuela and the natural disasters in the Caribbean. But democracy, despite some disillusionment, is holding firm and the region's economic policies, while under strain in some cases, are still on the right path towards greater openness and stability.

Latin American governments have implemented difficult reforms, but they have had help from their neighbours. Over the past decade hemispheric agreements covering everything from security to democracy and human rights have been approved. There is constant pressure on all governments to keep moving forward on political and economic reforms, since backsliding will bring censure from the entire hemisphere. The Argentina summit will be critical because, after some tough years, a firm commitment to further domestic and regional reforms will be especially important.

The experience in the Americas over the past ten years has important implications for some other regions of the world. Many Latin American countries were reluctant to move towards greater regional co-operation because they saw it as a threat to the nation state. In fact the opposite is true: we need strong states if our international systems are to function at all. Only strong states can make international commitments that they know they can live up to. Only strong states can effectively mediate between the rigours of the international economy and the needs of their citizens; states with good governance prosper, while states where governance is weak impose terrible costs on their people. Strong states today carry the confidence and support of their populations; repression is a sign of weakness. Latin American states are stronger today than ever, and there is no way to turn the clock back. The costs are simply too high.

> It comes down to this: how well are we doing in helping to make weak states stronger so that they can better fulfil their responsibilities to their own people and to others?

Mexico is a striking example. When NAFTA (the North American Free-Trade Agreement) began, many Mexicans worried that it represented a recolonisation of their country, this time by the gringos, while in Canada and the United States there were deep worries that cheap Mexican labour would wipe out our economies. Now, after 11 years, all three economies have grown much more competitive globally and Mexican politics has gone through a democratic transformation as dramatic in its way as those in eastern Europe. Inconceivable ten years ago, Canada's political relationship with Mexico today is one of our most intensive and important, not just bilaterally but also in our many joint efforts in the western hemisphere and beyond.

Beyond the rhetoric, the real question

There are lessons from the Americas that could work elsewhere, and not just regionally. The UN's Millennium Summit +5 in 2005 is supposed to review progress since the world's leaders agreed in 2000 that "we have a duty...to all the world's people, especially the most vulnerable and, in particular, the children of the world, to whom the future belongs." There will be heaps of rhetoric, but it comes down to this: how well are we doing in helping to make weak states stronger so that they can better fulfil their responsibilities to their own people and to others?

The world is moving in the right direction. On development, the UN's Monterrey conference agreed on the need for a broad approach by addressing such issues as debt, trade and market access, social investments, domestic economic policies and, perhaps most importantly, institutional capacities. All the aid in the world will have only a fleeting effect if a country does not have functioning public institutions and a rule of law. Development depends on good governance.

It also demands protecting the rights of individuals and communities. Almost all of the major conflicts have their genesis in the efforts of one community to disadvantage and persecute another, whether in the Balkans, East Timor or Central Africa. Where governments need and want our help, we must do everything we can to shore up the forces of tolerance and moderation.

But where governments are complicit in persecution, as in Darfur, we need clear international law that authorises multilateral action in situations of extreme humanitarian emergency. The UN Millennium Summit +5 should promote this "responsibility to protect" as a clear signal that sovereignty is not inviolable and that states will be held to account for their actions.

The international community has, with a lot of difficulty, established some important political, economic and social benchmarks for how well countries are meeting their responsibilities. And yet, each year, the divide between strong and weak states grows wider. In 2005 we will have several major opportunities, regionally and globally, to reverse this trend and act collectively to strengthen governance everywhere so that each person on earth is able to live in dignity and freedom. □

Asia

Japan redux

Robert Ward

2005

Japanese law firms will be able to merge fully with foreign ones. Previously, foreign firms operating in Japan had to form local joint-ventures, separate from their global practices. Similarly, as part of an agreement with the WTO, South Korea opens its legal market to foreign practitioners.

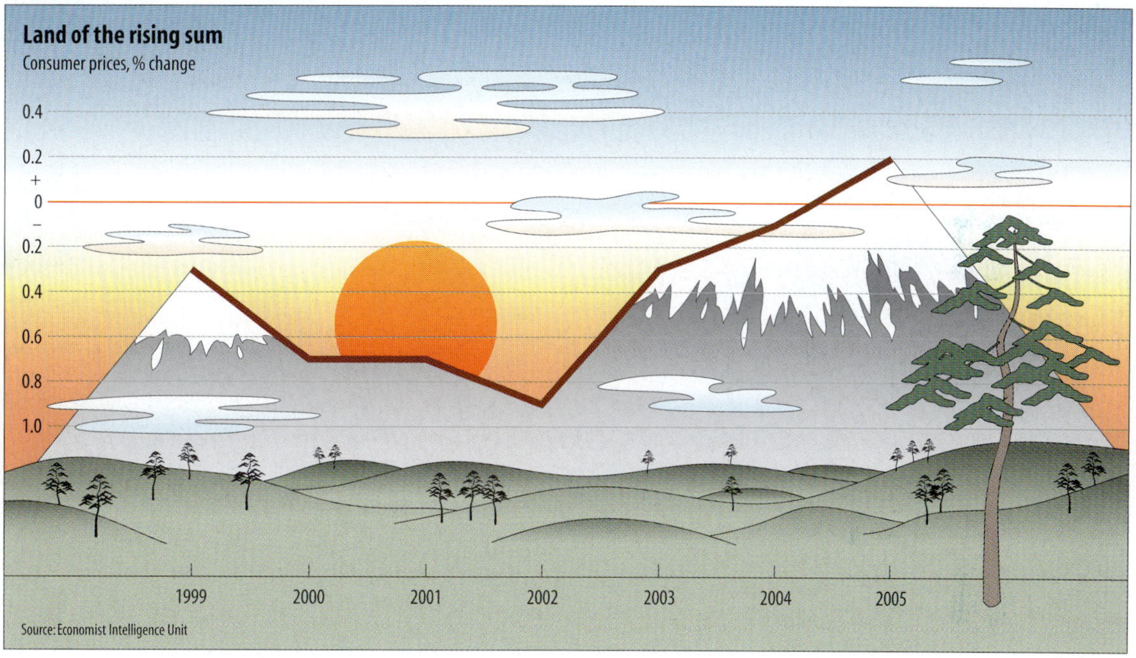

A force to be reckoned with again

Japan has put itself back on the map. Leaner and meaner following its "lost decade", Japan finally punched its economic weight in 2004. Military involvement in Iraq and an open push for a permanent seat on the UN Security Council even suggested Japan might be putting on political muscle too. In 2005 these gains will be consolidated. More important, however, 2005 will be a year of transition, in which Japan finally shakes itself free from many of the economic and political legacies of its recent past.

Most obviously, Japan will successfully wrap up the memory of the bubble era and its aftermath in 2005. Confidence in the banking sector will be boosted by the withdrawal in April of the government's final blanket guarantees on deposits at private-sector banks and by the merger in October of Mitsubishi Tokyo Financial Group, regarded as one of the strongest of Japan's mega-banks, with the weakest, UFJ Holdings. Wobbly regional banks will remain a concern, but stabilisation at the top of the sector and a readiness to use public cash if needed suggests that these will no longer pose a systemic risk.

Recent above-trend growth will also ensure that the most damaging symptom of Japan's economic ills, deflation, continues to ease. Even a modest overall increase in consumer prices in 2005 is possible, the first such rise since 1998. This will be a boon to companies, helping to improve their financial position and restore pricing power. Easing deflationary pressures may persuade the Bank of Japan (BOJ, the central bank) to push to normalise monetary policy. Although interest rates are unlikely to rise in 2005—memories of the bitter criticism of the BOJ's premature tightening in 2000 run deep—the BOJ may alter its policy framework, shifting from the targeting of current-account balances held with it by private-sector banks, back to interest rates.

> Watch for niche consumers such as the "bubble juniors": born in the early 1990s, brand-savvy and numbering around 7m, these are the world's richest tots

All this will take place against a background of yet another year of solid overall growth. Although not as whizzy as in 2004, expansion will be respectably above trend, at close to 2%. While business investment growth will experience a natural fallback from the blistering highs recorded in 2003-04, Japan's consumers will ▸

Robert Ward: Economist Intelligence Unit

Islands in the oil stream

Can Russia and Japan reverse 150 years of history?

Diplomatic relations between Japan and Russia began in 1855 with the signing of the Shimoda treaty. It's been mostly downhill from there. The two nations came to blows over Manchuria and Korea in 1904-05. The result: a surprise win for Japan. For most of the second world war Japan and Russia were on neutral terms. At the last minute Russia sided with the allies against Japan. When the war ended Russia occupied a group of islands north of the Japanese mainland. Japan has been asking for the return of those islands ever since. Russia won't budge. A formal peace treaty between the two countries has not been signed.

Lately, though, things have been looking up. At the 2004 G8 summit, Japan's prime minister, Junichiro Koizumi, and Russia's president, Vladimir Putin, agreed on a "plan of action" which, they say, will lead to a peace deal. The 150th anniversary of the Shimoda treaty seems an auspicious moment. The hope is that the details will have been thrashed out in time for a summit meeting of the two leaders in early 2005.

The diplomatic lubricant is oil. Japan has money and needs oil. Russia has oil and needs money. Messrs Koizumi and Putin will no doubt come to a mutually beneficial arrangement. Indeed, Japan has already invested heavily in Russian energy projects and has been lobbying Russia to direct a proposed $10 billion oil pipeline to the nearby port of Nakhodka.

The main obstacles to a Russo-Japanese peace treaty are not economic but political. Both leaders are populists who are mindful of their images at home. Noisily demanding the return of the islands would help Mr Koizumi. Sternly refusing to do so would help Mr Putin (and conceding the islands on the centenary of Russia's defeat by Japan certainly would not).

The most likely upshot of all this is stalemate. A trade agreement between Japan and Russia will probably be reached in 2005. But a peace treaty? That may be harder. □

continue to surprise. Watch in particular for niche consumers, whose spending power will ensure that Japan remains one of the world's most exciting markets for high-end goods.

One such will be the "bubble juniors": born in the early 1990s, brand-savvy and numbering around 7m, these are the world's richest tots, with annual disposable income reckoned to be in excess of ¥1m ($9,000) each. Or the "parasite singles", a growing number of single women still living at home with their parents, who spend around 10% of their income on luxury goods. Or even the *oyaji*, men in their 40s and 50s who, more confident now that the worst of the post-bubble restructuring is over and still enjoying seniority-based pay, became among the biggest spenders in 2004, particularly on high-end items such as digital televisions and luxury cars.

With no parliamentary elections due in 2005 and no obvious challengers, Japan's prime minister, Junichiro Koizumi, will have plenty of political room to push his pet projects. Top on the list is constitutional reform. Mr Koizumi has instructed his Liberal Democratic Party (LDP) to come up with a blueprint for refreshing the constitution—the world's oldest unamended constitution—in time for the celebrations in November to mark the 50th anniversary of the party's founding. Proposals are likely to include loosening the constraints on the operations of the Self-Defence Forces (Japan's de facto military), particularly outside Japan. As well as challenging the pacifist ideals that have underpinned Japan's security policy since the end of the second world war, such a revamp would also probe useful political holes in the largest opposition party, the Democratic Party of Japan, which is bitterly divided on the issue of constitutional change.

Mr Koizumi will also be looking elsewhere for his place in history. His proactive North Korean diplomacy suggests that he may push for the establishment of diplomatic relations with the regime. The likely return to Japan in 2005 of a handful of ageing Japanese Red Army terrorists holed up in Pyongyang since the 1970s would help facilitate this. A normalisation of relations with North Korea would dovetail nicely with celebrations at the end of 2005 to mark the 40th anniversary of the establishment of bilateral relations with South Korea. These celebrations will be still warmer if, as planned, Japan and South Korea manage to make some progress on a bilateral free-trade agreement by then.

Although Mr Koizumi will remain the LDP's most powerful figure in 2005, his star will fade. The LDP's lacklustre performance in the mid-2004 upper-house election suggested that Japan's voters have begun to tire of Mr Koizumi's Kabuki-like sparkle. This will, however, matter less in view of the party's factional shifts—a reassuringly Japanese constant, perhaps, in a year of otherwise encouraging economic and political change. □

2005

Solar-B, a Japanese spacecraft designed to observe the Sun, will be launched in September.

Chill, China

James Miles *BEIJING*

A need for cool heads and a cooler economy

China's rise in recent years has been exhilarating. But its challenge in 2005 will be to avoid becoming too exciting, both at home and in relations with its neighbours. As the country's leaders undertake the hazardous task of letting a little steam out of a searing economy, the coming year will also see them embroiled in tensions across the Taiwan Strait. The chances are that these difficulties will be managed without precipitating a crisis in 2005, but relations with Taiwan will need to be managed with care. America will watch nervously.

Fears that the efforts to cool the economy might bring about a sharp slowdown have subsided somewhat. Growth of some 8.9% in 2004 was only marginally lower than in 2003. It will slow a little more in 2005. The focus will remain on restraining investment in overheated sectors such as steel and car production and keeping a grip on the money supply. There might even be an increase in interest rates, the first in nine years.

Despite complaints from many of China's trade partners about what they regard as the undervaluation of the Chinese currency, there is little likelihood of a major adjustment in its link to the dollar in the coming year. Any shift will be small: China does not want to hit exporters or give a windfall to speculators. Full

> Mr Hu's toughest test of strength will be handling relations with Taiwan

convertibility will remain a distant goal. The first task will be to sort out the country's banking mess.

Coming soon, after much delay, should be the overseas listing of a state-owned commercial bank: the Bank of China and China Construction Bank are the leading contenders. China's hope is that the long-awaited sales will force the banks to adopt international standards of governance, in preparation for an expected onslaught of competition when the sector is opened to foreign competition at the beginning of 2006. But the corrupt and wasteful habits of decades will not change fast.

Taming the economy will tax the political skills of President Hu Jintao and the prime minister, Wen Jiabao—both approaching the halfway point of their (renewable) five-year terms of office. Provincial leaders are notoriously slow when it comes to reining in reckless investment. But Mr Hu should benefit from the extra authority that comes from having at last taken over as China's military chief from the ageing Jiang Zemin. He now combines the country's top three posts: president, general secretary of the Communist Party and head of the party's military commission.

His toughest test of strength will be handling relations with Taiwan. There President Chen Shui-bian, now in his second term, will be more emboldened in his efforts to assert Taiwan's independence, though he will still stop short of making it a legal fact (for all his bravado, Mr Chen knows that such a move could well mean war). Mr Chen will start fleshing out plans for a new constitution to be adopted in 2008 in place of the anachronistic one of 1948. Even if this does not include pro-independence language, China will find merely the process of drawing up a constitution for an island it considers a rebel province a challenge to its national pride. The Americans, fearful of being sucked into a war, will be urging Mr Chen to tread very warily.

As if 600-odd missiles pointing at Taiwan were not enough, China's leaders will try to pile on psychological pressure. The annual session of China's parliament in March will see calls for legislation that would oblige the ▶

2005

The first phase of new fuel-economy standards in China comes into force in July. The rules on the minimum mileage per gallon are more stringent than in America.

James Miles: China correspondent, *The Economist*

TAIWAN *FORECAST*

After several years that will be remembered more for incessant bickering and a mysterious political shooting than any serious policy debate, 2005 will bring a period of relative calm to Taiwan. The pro-independence "pan-green" alliance of the Democratic Progressive Party (DPP) is likely to win a majority for the first time in a parliamentary poll at the end of 2004, ending the gridlock that has plagued politics since the DPP's Chen Shui-bian became president in 2000. After its second national election in just nine months—Mr Chen narrowly retained the presidency in March in a vote overshadowed by that bizarre election-eve shooting, in which a bullet grazed the president—Taiwan can move on.

With only local elections in 2005, Mr Chen will face less pressure to invigorate his supporters with populist China-bashing. The respite, however, will be brief: polls for the high-profile mayorships of Taipei and Kaohsiung loom in 2006, when the DPP's controversial plans to rewrite Taiwan's constitution will also be ready. As a result, 2005 is perhaps the only time during Mr Chen's eight years in office when he will be willing to offer real concessions to improve cross-strait relations. The year will be no less important for the opposition Kuomintang, which was thrown into disarray by Mr Chen's re-election. The party and its "pan-blue" allies must show they can regroup and formulate a vision capable of competing with the DPP's Taiwanese nationalism.

The economy remains beholden to a global IT cycle that will turn downwards in 2005. But slowing headline rates of growth will hide more positive trends. The sophisticated display industry will expand rapidly, even as lower-end IT manufacturing moves to China. And a long-awaited high-speed rail link between Taipei and Kaohsiung will be inaugurated in October 2005.

KEY INDICATORS	2003	2004	2005
GDP growth (%)	3.3	5.8	4.8
Budget balance (% GDP)	-2.8	-2.9	-2.6
Unemployment (%)	5.0	4.5	4.5
Inflation (%, ave)	-0.3	1.7	1.4

Economist Intelligence Unit

2005

China will launch a $23m satellite to monitor the construction of venues for the 2008 Olympics—and the Beijing traffic, reckoned to be the greatest threat to the success of the games. It will provide information for urban planning, environmental impact, traffic control and disaster planning.

government to attack the island if it declares independence. But China's leaders are in no mood for war. They know that even something intended merely as a warning could escalate into an all-out confrontation that could cripple China's economy and devastate its reputation.

At a time of growing social dislocation caused by breakneck economic growth, the party's preoccupation will remain with preserving domestic stability and avoiding trouble internationally. The coming year might even see China broker a solution to the nuclear crisis on the Korean peninsula. That would be a huge diplomatic gain for China, which wants to cultivate an image as a responsible emerging great power.

To demonstrate its status, China will launch its second manned space rocket in 2005. This time it will involve two men at least, who will stay in orbit for several days longer than the 21 hours spent by Yang Liwei, China's first space traveller, in 2003. □

Forward march! Eyes left!

Simon Long *DELHI*

Can India's Congress party manage its partners?

Can a government that relies for its parliamentary majority on the votes of two Communist parties pursue liberalising economic reform? If it wants to fulfil its promises, India's Congress party will have to try. At worst, the government could fall, heralding a frustrating period of short-lived coalitions. More likely, it will survive, but find its hands tied.

The question will be most pressing—and the answer much clearer—at the end of February, when Palaniappan Chidambaram, the new finance minister, presents his budget. He has said he wants to be "minister for investment", recognising the shortage that explains the failure of the Indian economy to grow faster.

To stimulate investment, India needs to do a lot of things: reduce its huge fiscal deficit, improve public services, overhaul restrictive labour laws, bring more private capital into state-owned businesses and end the "inspector raj" of licensed bureaucratic harassment of business. That is a tall order, especially since Congress's partners will oppose many of the necessary reforms.

Simon Long: South Asia correspondent, *The Economist*

The tussle between Congress and its allies is one that none of them expected to face. They were as surprised as were their opponents and the pollsters by their victory in the general elections in April and May 2004. The shock defeat of the coalition led by the Bharatiya Janata Party (BJP) was interpreted in a number of ways: as a rejection of the "communalism" of the Hindu-nationalist BJP, whose rule had been scarred in 2002 by an anti-Muslim pogrom in Gujarat; as a cry of pain from the dirt-poor countryside, home to 700m Indians angered by the BJP's campaign advertising India's "shining" economic success; and even as a repudiation of economic reforms, introduced in 1991 by Manmohan Singh, then the finance minister and now prime minister.

In truth, India is too big a country for such simplification. In most places, voters threw out the party in power at the state level—the "anti-incumbency factor" that dominates Indian elections. So, if a national "mandate" was given, it makes more sense to describe it as a demand for more reform, not less.

There were two big exceptions to the anti-incumbency rule: Communist-run West Bengal, and Bihar, whose Rashtriya Janata Dal (RJD) is the second-largest party in the ruling coalition. Those exceptions, essential to Congress's majority, also bring it its biggest headaches. The RJD is led by Laloo Prasad Yadav, a charismatic, folksy politician, who makes much of his lower-caste origins. But Mr Yadav, who is the railways minister, is one of several RJD ministers who have had criminal charges filed against them (which they strongly deny). Bihar, which he and his wife have ruled as chief ministers since 1990, is notorious as India's poorest and worst-governed state. A campaign against what it calls "tainted" ministers will give the BJP one of the main themes in opposition.

Outside looking in

By March 2005 state elections are due in Bihar, along with neighbouring Jharkhand, and Haryana, near Delhi. Mr Yadav will want to use his power at the centre for electoral gain at home. Throughout 2005, West Bengal's Communists, vital "outside supporters" of the Congress coalition, will have their eyes on state elections due in 2006. They will oppose every reform likely to upset their grass-roots activists.

However, the looming elections make it even less likely that the Communists will topple the government. Nor is the opposition capable of bringing it down. The BJP will return closer to its roots. Power blunted its sharper edges. They will be honed again, as the BJP seeks to enthuse its demoralised activists by raising "Hindu" issues. It will also harp on the Italian origins of Sonia Gandhi, Congress's leader. The BJP's alarming tendency to resort to extra-parliamentary mass campaigns will pose a threat to social harmony. ▶

Indian summer GDP % real change

Source: Economist Intelligence Unit

The Chindia story

Christopher Lockwood

China and India begin a new chapter

In 1962 China and India fought a brief but bloody border war. In the decades that followed the two countries took a perverse delight in infuriating each other. Both countries shared two things, though: a tendency towards economic isolationism and a proud commitment to self-sufficiency. In both cases it led to stagnation and widespread poverty.

Roll the film forward 40 years and see how much has changed. Both countries have opened their economies and are now growing at roaring rates. And the long hostility between the two has been set aside, even if lingering mutual suspicions still act as a significant restraint. In 2002 (precisely 40 years after the war) the then Chinese premier, Zhu Rongji, visited India and told his hosts: "You are the first in software, and we are the first in hardware. When we put these two together, we can become the world's number one." At the time it seemed a ludicrous conceit, but it is starting to come true.

Total, or bilateral, trade between the two countries (including Hong Kong) could top $15 billion for the first time in 2005. That is small beer beside, say, China's total trade with America. But the key thing is the rate at which it has grown. A decade ago it was only around $300m. A virtual Chindia, a loose economic link-up, is taking shape.

If ever two economies were designed to complement each other, they are India's and China's. China, with a seemingly inexhaustible pool of cheap labour and an infrastructure that is startlingly good for a developing country, excels at manufacturing. But it is weak in services. Blame the absence of democracy for that, in part: information flows are still tightly restricted in a country that views the internet with suspicion and censors foreign publications. Language skills, too, are an issue.

India is the reverse. Its economic renaissance has come primarily from services. Manufacturing makes up a paltry 15% or so of India's GDP. Its infrastructure is famously terrible. But India is starting to make a good living by targeting areas that do not depend on efficient ports and highways. Call centres are only the beginning. India, in particular Bangalore in the south and two new "cyber-cities" that have sprung up just outside Delhi, is also hoovering up jobs in back-office processing and software development.

The truly fascinating twist, though, is that the two countries are not just dividing the world market between them along hardware/software lines. They are starting to invest in each other as well. When Mr Zhu visited Delhi and the then prime minister of India, Atal Behari Vajpayee, made his return visit to China the following year, the headlines might have all been about diplomacy, but dozens of business and investment agreements were signed in the margins. Politics permitting, the Chindia story has much further to run. □

Christopher Lockwood: Asia editor, *The Economist*

A great match

But not to Congress rule. It will survive and its impressive economic team will do what it can to lift India's long-term growth rate to 8% a year, as was achieved in 2003. The international standing of Indian business will continue to rise, partly because of the astonishing growth of its remote-services businesses. These will face challenges in 2005. The protectionist ballyhoo against outsourcing and the jobs lost in America and Europe will be replaced by concerns about the quality of service, the security of data and the sky-high rates of staff attrition in Indian call centres. There will be bad publicity and many smaller firms will go out of business. The bigger, longer-established information-technology firms, however, will go from strength to strength.

The reformists in the government want to extend the lessons of the success of the IT industry to the rest of the economy: keep government out of the way and allow Indian entrepreneurs to flourish. But politics will impede them. Progress will be slow.

The same can be forecast for the big foreign-policy initiative India has inherited from the BJP, the effort to make a lasting peace with Pakistan. A second round of their "composite dialogue" will culminate in meetings between the foreign ministers in May or June. They will take note of modest progress on almost every bilateral

India will have to engage in a serious dialogue on Kashmir, or risk throwing away the best chance in a generation of a settlement

issue, apart from the one that really matters: the disputed territory of Kashmir. The second half of 2005 will then bring increasing pressure at home on Pakistan's president, Pervez Musharraf, to show evidence of Indian flexibility. India will have to engage in a serious dialogue on Kashmir, or risk throwing away the best chance in a generation of a settlement—a settlement, moreover, largely on its terms. □

2005

The World Health Organisation will closely monitor the possible emergence of a deadly human-to-human strain of "bird flu".

Work in progress in Pakistan

Najam Sethi *LAHORE*

And it won't get any easier in 2005

When General Pervez Musharraf seized power in October 1999 from the discredited civilian regime of Nawaz Sharif, Pakistan was variously described as a "failing", "failed" or "rogue" state. Its economy was in the dumps. The army had stirred up Islamist insurgency to the east in Indian-held Kashmir and propped up the Taliban regime in Afghanistan to the west. After the coup, Pakistan was kicked out of the Commonwealth. It had to endure a sermon from Bill Clinton during a niggardly five-hour stopover in Islamabad after a highly successful five-day trip to India. And its people were squeezed by the International Monetary Fund's structural-adjustment programme.

But September 11th 2001 changed all that. Mr Musharraf swiftly facilitated the downfall of the Taliban and joined the war against al-Qaeda. This about-turn in a country awash with Islamist sentiment and with an army motivated by Islamic *jihad* provoked widespread anti-Americanism and posed a grave risk to Mr Musharraf. But it did afford an opportunity to rehabilitate Pakistan internationally and revive its economy.

As a reward for Pakistan's support in the war on terrorism, billions of dollars of debt were written off or rescheduled. Access to western markets for Pakistani products was eased. The IMF's belt-tightening programme was terminated. And growth has recovered strongly. The Karachi stockmarket, which grew by 55% in 2003-04, became one of the world's best performers.

Mr Musharraf has also revived "guided democracy". He held elections in 2002. He has acquired a degree of legitimacy by doing a deal with the Muttahida Majlis-i-Amal (MMA), an alliance of six religious parties, to amend the constitution and make himself president of Pakistan for five years. And he has encouraged a remarkable thaw in relations with India. Pakistan was also readmitted to the Commonwealth in 2004.

Therefore Pakistan in 2005 under Mr Musharraf may be described as a work in progress. This involves creating a stable and representative political system, turning back the tide of extremist Islam, nurturing a buoyant economy, sustaining the peace process with India and consolidating a co-operative relationship with the wider world, especially America. That is a challenging task in view of the stumbling blocks ahead.

Mr Musharraf's guided democracy depends on forcing two former prime ministers and mainstream leaders, Benazir Bhutto and Mr Sharif, to stay out in the cold. Mr Musharraf has filled the political vacuum left by their pro-West parties with the anti-West religious parties of the MMA—whose leader, Maulana Fazlur Rehman, has been duly nominated by the government as leader of the opposition. The MMA has also been nudged to form governments in two out of the country's four provinces. Thus Mr Musharraf is relying for political stability on the very MMA whose Islamic extremism poses the greatest challenge to his rule and to good relations with the West. There have been two assassination attempts on Mr Musharraf and one on the current prime minister, Shaukat Aziz. These were carried out by Islamic zealots linked to both the MMA and al-Qaeda. If Mr Musharraf were to be suddenly removed, Pakistan would plunge into turmoil.

Contradictions between the MMA and Mr Musharraf will sharpen in 2005. The MMA will insist he stop assisting the war against al-Qaeda. Mr Musharraf's refusal will make him a target in more ways than one for the Islamists. The same sort of problem besets his bid to normalise relations with India and exploit the peace dividend. The dialogue is rigidly held hostage by the Kashmir dispute. India wants to build confidence by resolving the less contentious issues first and the intractable problem of Kashmir later. But Mr Musharraf cannot pack up the Islamic *jihad* (based in Pakistan while waging war in Kashmir at the behest of the Pakistani army) until India agrees to resolve Kashmir.

Mr Musharraf's reform agenda is caught squarely between the rock of keeping out the mainstream pro-West parties for personal reasons (they want a restoration of unbridled democracy) and the hard place of allying with the religious groups to safeguard the army's vested interests vis-à-vis India. In short, his foreign-policy commitments are in conflict with his domestic political compulsions. These tensions will mar Pakistan's stumbling quest for stability and growth in 2005. □

> If Mr Musharraf were to be suddenly removed, Pakistan would plunge into turmoil

Najam Sethi: editor of the *Friday Times* and *Daily Times* in Pakistan

Delightfully dull in Indonesia

Edward McBride

Under its new president, the world's biggest Muslim country should enjoy a welcome return to stability

For the past seven years Indonesia has produced nothing but surprises. First came the Asian crash of 1997, which put a halt to the country's miraculous economic growth. The fall of Suharto, Indonesia's strongman of 30 years, followed soon after. Next came a remarkably rapid series of democratic reforms, including free elections, the ejection of the army from politics and the unleashing of a free press. But there was also instability: various restive provinces attempted to secede and Islamic radicals started setting off bombs, even as Indonesia churned through three more presidents in quick succession. After all this drama, 2005 may herald the biggest surprise of all—a return to relative stability.

A first indicator of things to come will be a handful of high-profile corruption investigations, designed to highlight the reformist instincts of Susilo Bambang Yudhoyono, the new president. The general-turned-politician—universally known as "SBY"—won a handsome victory in Indonesia's first direct presidential election in September 2004. He has expressed determination to improve Indonesia's investment climate. But the reforms he has in mind, including an overhaul of the police and courts, will take years to bear fruit. In the meantime he is counting on a tough attorney-general and energetic prosecutors to impress potential investors.

Mr Yudhoyono himself will concentrate on easing tensions in Indonesia's many troublespots. His hearts-and-minds policy will help restore order in the islands of Maluku and Sulawesi, where a weak economy and widespread unemployment has prolonged a bloody feud between local Christians and Muslims. But he will struggle to improve the conduct of the army and thus to win over the inhabitants of Aceh and Papua, two oil-rich provinces wracked by separatist insurgencies. Nonetheless, there will be fewer embarrassing reports of remote provinces going up in flames, and no more talk of Indonesia's imminent disintegration.

Businessmen were so disappointed by the previous government's indifference that even these small steps will cheer them up. So 2005 will also be the year that foreign investment in Indonesia starts to flow again. Many Indonesians who have salted money away overseas in recent years will start to bring it home. A clarification of murky regulations should also prompt investment in power plants, toll roads and other badly needed infrastructure.

But the news will not all be good. Growth may climb somewhat, but will not reach pre-crisis levels. Unemployment will continue to rise, as millions of young Indonesians enter the job market. Demonstrations will break out when the government cuts subsidies and so raises the price of fuel. Budget strictures will prevent Mr Yudhoyono from implementing his most ambitious policies; many voters will feel short-changed.

Nor will the other branches of government necessarily co-operate with the new leader. Mr Yudhoyono's Democrat Party only controls a tenth of seats in the lower house of parliament—so he will spend much of his time cajoling recalcitrant legislators. But he might manage to engineer friendlier regimes in Golkar and the Indonesian Democratic Party of Struggle, the two biggest forces in parliament, which will soon pick new leaders. The upper house, consisting of non-partisan regional representatives, is an unknown quantity which convened for the first time in October. A new constitutional court will throw some spanners in the government's works, as will uppity local parliaments.

Terrorism, too, remains a worry. More bombs will no doubt go off in 2005. When a car bomb blew up outside the Australian embassy in Jakarta in September 2004, killing the driver and nine others, the police warned that the same terrorists might have another such device ready to deploy. Two expert bombmakers suspected of involvement in many of Indonesia's recent attacks are still at large. But the police are getting better at tracking them down, while the terrorists are getting

There will be fewer embarrassing reports of remote provinces going up in flames

worse at penetrating the defences of likely targets. That reduces the odds of an atrocity akin to the Bali bombings in 2001, which claimed 202 lives.

So the world's biggest Muslim country (estimated population: 227m) will grapple with many of the same workaday problems faced by more sedate places: improving the economy, coping with partisan politics, streamlining the bureaucracy. Much more important, however, are the problems it has put behind it: runaway inflation, near insolvency, financial-sector meltdown, incipient break-up, military meddling in politics and an archaic, authoritarian system of government. Even the struggle against terrorism will begin to seem more manageable. By the country's recent standards, 2005 will be a reassuringly dull year for Indonesia. □

2005

Jung Chang, the Chinese-born author of the bestselling "Wild Swans", together with her husband and co-author Jon Halliday, will publish a biography of Chairman Mao. The book will be released worldwide, except in China, where (like "Wild Swans") it will be banned.

Edward McBride: South-East Asia correspondent, *The Economist*

More jobs, please

Recorded unemployment

% of total labour force

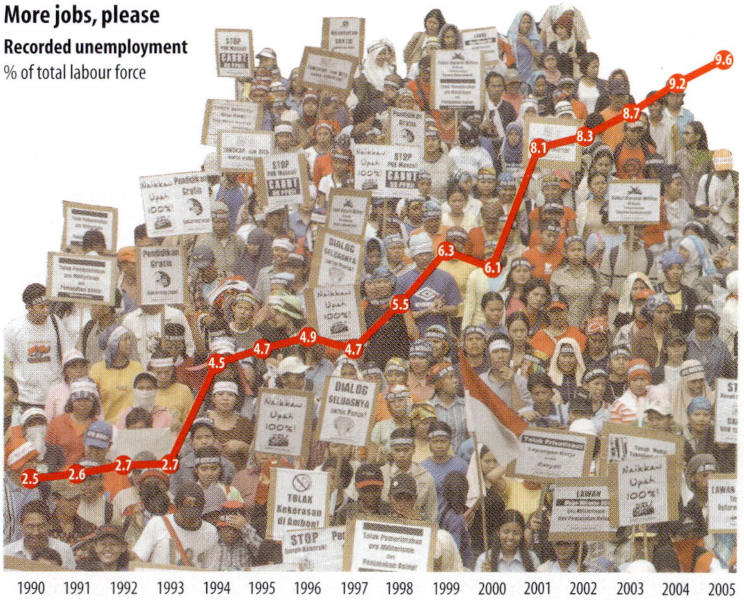

VIETNAM *FORECAST*

Vietnam is on the cusp of becoming a bona fide part of the global economy by acceding to the World Trade Organisation (WTO). Unfortunately, the government will probably have to put on hold its celebrations to mark this lofty achievement. Although coming close, it is unlikely to meet its target of joining the WTO by the end of 2005.

In its quest for WTO entry, the government has stepped up the pace of trade reform. In other areas its reform rhetoric has not been matched by actual changes on the ground. A few large state-owned enterprises may be partly privatised in 2005, and the private sector may enjoy a slightly easier operating environment, but the Communist Party's controlling mentality remains in force. Still, foreign investors are attracted to Vietnam's thriving economy, with its rapidly growing private sector and buoyant consumer demand. Investors also like the relatively stable political environment, devoid of the security risks looming over some other countries.

Vietnam's economic competitiveness—or rather, the lack of it—will be a cause for concern in 2005. The expiry of the Multi-Fibre Arrangement at the end of 2004 permits WTO members, including China, to begin exporting garments around the world, quota-free. Vietnam's largest and most efficient manufacturers should survive this onslaught of global competition, but others will struggle to keep their export orders.

Robust economic growth and falling poverty rates have helped Vietnam become a darling of foreign-aid donors. However, western governments regularly berate the Communist Party for its poor record on human rights. America has been particularly vocal. But, reflecting Vietnam's emerging status in the global economy, in 2005 friction between the former foes will be over trade in shrimp, not political ideology.

KEY INDICATORS	2003	2004	2005
GDP growth (%)	7.2	7.0	6.8
Budget balance (% GDP)	-2.6	-3.5	-4.1
Unemployment (%)	1.7	2.2	2.4
Inflation (%, ave)	3.1	8.0	6.8

Economist Intelligence Unit

Still feeling lucky?

Robert Milliken *SYDNEY*

Time for Australia to re-examine its priorities

Having lived beyond their means through so many boom years, Australians can expect a rude shock in 2005. Much of the boom has been driven by soaring house prices and cheap credit. Neither will last. A bumpy landing for some lies ahead in the lucky country's 14th year of uninterrupted growth.

Household debt doubled over the past five years and stood at a record 150% of disposable income by the end of 2004. The Reserve Bank of Australia, the central bank, muttered dark warnings during 2004 that credit growth was unsustainable. But it delicately held off raising interest rates in the charged political climate building up to Australia's general election in October. The conservative coalition government of John Howard fed the feelgood factor by throwing money at voters on the back of a budget surplus.

Now for the reckoning. With the election out of the way, the bank will move quickly to push interest rates up. But despite the dampening of domestic demand, Australia's economy will grow by about 3.5% in 2005, driven by businesses investing and exports picking up after a worrying slump. China cannot get enough of Australia's gas, iron ore, nickel and copper.

Robert Milliken: Australia correspondent, *The Economist*

Starting to wobble

Having won a fourth term, Mr Howard must now make good his promises to keep the good times rolling. The margin of his victory surprised even his supporters: it gave the coalition effective control of the Senate, the upper house of federal parliament, where minor parties have held the balance of power for almost 20 years. When the new Senate convenes in July 2005 Mr Howard will start pushing through some of his more contentious economic reforms that the old Senate had stalled. Expect the government to sell its 51% share of Telstra, the country's biggest telecoms company, to weaken union powers and abolish laws that restrict foreign ownership of media companies. And don't expect Mr Howard, at 65, to stand aside gracefully for Peter Costello, his 47-year-old deputy and the man tipped to succeed him as leader of the conservative Liberal Party.

The post-invasion mess in Iraq and a huge bomb blast outside the Australian embassy in the Indonesian capital, Jakarta, in September 2004 showed that Australia has much thinking to do about redirecting the focus of its policy closer to home. One challenge will be to balance Australia's strong commercial relationship with China against its close ties with Washington in the event of any crisis between China and America over Taiwan. Another will be to change the lukewarm relationship with Indonesia. The excellent co-operation between Australian and Indonesian police since the 2002 Bali bombing shows the potential for the two neighbours to work together more closely. A change of leadership in Jakarta after the Indonesian presidential election in September 2004 offers Canberra a much-needed circuit-breaker.

The 120,000 immigrants who arrive in Australia in 2005 will find a country divided over how much public money should underwrite schools, universities, hospitals and other infrastructure, to say nothing of water conservation in the world's second-driest continent (after Antarctica). With A$8.6 billion ($6.4 billion) available from the 2003-04 budget surplus, it seems a curious quandary. John Edwards, chief economist of HSBC in Australia, suggests this shows how Australia has failed to build on its long period of prosperity by re-investing in its future. The lucky country's biggest challenge in 2005 could be how to re-invent itself before the luck runs out. □

Building the Unified Economic Space within the CIS in 2004 and 2005

Results of 2004 and development plans for 2005

presented by Yerzhan Tatishev, Bank TuranAlem
Chairman of the Management Board

Strengthening of economic integration of CIS countries

- Presidents of Kazakhstan, Russia, Ukraine, and Belarus agreed to intensify the building of the Unified Economic Space within the CIS countries
- The aggregate real GDP growth of CIS countries increased to 8%
- Current account surplus of CIS countries increased to 8.3%
- Aggregate CPI of CIS countries in 2004 moderated to 9.9% in 2004 from 13.8% in 2002
- Russia and Kazakhstan ratified the Convention on double taxation.

Bank TuranAlem's contribution into the economic and financial development of CIS countries

- The Bank continues implementing its development strategy within the CIS region and connecting CIS economies through banking system.
- BTA established representative offices in Kyrgyz Republic, China, Ukraine, Belarus and certain regions of Russian Federation in 2004. Next year the Bank plans to open representative offices in Armenia, Azerbaijan, Tajikistan and other CIS countries.
- Total BTA loans and Trade finance volumes in the Russian banking and corporate sectors exceeded USD 500 million, as at fourth quarter 2004.
- As at 1 November 2004 BTA became the 6th largest private bank in CIS in terms of assets size – USD 4 bln.
- BTA signed Memorandum of collaboration with 8 regional administrations of CIS countries

Financial Information:
Total assets: $4 bln
(as at 1 November 2004)

Ratings:

Standard&Poors's	
Senior debt	BB-
Outlook	positive

Moody's	
Senior debt	Baa2
Outlook	positive

We have much in common.

Bank shareholders: RZB, FMO FINANCE FOR DEVELOPMENT, European Bank for Reconstruction and Development, IFC, DEG Development is our business, KAZAKHSTAN SHAREHOLDERS

Republic of Kazakhstan, Almaty, 480051, 97 Zholdasbekova str., Samal-2, tel: +7(3272) 505100, fax: +7(3272) 500224
Russian Federation, Moscow, 129110, 62 Mira ave., building#1, tel: +7(095) 7756690, fax: +7(095) 7756693
Ukraine, Kiev, 01004, 9/2 Bolshaya Vasilkovskaya str., office 14, tel: +380(44) 2475759, fax: +380(44) 2273604
Republic of Belarus, Minsk, 220123, 20 V.Horuzhei str., tel/fax: +375 17 2895841

BankTuranAlem
ESTABLISHED IN 1925

www.bta.kz/en/

Asia's era of change and promise

Lee Hsien Loong, prime minister of Singapore, sees great opportunity in the rise of China and India

Asia is poised at a moment of great change and promise. The rise of China and India in the coming decades, and how the world responds to their rise, will define this century.

The transformation and opening up of these two economies is already the central reality for Asia. China has become Japan's second-largest trading partner and South Korea's largest. Asian businessmen are pursuing projects and contracts all over China. Chinese companies are venturing abroad, starting a reverse flow of foreign direct investments. Millions of Chinese tourists swarm the region.

India started opening up later, but it too offers many opportunities. The expanding Indian middle classes have fast-growing needs for everything from education and medical care to financial services. India's economic reforms have seen many false dawns and are far less entrenched than China's. But there is a sense that this time the reforms are irreversible, whichever party is in power in Delhi. The new Congress government has promised to liberalise India's economy further and double its share of global trade within five years.

South-East Asia has a large market of half a billion people, abundant natural resources, and ample land and labour juxtaposed with cities offering first-world conditions. It is well placed to prosper along with China and India. At the same time, members of the Association of South-East Asian Nations (ASEAN) maintain broad and diversified relations with the United States, the European Union and Japan. They are negotiating free-trade agreements with major trading partners around the world and enhancing economic co-operation among themselves.

> Countries which prepare their peoples for the changes, and move early to anticipate the strategic shifts, will have the advantage

It is far better for Asia to have two prospering and stable giants, rather than two backward and troubled ones. A vibrant India will complement an emerging China and broaden the basis for prosperity in Asia. But it means major adjustments for the other economies. It is not just cheap unskilled workers; China and India supply many of the world's scientists and engineers. A new division of labour is emerging, as other countries find ways to grow alongside China and India and develop strengths of their own. Shifting to this new pattern will take time and effort, and there will be winners and losers. Countries that prepare their peoples for the changes, and move early to anticipate the strategic shifts, will have the advantage.

China's economic weight is already having an impact on the strategic balance in Asia. In an earlier period, the rise of Japan after the Meiji restoration created massive upheavals which led eventually to the Pacific war. China and India will create even bigger reverberations. Managing their peaceful emergence requires wisdom and statesmanship by all the major powers.

A time for statesmanship in the Pacific

Since the second world war the United States has been a major power in Asia. The *Pax Americana* has enabled Asian countries big and small to grow in peace. Now a new balance will have to be struck. The legitimate, growing interests of China and later India will have to be accommodated. Their relations with the United States should be based on mutual benefit, rather than containment or rivalry. Europe too has an interest in building up its stake in Asia, so as not to be at a grave disadvantage compared with the United States. Many Asian countries will welcome the deep engagement of America and Europe in the region.

There are security threats to the benign scenario. The most dangerous is tension across the straits of Taiwan. Taiwan's economy is steadily integrating with China's, but politically the two are drifting apart. In Taiwan consciousness of the island's separate identity is growing. The ruling party rejects One China and talks about "one country on each side of the straits". Pro-independence elements are increasingly adventurous. However, they can only go as far as the United States allows, for ultimately cross-straits relations depend on Sino-American relations.

China is determined to prevent Taiwanese independence, but the Taiwanese have not fully grasped this. There is a real risk that a miscalculation or mishap could spark an armed conflict, which would become a confrontation between China and America. This would of course be a grave setback for the whole region, and the world.

Extremist Islamic terrorism is another long-term problem. In South-East Asia the Jemaah Islamiah group, which is linked to al-Qaeda and perpetrated the Bali and more recent bombings, remains active. The terrorists will fail in their Utopian aim to establish an Islamic caliphate. But countries need vigilance and resolve to prevent attacks that will undermine confidence, investments and growth. Dealing firmly with extremist groups and their support networks without antagonising moderate Muslims will be a major challenge for governments.

In this dynamic environment, small countries such as Singapore have to position themselves carefully. The challenges loom larger for us than for bigger countries. But it is also easier for small countries to persuade their people of what needs to be done, set clear directions and change policies when new situations arise. The starkness of our situation leaves no room for complacent delusions.

For all the risks and uncertainties, Asia today is one of the world's most dynamic and promising regions. It is our fate to live in exciting times and our good fortune to have the chance to shape a better future for ourselves. □

Middle East and Africa

Also in this section:

Israel's countdown to disengagement

David Landau *JERUSALEM*

Out of Gaza, into political turmoil

The 12 weeks that, with luck, will change the Middle East are to start in the summer of 2005. By mid-autumn, under Ariel Sharon's disengagement schedule, the last Israeli soldier will have withdrawn from the Gaza strip and from the northern tip of the West Bank. The last Israeli settlers will have left too, voluntarily or dragged out by the army, two weeks earlier.

The timing, then, is clear. So is Mr Sharon's determination to go through with the disengagement. The widespread scepticism that first greeted the prime minister's plan has largely dissipated. What remains in doubt is his ability to force his political will on a querulous cabinet and a restless, fragmented parliament.

If Mr Sharon succeeds, 2005 will certainly be the most momentous year for Israelis and Palestinians since the Oslo agreement of 1993, arguably since the Six Day War in 1967 when Israel first occupied the Palestinian territories. The dismantling of settlements will signify the beginning of the end of occupation. That is why the settlers throughout the West Bank and Gaza and their political allies inside Israel have turned the full force of their ideological fervour against Mr Sharon, their longtime leader and champion.

2005

The UN's arms embargo against the Democratic Republic of Congo expires at the end of July.

Down the road, a viable Palestinian state?

They could have decided to downplay the disengagement from Gaza and the tip of Samaria. After all, barely 10,000 settlers are to be evicted, out of a total of more than 250,000 in the West Bank and Gaza. Gaza, moreover, is not the historical heartland. It belonged to the Philistines, not the Israelites, for much of the biblical era. And the modern-day occupation is thoroughly unpopular with most Israelis, whose soldier-sons are sent to guard the Gaza settlements.

Nevertheless, the settler movement's rabbis and lay leaders resolved to draw their line in the sand around Gaza. They recognise—even though he himself publicly denies it—that Mr Sharon (or whoever succeeds him) will not be able to stop at this disengagement. If the Palestinian Authority can provide a modicum of order in liberated Gaza, international pressure will quickly mount for further withdrawal and the creation at last of a viable Palestinian state in Gaza and the West Bank. The conflict will narrow to three or four strips of West Bank land close to the 1967 line, now densely populated by settlers, which Israel will try to keep under an eventual peace treaty, perhaps swapping them for Israeli territory abutting Gaza. The false messiah of Greater Israel will finally give up the ghost.

It is the far right's decision to fight Mr Sharon that makes the Gaza disengagement a political cataclysm for Israel. It has driven the centre and much of the left, however reluctantly, into Mr Sharon's camp. The man the liberals loved to loathe is now their unlikely champion. Peaceniks would ideally prefer negotiations to the prime minister's unilateralism. But the collapse of the Labour government's negotiation with Yasser Arafat in 2000-01 left many in the Israeli peace camp permanently disenchanted with the Palestinian leadership. Unilateral withdrawal from Gaza, however deficient, is better than staying there.

Whoever wins the disengagement battle, Israeli poli- ▶

If Mr Sharon succeeds, 2005 will certainly be the most momentous year for Israelis and Palestinians since the Oslo agreement of 1993

David Landau: editor, *Haaretz*

tics will emerge unrecognisable. The Likud party could well split. Mr Sharon will be hard put to win re-election as leader of the party in its present, militant mood. The party's central committee has repeatedly spurned the disengagement plan. The parliamentary faction is divided. Mr Sharon will need the votes of the opposition Labour Party to stave off defeat in the House during the months leading to the disengagement. But even they may not be enough. By law, he must carry the budget by March 31st, or else face elections by the summer.

With Mr Sharon a spry but slowing 76 and the leader of the Labour opposition, Shimon Peres, an indefatigable 81, the prospect of a hung parliament and early elections might have been expected to open the way for new blood at the top. In fact, say the polls, many voters would like to see some sort of fusion of Labour and the Likud moderates, with the two old men, whose 50 years of personal friendship transcend their political differences, ruling jointly over a new super-party. Its central policy plank would be to implement the Gaza disengagement. To complete this geriatric dream-team, some suggest attaching the head of the third-largest party, Shinui: the justice minister Yosef Lapid, a sprightly 73.

Mr Peres, though, is dubious. He says Mr Sharon is too old and tired to embark on so radical a transformation of the party-political alignment. In fact, Mr Peres's position in his own party is less than secure. In pre-election primaries he might well be toppled.

The depth of the crisis affecting the two major parties is reflected in the fact that both elderly incumbents are threatened chiefly by discredited former prime ministers. Binyamin Netanyahu, prime minister from 1996 to 1999, was swept away by Labour's Ehud Barak (1999-2001), who in turn was crushed by Mr Sharon. Mr Netanyahu slowed the post-Oslo negotiations with the Palestinians to the point of virtual paralysis. Mr Barak boldly tried a leap to peace at Camp David in the summer of 2000. That failure brought on the *intifada*—which, close to 4,000 deaths later, is still not over.

Mr Netanyahu is the powerful minister of finance in Mr Sharon's cabinet. He has been steadily undermining the disengagement plan. Mr Barak, ostensibly on a time-out from active politics, is chipping away at Mr Peres's support for the Sharon government. Each of them hopes to end 2005 as prime minister. Mainstream Israelis and Palestinians can only hope the old men hang in long enough to get the disengagement done. □

2005

Welcome telecoms competition will expand in South Africa, eroding the monopoly of Telkom, previously the country's only fixed-line provider.

Bullets or ballot boxes in Iraq?

Xan Smiley

Either way, it won't be pretty

As the CIA accurately reported in late 2004, the three-fold choice for Iraq in the coming year is "tenuous stability", "further fragmentation and extremism" and a "trend towards civil war". The worst outcome—civil war—is not inevitable. But the most unlikely result of all is that which George Bush and his advisers heralded when American forces were sent in to topple Saddam Hussein in March 2003: a liberal, secular democracy, setting an example to the Arab world.

The most hopeful start to the year would be a general election, scheduled by the end of January, in which, say, 60% of the electorate cast votes, despite the inevitable threats and intimidation of the insurgents. That would give the ensuing government a measure of legitimacy. More than 100 parties may compete in the election, which will be contested by national lists. A more-or-less nationwide election will be seen as a triumph.

There are two vital prerequisites. One is that the

Xan Smiley: Middle East and Africa editor, *The Economist*

SAUDI ARABIA *FORECAST*

In 2005 Saudi Arabia will be entering uncharted political waters. The election of half the members of the country's municipal councils, although a modest experiment in democracy by the standards of even some Middle Eastern neighbours, will be an unprecedented nationwide electoral process for the kingdom. It is due to be conducted in three phases, starting in February and ending in April. If successful, direct election of half the members of regional councils will follow by 2006, with a partly elected national legislative body sometime after that.

A "Riyadh spring" this is not. Electing councillors across the country will be a quantum leap for the kingdom, but the candidates will be drawn from a carefully selected shortlist—and it seems the process will not extend to women, even as voters. However, the government is serious and also plans further rounds of a national dialogue with key Islamic and liberal constituencies demanding accountable and transparent decisions. The test will be whether the political thaw can meet the concerns of the mass of increasingly alienated Saudi nationals.

The country's rulers badly need to improve their public reputation. A political process that encourages decision-making to be open will be uncomfortable for the ruling family, but it is part of a series of steps needed to isolate the small band of militants who threaten security in the kingdom.

Equally important will be increasing economic opportunity for the burgeoning population. Rising oil output and foreign investment will stimulate economic growth of over 2% in 2005, but the population will expand by some 3%. A series of gas and petrochemical projects with foreign partners should get properly under way in 2005. These will represent a foreign vote of confidence for the kingdom's rulers. But the challenge of creating sufficient jobs and ending security threats will take longer.

KEY INDICATORS	2003	2004	2005
GDP growth (%)	7.2	3.3	2.3
Budget balance (% GDP)	5.6	3.5	-0.3
Inflation (%, ave)	0.6	0.4	0.3

Economist Intelligence Unit

Sunni insurgency, affecting Baghdad and the "Sunni triangle" to the west and north of the capital, be restricted to those areas. The UN-appointed interim government of Iyad Allawi would like to smash the insurgency in Fallujah, the city at the heart of the Sunni rebellion, before the election.

> Do not rule out the prospect that a new government might ask the Americans to leave earlier than expected

The second prerequisite is that the Shias, who represent about 60% of Iraqis compared with 20% for the Sunni Arabs and 20% for the Kurds, include the radical Shias among the voters. An election with only minimal participation from the rebel Sunni areas would be credible, at a pinch; but the refusal of those many Shias who follow a turbulent clergyman, Muqtada al-Sadr, to go to the polls would virtually invalidate the result. A big hope for 2005 is that Mr Sadr, who has blown hot and cold on whether to be a man of violence or a peaceful politician, will choose electoral politics.

If he does, he will do far better than the Americans and their protégés would like. For a start, a majority of poor Shias in Baghdad (particularly in the 2m-strong al-Thawra slumland of north-eastern Baghdad, known after his father as Sadr City), as well as in Shia towns across central and southern Iraq, are likely to vote for him. A main plank of his policy is the immediate expulsion of the Americans. Still, the Americans would rather he did join the electoral fray than go back to fomenting outright rebellion. And do not rule out the prospect that a new government might ask the Americans to leave earlier than expected; the Americans have promised that if asked to go, they will go.

However, the national-list system should favour a coalition of half a dozen establishment parties, most of them Shia-oriented, including Mr Allawi's Iraqi National Accord and Ibrahim al-Jaafari's more popular Dawa party. The perennial enigma of Shia politics, and the man who can still make or break almost any plan for Iraq, is Grand Ayatollah Ali Sistani, by far the most influential Shia cleric. He will continue to disavow an active political role for himself, will probably refuse to bless any particular party, and will advise against the establishment of an Iranian-style Shia theocracy. But if, for whatever reason, he were to declare an election void, that would almost certainly kibosh any government that emerged from a disputed ballot.

Only in Kurdish parts of the country are the two main political parties—run respectively by the Barzani and Talabani clans—both pro-American and popular. Whether or not they team up to form a single list in the three of Iraq's 18 provinces that they run, they will win in those provinces overwhelmingly in any election.

But this raises the question of Iraq's continuing viability as a country, even if Mr Allawi does manage to bring it to a more or less credible election. For the emerging government's biggest task will then be to write a new constitution. The Shias, backed by Mr Sistani, seem determined to bin the much-vaunted Transitional Administrative Law (the TAL) which the Americans wrote as an embryonic constitution, entrenching all sorts of human rights and a federal ethos, before they handed over formal sovereignty to Iraqis in June 2004.

This enrages the Kurds. If a half-credible new government manages to emerge out of an election in early 2005, an intense struggle between the Kurds and the Shias is likely to ensue over the constitution and electoral system that are due to be endorsed by referendum and then provide a basis for a final, full-blooded election in late 2005 or early 2006. The divided city of Kirkuk will again be a flashpoint. The Kurds insist it is theirs, as fiercely as Arab Iraqis and Turkomen (related to the Ottoman Turks who ran most of the country until 1920) say it is theirs.

Even if a compromise is struck (giving Kirkuk a special status and finding some arrangement to share out its oil wealth), the longer the chaos continues in the Shia- and Sunni-dominated parts of Iraq, the stronger the pro-independence sentiment will swell the hearts of ordinary Kurds. And if things get still worse in the rest of Iraq, the Americans may think of giving their backing to an ultra-autonomous Kurdistan—while the rest of the country slides into civil war. □

2005

Ethiopians hope to see the return of a magnificent 24-metre obelisk, looted from Aksum by the Fascists in 1935. Until 2003 the monument stood at a busy intersection in Rome.

Tall story

Dubai's dream, every vertigo sufferer's nightmare

The human soul, Arabs say, moves at the pace of a trotting camel. But multi-billion-dollar property developments can move a lot faster than that. By late 2007 Dubai—a city which barely existed 40 years ago—will boast yet another architectural curiosity to add to its already impressive collection: the world's tallest building.

Work on the skyscraper, known as Burj Dubai ("burj" means tower in Arabic), will get into full swing in 2005. Emaar, the company behind the project, won't say exactly how high it's going to be. Something over 700 metres is likely. That's 200 metres higher than the current record-holder, Taipei 101 (508 metres). Plans for megatowers in Shanghai and New York (on the site of the former World Trade Centre) have also been announced. But Emaar promises that its building will not be outdone.

Burj Dubai's design, by a Chicago-based firm, Skidmore, Owings & Merrill, is meant to reflect certain "historical influences of the Gulf". To the untutored eye, it looks like a whopping great icicle, surreally plonked down in the middle of a theme park. The building is part of a 200-hectare (500-acre) development that also includes the Dubai Mall, a shopping centre which, at nearly 1m square metres, will be—no prizes for guessing—the world's biggest. □

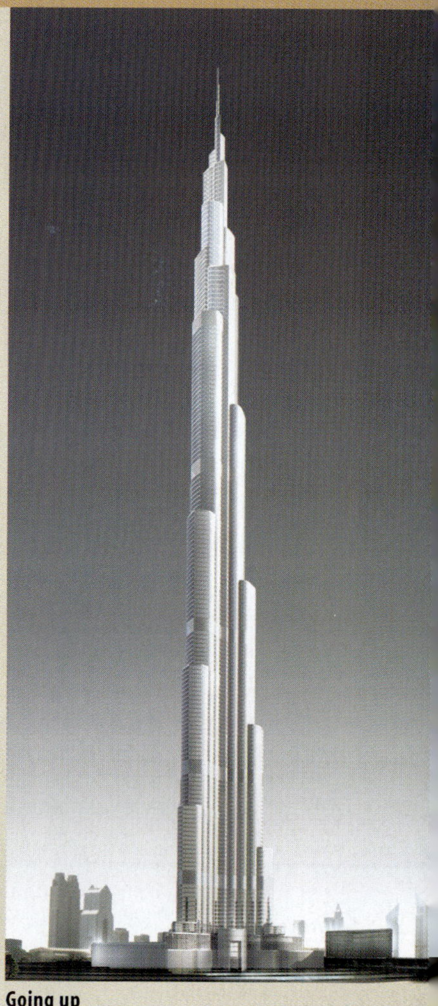

Going up

Mushrooming

Xan Smiley

The quest to stop the spread of nuclear weapons

No weapons of mass destruction (the famous WMD) may have turned up in Iraq, but that does not mean the world can relax—especially when it comes to WMD of the nuclear sort. The hunt for nukes, and the search for a way to limit and control their spread, will be as intensive in 2005 as it has ever been.

The most active diplomacy will focus on Iran, which was discovered two years ago by the International Atomic Energy Agency (IAEA), the UN's nuclear watchdog, to have lied for 18 years about its nuclear programmes; and on North Korea, which has boasted that it already has nuclear bombs. The European Union in the shape of its three leading countries—Britain, France and Germany—will be increasingly frustrated in its efforts to persuade Iran to come clean, desist from its troubling activities and give up its uranium-enrichment technology; it has accepted IAEA spot checks so far, but may continue to refuse to ratify a promise to accept them indefinitely. Iran will seek to spin out the diplomacy but could find itself facing economic sanctions from the EU and Japan if its lack of co-operation continues. If diplomacy fails, do not rule out the possibility of Israel striking at several of the sites—such as Bushehr in southern Iran.

Shocking new discoveries of nuclear programmes elsewhere are likely to be made in 2005, revealing the scale of the illicit network woven by Abdul Qadeer Khan, a Pakistani nuclear scientist belatedly exposed by the Pakistani authorities. It will probably become plain that Pakistan also sold its nuclear wherewithal to Saudi Arabia, which will find itself subjected to embarrassing scrutiny, as well as to Iran and others. Contrite Libya will help the West to unravel Mr Khan's web.

The biggest and more predictable event on the global WMD calendar will be the meeting in May that is due every five years, gathering the 190-plus countries that have signed the Nuclear Non-Proliferation Treaty (NPT). North Korea says it has withdrawn from it, Iran is threatening to leave, while three other countries with nuclear weapons—India, Pakistan and probably Israel—refuse to join. The hope is that the NPT will be toughened up. Countries seeking to withdraw would face heavy penalties; and more countries would sign an "additional protocol" that allows for intrusive, random inspections to ensure that those countries that do enrich uranium for peaceful reactors are not tempted to sell on their wares or to switch from peaceful purposes to weapons. The fear, as ever, is that countries, or bad people in them, might be tempted to sell on either their knowledge or nuclear material to rogue states or rogue groups, such as al-Qaeda.

"The present nuclear arms-control regime is looking battered," says Mohamed ElBaradei, head of the IAEA. He will be arguing that the processing of weapons-usable material (separated plutonium and highly enriched uranium) in civilian programmes should be restricted to facilities under multinational control. A debatably good idea, easier said than done. □

The good news in Africa

Robert Guest

Fewer wars, greater efforts to resolve conflicts

Robert Guest: Africa editor, *The Economist*; author of "The Shackled Continent: Africa's Past, Present and Future" (Macmillan)

In 2004 the big stories from Africa were the genocide in western Sudan and the tenth anniversary of the genocide in Rwanda. Other news included war in Burundi, communal street fighting in Nigeria and mass displacement in northern Uganda, where 1.8m people have fled their homes to avoid being murdered by an army of child soldiers led by a man who thinks he is the Messiah. All this obscures a surprising trend: as Jean-Marie Guéhenno also notes in *The World in 2005*, Africa has actually grown more peaceful in recent years.

As recently as 1999 a fifth of Africans lived in nations tortured by war. But civil wars in Sierra Leone, Liberia and Angola appear to be over. A ceasefire ending the pointless border conflict between Ethiopia and Eritrea, in which massed ranks of infantrymen were scythed with machine-gun fire, is still holding. Even the Democratic Republic of Congo is looking better. Though not exactly at peace, it is not gripped by the furious fighting that claimed 3m lives between 1998 and 2003. (As in all African wars, most of these deaths were from war-induced starvation or disease, but hundreds of thousands of people were also killed with bullets or farm tools.)

What has prompted this sudden outbreak of peace? Some wars ended because the combatants were exhausted. In Angola, for example, after the rebel chief Jonas Savimbi was shot in 2002 his bedraggled followers gave up and formed a political party. Other wars ended because of skilful diplomacy. Liberia was pulled from the inferno when Nigeria persuaded its warmongering president, Charles Taylor, to accept asylum. And outside military intervention has calmed some troublespots. ▸

SOUTH AFRICA *FORECAST*

South Africa has achieved much to be proud of in the ten years since its first all-race elections in 1994. Multi-party democracy, dominated by President Thabo Mbeki's African National Congress (ANC), is firmly established, racial tensions have largely receded and overall management of the economy is sound.

Still, 2005 will not be an easy year for Mr Mbeki. For one thing, South Africa needs more jobs. The country's massive unemployment problem (one in four South Africans is officially out of work) will not get better any time soon. Although the economy looks set to grow by 3.3% in 2005, this is well short of the 5% a year needed to make a serious dent in unemployment. And until that happens, it is hard to see how the government hopes to bring crime under control—essential if South Africa is to remain an attractive destination for foreign investors and tourists.

Although the government will remain broadly prudent, state spending on infrastructure (notably the development by September of the $500m deep-water port of Coega near Port Elizabeth), on the HIV/AIDS programme and on other social services will increase. After procrastinating for many years, Mr Mbeki and the ANC leadership have a lot of catching up to do in fighting the HIV/AIDS pandemic. Its social and economic impact will be limited in 2005, but the long-term consequences will be disastrous if the government fails to tackle the matter vigorously.

Armed with a two-thirds parliamentary majority following its landslide election victory in April 2004, the ANC can brush off criticism from an increasingly weak and fragmented opposition at home. But the mess in neighbouring Zimbabwe, where South Africa's softly-softly policy towards President Robert Mugabe has been an abject failure, could still come back to haunt Mr Mbeki.

KEY INDICATORS	2003	2004	2005
GDP growth (%)	1.9	2.8	3.3
Budget balance (% GDP)	-2.2	-2.7	-3.2
Unemployment (%)	29.7	26.2	24.8
Inflation (%, ave)	5.9	4.5	4.7

Economist Intelligence Unit

▶ British soldiers helped to rescue Sierra Leone from its hand-chopping rebels, and French and west African peacekeepers have done a reasonable job of keeping the two parties to Côte d'Ivoire's civil war apart.

For many Africans, peace has brought hope. Refugees are returning home, peasants are planting crops without fear that they will be stolen by passing armies. For the first time in a generation, Angolans can travel around their country without fear of being killed.

> Africa will be less bloody than news footage suggests, but bloodier than Africans would wish

But two grave worries remain. One is Sudan, where the atrocious campaign of ethnic cleansing in the western region of Darfur threatens to tear apart Africa's largest country. The other is that, even in the countries now at peace, the underlying causes of war have often not been addressed. Studies show that civil wars are more likely to occur in countries with bad governments, stagnant economies and lots of valuable minerals. Tyranny gives people cause to rebel. Poverty makes soldiering seem an attractive career option. Mineral wealth makes power lucrative to those who seize it.

Africa has all these problems in truckloads. Several wars that seem to have been extinguished are in fact only waiting to re-ignite, argue the pessimists. The skirmishing that continues in eastern Congo, for example, could easily re-escalate into all-out war. And since western powers are over-stretched in Iraq, Africans may find that they receive little help in putting out any new fires.

Optimists counter that Africans themselves have started to make more serious efforts to resolve their own conflicts. The two key peacemakers are the presidents of Africa's richest and most populous nations respectively: Thabo Mbeki of South Africa and Olusegun Obasanjo of Nigeria. Mr Mbeki has worked hard to cajole warring factions into patching up their differences, with some success in Congo and Burundi. The affable Mr Obasanjo has acted as an honest broker between warring parties in Darfur, though without much yet to show for it.

The problem for Africa's peacemakers is that no African army has the cash or planes to fly a large military force into hostile territory. They can deploy peacekeepers to neighbours that welcome them, or act as bodyguards for rebel leaders who lay down their arms and try to become politicians. But they cannot keep the peace where there is no peace to keep. For this, they would need substantial funding from abroad. At present they receive only dribs and drabs of cash, for example to help with the African Union's mission to Darfur.

What to expect in 2005? The best guess is that Angola, Sierra Leone and Liberia will remain peaceful, and an uneasy stalemate will hold in Côte d'Ivoire. Despite forecasts to the contrary, Zimbabwe will not collapse into civil war, since only one side (the government) is armed. If Guinea's ailing President Lansana Conté dies, there may be a coup there. Sudan will remain utterly wretched, as international efforts to halt the killing in Darfur will amount to a tiny fraction of what is needed. Congo will hang together, but only just.

Most African countries will remain stable, including the two most important: Nigeria and South Africa. Predictions that Nigeria's ethnic violence could lead to civil war seem wildly implausible, and South Africa faces no visible threats. Africa will be less bloody than news footage suggests, but bloodier than Africans would wish. □

Down, but not out

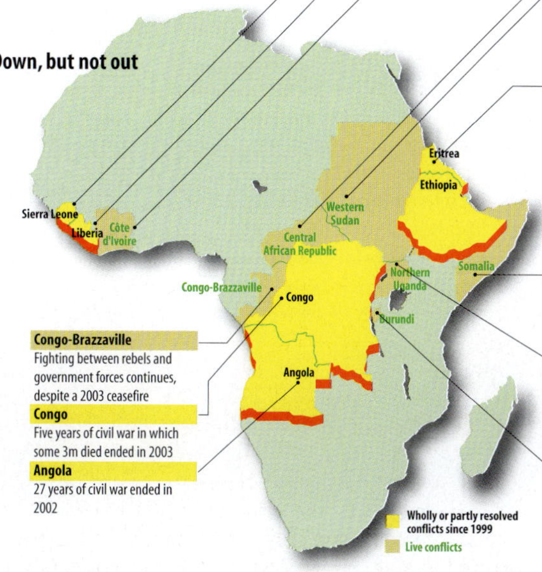

Sierra Leone Ten years of civil war ended in 2002. The tentative peace is maintained by UN troops, due to withdraw at the end of 2004

Liberia 14 years of civil war ended in a shaky truce in 2003

Côte d'Ivoire Ongoing clashes between the rebel-held north and army-held south

Central African Republic Internal political instability and violent border skirmishes over water and grazing rights

Sudan Ruthless ethnic cleansing in the Darfur region, leaving 1.5m homeless, 50,000 dead and 200,000 in refugee camps in neighbouring Chad

Eritrea and Ethiopia The precise demarcation of the violently disputed border between the two countries has yet to be finalised, despite a formal agreement in 2000

Somalia Anarchic country controlled by feuding warlords. Central government unable to exercise sway even over the capital city, Mogadishu. Two slices of the country, "Somaliland" and "Puntland" have de facto seceded

Uganda A brutal campaign of abduction and murder by the mystical Lord's Resistance Army has forced as many as 1.8m people from their homes

Burundi Civil war in Burundi, and sporadic fighting between ethnic militias that spills across borders in the Great Lakes region: Rwanda, Burundi and eastern Congo

Congo-Brazzaville Fighting between rebels and government forces continues, despite a 2003 ceasefire

Congo Five years of civil war in which some 3m died ended in 2003

Angola 27 years of civil war ended in 2002

International

A turning-point for terrorism

Michael Clarke

The weaknesses of the al-Qaeda franchise will become more apparent

International terrorism will generate scary headlines as long as the "war on terrorism" remains near the top of the agendas in Washington and Moscow. And the sheer number of groups now operating, however inefficiently, will produce frequent minor incidents and occasional major ones that will reinforce the siege mentality among the western public.

Al-Qaeda will remain on the run in 2005, its leadership depleted and dispersed, its communications compromised, its most spectacular operations more difficult to mount than ever. But al-Qaeda has evolved since 2001 and has achieved the holy grail of all such franchised operations—notoriety and a powerful brand to inspire legions of amateurs to act in its name. The current al-Qaeda "network of networks" encompasses around 40 different Islamic terrorist groups around the world.

The franchising of the al-Qaeda brand will tend to create common cause between the new global jihadists and erstwhile nationalist and separatist groups. This potent mixture will draw on anti-western sentiment wherever it can find it: in Iraq, Iran, the West Bank, Chechnya, Afghanistan, Pakistan, Indonesia, the Philippines and many other countries.

With 9/11-style strikes harder to organise, the style of attempted attacks will move in the direction of co-ordinated smaller incidents for maximum impact, always with an accent on novelty of technique. We can expect more experimentation with chemical, biological and even radiological devices. There are great technical difficulties for a terrorist in using such deadly elements in a spectacularly lethal way, but they promise a powerful psychological effect.

The world has to live with the fact that the new international terrorism—particularly the jihadist sort—does not see it as self-defeating to be wilfully indiscriminate. More than half of all the current targets of international terrorism, and 90% of its casualties, are "random civilian", as opposed to military/governmental, or business. Such terrorism will appear to thrive in 2005, since the ideological base for jihadism is broadening.

Even so, western society need not despair. For 2005 could mark a turning-point, as terrorism's emerging weaknesses become apparent.

First, although international terrorism may now seem more frightening and indiscriminate, it was almost twice as bad in the 1980s, when in most years there were over 600 significant incidents that annually killed up to 1,000 or more people worldwide. In the current era of terrorism there are normally fewer than 300 such incidents, causing 600-700 deaths in most years. This may be cold comfort to those living with high levels of domestic terrorism—for example, in Israel or Iraq—but

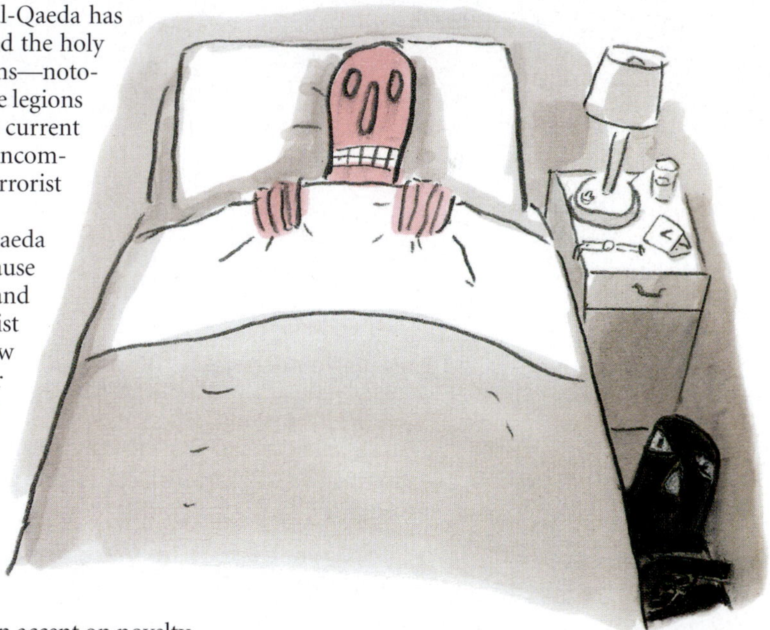

international terrorism will not destabilise the world, unless the world somehow frightens itself into a crisis.

Second, al-Qaeda's unity of purpose and the principle of discipline among its top leadership will be sorely tested by enthusiasms further down its franchise chain. Jihadist groups will compete with each other for power and ideological purity. Al-Qaeda's inspiration will be weakened and feuding groups will be more easily ▶

> Terrorism will not destabilise the world, unless the world somehow frightens itself into a crisis

2005

Proposed reforms to the structure of the UN Security Council will be hotly debated, as India, Germany, Japan and Brazil (among others) lobby for permanent seats.

Michael Clarke: director, International Policy Institute at King's College London penetrated. The fierce, inept amateurs at the base of the pyramid may start to alienate potential supporters of anti-western terrorism. Certainly, they raise alarms in governments from Morocco to Indonesia and encourage more efficient international co-operation against terrorism, as well as domestic clampdowns.

Not least, more traditional terrorist groups are already on the defensive. The Madrid bombing of March 2004 was a jihadist attack that bore some fingerprints of the Basque separatist group ETA; the Beslan school atrocity in September 2004 was a Chechen nationalist attack that bore jihadist fingerprints. Both ETA and the Chechen separatists lose hugely by these associations.

The al-Qaeda jihadist wave is neither as powerful nor as monolithic as it appears. Whether it begins to break and lose momentum in 2005 will depend more than anything else on the way America and its allies handle their self-proclaimed war. Can they make it easier for Islamic governments and mainstream Islamic institutions to speak out clearly against jihadist terror, can they prevent Iraq and Guantánamo Bay being such distractions? If so, they could begin to isolate the jihadists from much of the anti-western discontent they have so successfully mobilised in just three hectic years. □

Here's to health and happiness

Our global poll of expectations for 2005

Optimism about the state of the world in 2005 is plentiful—though not about Iraq. Only 35% of respondents in our annual global poll of Economist.com readers think the security situation in Iraq will improve in 2005; 65% think it won't. And Iraq (picked by 37% of respondents) easily outscores all rivals as the country where people would least like to live in 2005, well ahead of next-worst Afghanistan (12%). In the same survey a year ago, 15% chose Iraq as the least-liveable country, while 19% opted for Afghanistan.

The broad barometer of expectations for the year ahead still points to "fair", even if the outlook has clouded a bit since last year's poll. Optimists outnumber pessimists by nearly two to one: all things considered, 34% think 2005 will be better than 2004, compared with 18% who think it will be worse and 48% who reckon it will be about the same. But a year ago, 44% were optimists and only 12% were pessimists.

The slightly more wary mood has more to do with developments in the wider world than with respondents' expectations for their own personal circumstances, which remain broadly unchanged compared with a year ago: 52% expect to be better-off in 2005, compared with 40% who think their personal economic situation will be about the same and just 8% who expect to be worse-off. The global economy is thought likely to improve, but by a less hefty margin (38% say it will be better in 2005, 21% say it will be worse). As for the stockmarket, there are also twice as many bulls as bears—39% think the market will rise in 2005 and 18% expect it to fall.

What about the risks ahead? Fears of an epidemic such as SARS have eased (only 19% think this likely in 2005, down from 33% a year ago). Worries about terrorism are more or less unchanged, with nearly one respondent in four expecting a major attack on the scale of September 11th 2001 in the year ahead. But a dollar collapse and, especially, a property bust are reckoned to be likelier. The share of respondents expecting the dollar to tumble has risen from 24% to 29%, while the number predicting a house-price collapse has edged up to 41% from 39% a year ago.

The online poll for *The World in 2005*, with 3,160 responses from around the world (40% of them from America and Canada), was taken between September 23rd and 28th 2004, before the American election. In line with their gloomy views on Iraq, perhaps, respondents have low expectations about attitudes towards America. Fully 44% think America's reputation abroad will deteriorate in 2005; only 18% think it will improve. America was picked by 7% even of those who log on to Economist.com as the country where they would least like to live.

Economist.com users, of course, are not an entirely representative sample of world opinion. They are English-speaking, globally minded, predominantly male—and relatively rich. Perhaps that explains why material well-being comes quite low on the list of factors they say matter most for their personal happiness in 2005; only 14% view this as very important. What really counts are job satisfaction (considered very important by 38%), political and civil liberties (45%), family relations (64%) and, above all, health (77%). But the results are surprisingly consistent across countries, gender and age groups. The global elite, it seems, share global values. □

All things considered, do you expect the world next year to be:

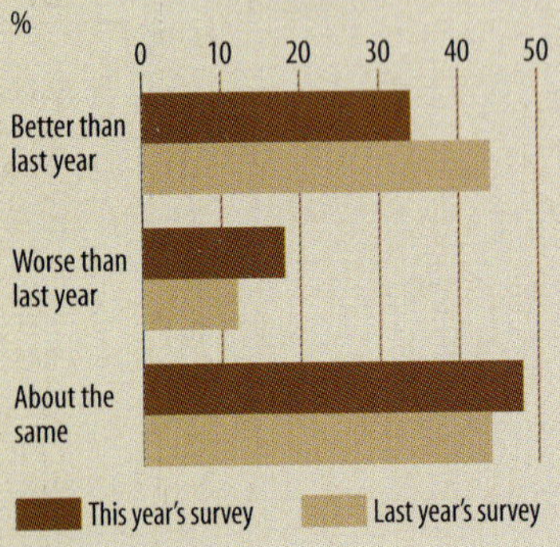

Source: Economist.com survey

How important are the following likely to be to your personal happiness in 2005?

% responding "Very important"

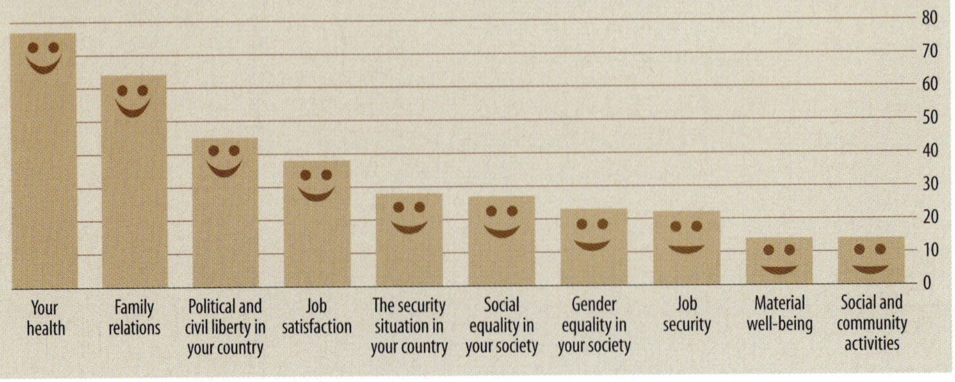

Giving peace a chance

Jean-Marie Guéhenno

Contrary to popular belief, the world will continue to get safer

Fewer people are dying as a result of war now than at almost any time since the 1920s. According to the forthcoming Human Security Report (to be published by Oxford University Press), there were some 27,000 deaths from all forms of political violence in 2003, the most recent year for which we have data. During the 1990s the average annual figure was more than five times as high, mainly concentrated in Africa—Angola, Congo, Sudan and, of course, Rwanda. The 1980s were bloodier but the 1950s, 1960s and 1970s were the deadliest decades, with most of the fighting and dying concentrated in East and South-East Asia.

As war goes down, peacekeeping goes up, at least for a while. Most peacekeeping operations—more than half—take place as old wars go out of business. As more wars end, with fewer new ones breaking out, as is happening now, there is a short-term surge in peacekeeping activity.

The number of UN peacekeepers will reach a peak in early 2005, when peacekeeping forces deployed in Haiti and possibly Sudan come to full strength. Their number will then decline slowly as nations with peacekeeping operations become gradually more stable. UN peacekeepers will probably leave East Timor and Sierra Leone later in 2005. These two countries can then join a list of states, from El Salvador to Mozambique and Namibia, which have successfully managed to move from war to peace.

The current surge has stretched the UN's capacity to its maximum. By mid-2004 there were more than 60,000 men and women wearing the United Nations blue beret in the field, compared with 38,500 four years earlier. Almost half the UN's 17 peacekeeping missions are in Africa, with the remainder on three other continents, covering 12 time zones. The costs of all this are increasing, too, and now run at more than $3 billion a year.

But this current wave of peacekeeping is an exceptionally good investment. Recent research by Paul Collier and Anke Hoeffler of Oxford University looked at

> As more wars end, with fewer new ones breaking out, as is happening now, there is a short-term surge in peacekeeping activity

the challenge of reducing the global incidence of civil war, which presently costs the world some $128 billion per year. Five options were considered, including aid as conflict prevention and aid post-conflict to reduce the risk of sliding back into war. Among the cases examined, by far the most cost-effective was external military intervention under Chapter VII of the United Nations Charter to enforce peace and to maintain it throughout the prolonged period—up to a decade—during which the risks of reversion to conflict are very high.

The research looked, in particular, at Sierra Leone. Thanks to a timely intervention from Britain and a good follow-on from the United Nations, the limb-hacking Revolutionary United Front is out of business. There is an enduring human cost, to be seen with the thousands of armless children, and there is no magic solution for the country's future economic development. But a horror has been stopped and people have returned, as far as they can, to normal life, planting crops, fixing their homes, educating their children.

Recent evidence from Liberia makes the same point. More than anything else, Liberians have reported to pollsters, they value the security that the UN force has brought them since it deployed in October 2003. In 17 operations around the world peacekeepers are working to create a halfway house of stability between the chaos of war and the rule of law. While the conditions for ultimate peace vary in each case, one aim remains constant—to allow people who could otherwise be trapped in hopeless conflict to get on with their lives and contribute, themselves, to an enduring peace.

Blue tide
Number of UN peacekeepers

Figures include troops, military observers and police

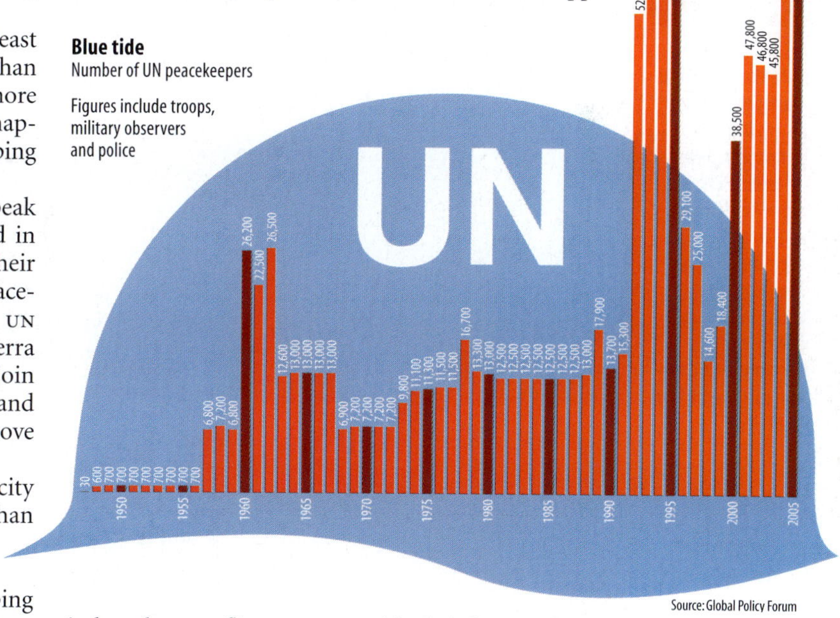

Source: Global Policy Forum

None of this is to say that there are not major lessons to be learnt in conflict management. Getting both the timing and level of forceful intervention right, for example, has too often proved to be an inexact science. Sometimes, as happened in Rwanda, we use no force at all, even in the face of genocide. Sometimes we intervene too early, when there is no peace to keep, or use the wrong tools altogether, as we did with lightly armed peacekeepers in Bosnia. Sometimes, as in Congo, the scale of the international effort is simply not proportional to the scale of the place or the problem. Iraq, too, offers a whole range of lessons, including that of planning for post-conflict operations.

Some of those lessons are being learnt. The European Union's quick intervention in eastern Congo in 2003 interrupted a cycle of violence that would almost certainly have claimed thousands of lives. Buoyed up by that success, the EU is now expanding the concept and aims to have up to nine "battle groups" available for deployment in support of a UN mandate by 2007. The robust United Nations force in Liberia has enough ▶

Jean-Marie Guéhenno: under-secretary general for UN Peacekeeping

We were right—and wrong

Daniel Franklin

You misread it first here

"So, were your predictions accurate?" That's the question most commonly put to the editors of this publication. You deserve an answer.

The question is not as simple as it sounds. For one thing, being "right" or "wrong" is moot when, say, an article is pointing to the risks of things that may or may not happen, or identifying a new trend. For another, cautious hedging words—perhaps, probably, possibly—survive our vicious editorial purges, as our writers sensibly take a nuanced view of the likely course of events. Even a clear prediction that eventually proves mistaken may have been the best possible analysis before the facts and the available information changed, so in a sense "right" at the time.

Besides, much of the mission of this publication is to provide early warning or assessments of things that we know will happen, whether it be the European Union's enlargement, a smoking ban in Irish pubs or the first Formula One grand prix in China. It is simply interesting to point out, as we did in last year's magazine, that 2004 would be a record year for the number of people with the opportunity to take part in elections around the world.

Not that we shone in forecasting the results, for (happily) democracy still has the power to surprise. *The World in 2004* picked the wrong winner in Indonesia. We expected President Chen Shui-bian to lose in Taiwan, and we were confident Mariano Rajoy would win in Spain; last-minute swings prompted by bombs and bullets helped to prove us wrong in both cases. India's prime minister, Atal Behari Vajpayee, would surely delay the election until October, we thought, and he would win; he went to the country early, and lost.

Our most hotly contested prediction was on Turkey. Turks complained in droves about our decidedly gloomy forecast that a currency crisis and debt problems would cause their economy to shrink by more than 4% in 2004. They were right and we were spectacularly wrong: far from going into recession and being one of the world's worst performers in 2004, the Turkish economy has been among the world's fastest growers, expanding by 9%.

On the record

Fortunately, we were right about quite a few things too—including election results from Greece to Panama. In Russia, Vladimir Putin's re-election as president was a foregone conclusion, but predicting his slippage into Soviet ways was prescient. We rightly drew attention to the tax competition that would come from the EU's new members, forecast sprightlier growth in Latin America, suggested the dollar's further slippage would be limited and looked forward to the spread of the tiny computers known as "smart dust". Some readers complained that we were wrong to publish an article by Anwar Ibrahim, Malaysia's jailed former deputy prime minister; Mr Anwar was released from prison in September.

We will, of course, continue to make howlers. And from now on they will be that much easier to track, since the archive of editions starting from *The World in 2004* will in future remain posted at Economist.com. Subscribers can conduct learned research on our triumphs and goofs, and ponder the wisdom of the movie mogul Sam Goldwyn's dictum: "Never prophesy, especially about the future." □

Daniel Franklin: editor, *The World in 2005*

2005

A $3.6bn, 1,760km pipeline transporting up to 1m barrels of Caspian Sea oil every day from Azerbaijan to a new terminal on the Mediterranean coast in Turkey is expected to be completed by the middle of the year.

military muscle to ensure that rebels won't overrun it, as they nearly did a much lighter force in Sierra Leone in 2000.

Effective peacekeeping can help lay the foundations for the future. But where war has torn apart a state, lasting peace depends on the emergence of a framework for security, justice and economic development that is both functional and legitimate. This takes time. To help, the outside world has to stay the course with diplomatic stamina and financial commitment. We don't yet have all the tools needed to help rebuild broken legal, financial and security systems, and we need to invest in developing them. After all, one of the lessons of September 11th 2001 is that weak states can incubate strategic threats with global implications.

It would be premature to predict that current efforts to "manage down" the level of conflict in the world will continue. Major drivers of conflict—under-development, weak governance, systemic corruption, plunder of natural resources, closed markets—continue to be very present both in Africa and in the greater Middle East. But where there are conflicts, and conflicts ripe for settlement, we do seem to be getting slowly better at stabilising them. □

Jointly does it

Javier Solana, secretary-general of the Council of the European Union and high representative for the Common Foreign and Security Policy, describes how international collaboration will flourish in 2005

The year to come will be marked by the restoration of a sense of common endeavour in international relations. That is not just my hope, but also my judgment and the European Union's objective as we pursue our goal of a secure Europe in a better world.

International divisions have fostered instability and uncertainty. The EU has an overwhelming interest in reversing this. Restoring international unity will allow us to harness common efforts to address common threats, strengthen international institutions and make progress on a number of pressing issues in 2005.

Renewed common endeavour requires a re-invigorated transatlantic partnership. With the American presidential election behind us, we can draw a line under a period of tension. Divisions were regrettable, but perhaps we understand one another better. Leaders on both sides of the Atlantic should look to the future rather than dwell on the past. So in 2005 expect a new phase in transatlantic relations, one with more emphasis on early and deeper dialogue on issues of shared strategic concern. Europe and America must work harder at understanding each other before issues become critical.

Iran will be a key test. The EU and America may have different approaches to Iran but we share the same goal: to avoid a proliferation of weapons of mass destruction (WMD). The EU cannot accept the acquisition by Iran of a nuclear-weapon capability. To achieve their shared goal, the EU and America must agree a balanced and comprehensive package of incentives and disincentives depend-

> With a broad majority of Israelis in favour of withdrawal from Gaza and with Palestinian society impatient for real reform, now is the time to move decisively forward

ing on which course of action Iran chooses to take.

There is a broadening transatlantic consensus that the quality of international society depends on the quality of the governments that are its foundation. Whereas the security threats of the past century came from strong states, those of the 21st century come from weak and failing ones. Addressing these new threats requires a mix of instruments best assembled and deployed as part of a collaborative international venture. Whether we choose to call it "nation-building" or "stabilisation and reconstruction", the tasks we face are substantial.

In Iraq the Union will focus its efforts on providing support ahead of and during the elections. We will participate in the reconstruction of key infrastructure. And we will help in efforts to ensure that the elections are as free and fair as possible.

In Afghanistan there is much work still to be done if the progress achieved so far is to be consolidated. After the success of the presidential elections in October 2004, it will be the turn of parliamentary elections. The international community must maintain its focus on achieving a complete and enduring stabilisation.

In Bosnia the new year sees a change of command for the stabilisation force, with responsibility passed from NATO to the EU. This is a milestone for both Bosnia and the Union. For Bosnia it is a sign of steady progress towards a normalised, European future. For the EU it is a sign of our increasing maturity as a security actor.

The violent eruption in March 2004 reminds us why Kosovo is the greatest challenge to security and stabilisation in the Balkans. Beginning a process that leads to a settled future in Kosovo requires the Provisional Institutions of Self-Government to deliver on the implementation of certain standards. In particular, they will have to demonstrate their commitment to peaceful coexistence between all communities. Creating a democratic and multi-ethnic society and ensuring the full protection of all minorities is the cardinal challenge and the test of success.

A push for peace

There is another nation that needs to be built if international peace is to be secured. The international community set 2005 as the deadline for the completion of the process leading to a viable, peaceful and democratic Palestinian state. Much time has been lost, and the calendar has slipped. But the principles for peace set out in the road map remain valid. With a broad majority of Israelis in favour of withdrawal from Gaza and with Palestinian society impatient for real reform, now is the time to move decisively forward. A complete and successful Israeli disengagement from Gaza, accomplished as part of a collaborative international process and in tandem with a responsible, reforming Palestinian Authority, would be a significant first step—but only a first step—towards lasting peace in the region.

The year to come will be decisive in terms of equipping ourselves with global institutions with the effectiveness to tackle contemporary challenges. The report of the UN secretary-general's high-level group could be the catalyst for a stronger, more collective effort at international security. I hope it allows us to devise workable and widely accepted responses to the new challenges of failing states, terrorism and the proliferation of WMD.

Global security, not just common humanity, demands that we renew the vigour with which we address poverty, the environment and disease. In 2005 the world must remind itself of the goals set in the Millennium Declaration and why they were set. Crucially, we must focus on better ways of achieving them. Restoration of common endeavour will require some give and take on all sides. It will, inevitably, be punctuated by disagreements. But it will be propelled forwards by the ever-greater awareness of global interdependence. □

2005

Richard Branson's Virgin Galactic, the world's first space-tourism operator, is expected to start taking bookings from would-be astronauts. Be patient, though: blast-off is not until 2007.

The world's best country

Laza Kekic

Why Irish eyes are smiling

Where will be the best place to live in 2005? *The World in 2005* turned to the Economist Intelligence Unit, which has devised a 2005 "quality of life" index for 111 countries. Result: Ireland comfortably tops the league. America, though the second-richest country (behind Luxembourg) in GDP per head, slips to 13th in quality of life. Britain languishes in 29th place.

It has long been accepted that material well-being alone does not adequately measure quality of life. Money matters, of course, but surveys suggest that over the decades big increases in income have translated into only a modest rise in satisfaction. Although rising incomes and expanded individual choice are highly valued, some of the factors associated with modernisation—such as the breakdown of traditional institutions and the erosion of family values—in part offset its positive impact.

But how to combine in a single, comparative statistic the factors believed to influence people's happiness? There have been many attempts, none entirely successful: the factors selected, and the weights assigned to them, tend to be arbitrary. Subjective surveys of "life satisfaction" have been attracting growing interest—especially since the evidence is that people in different countries and cultures cite similar criteria for being contented—but getting comparable surveys across many countries is hard and there is too much margin for error for a truly objective quality-of-life index.

So ours takes a new approach. We use life-satisfaction surveys (assembling the average scores for 74 countries) as a starting point for weighting the various factors that determine quality of life. A regression analysis suggests that as many as nine indicators have a significant influence, and can be turned into an equation explaining more than 80% of the variation in countries' life-satisfaction scores. The main factor is income, but other things are also important: health, freedom, unemployment, family life, climate, political stability and security, gender equality, and family and community life. We feed the factors into the equation, measuring them using forecasts for 2005 where possible (in four cases) and latest data for slower-changing indicators, such as family life and political freedom. The resulting score, on a scale of one to ten, gives the quality-of-life index.

Ireland wins because it successfully combines the most desirable elements of the new (the fourth-highest GDP per head in the world in 2005, low unemployment, political liberties) with the preservation of certain cosy elements of the old, such as stable family and community life. Offsetting its poor climate and, by rich-country standards, gender inequality are a higher political stability and security. Even if GNP—not available for all countries, but in Ireland's case significantly lower than GDP—is used to measure income, Ireland still wins.

Britain, by contrast, mixes high income per head with high levels of social and family breakdown; it comes bottom among the 15 countries of the pre-enlargement European Union. America ranks above the EU-15 average. Italy performs well but Germany and France do not—belying the notion that big euro-zone nations compensate for their economic sluggishness with a better quality of life than America.

China, for all the excitement over its development, still falls in the lower half of the league. Proud Russians will be disturbed to find themselves at the wrong end of the table. Bottom of the lot is Zimbabwe, where things have gone from bad to worse under Robert Mugabe.

In 1986, in response to an early attempt to measure well-being across countries, *The Times* scoffed: "Can anyone really assess, in mathematical or other terms, the value of living in Britain?" Well, they can try—on the basis of what people around the world themselves say about life satisfaction. No doubt critics will poke holes in this index too. Except, of course, in Ireland. □

Laza Kekic: director, country forecasting services, Economist Intelligence Unit

Top quality... ...and bottom

Worldwide quality-of-life index, 2005 (Score on a scale from 1 to 10)

Rank	Country	Score	Rank	Country	Score	Rank	Country	Score	Rank	Country	Score	Rank	Country	Score
1	Ireland	8.33	11	Singapore	7.72	21	Taiwan	7.26	31	Chile	6.79	60	China	6.08
2	Switzerland	8.07	12	Finland	7.62	22	Greece	7.16	32	Mexico	6.77	65	Morocco	6.02
3	Norway	8.05	13	United States	7.62	23	Cyprus	7.10	33	Barbados	6.70	71	Indonesia	5.81
4	Luxembourg	8.02	14	Canada	7.60	24	Belgium	7.10	34	Czech Republic	6.63	80	Egypt	5.61
5	Sweden	7.94	15	New Zealand	7.44	25	France	7.08	35	Costa Rica	6.62	92	South Africa	5.25
6	Australia	7.93	16	The Netherlands	7.43	26	Germany	7.05	36	Malaysia	6.61	93	Pakistan	5.23
7	Iceland	7.91	17	Japan	7.39	27	Slovenia	7.00	37	Hungary	6.53	105	Russia	4.80
8	Italy	7.81	18	Hong Kong	7.35	28	Malta	6.93	38	Israel	6.49	108	Nigeria	4.51
9	Denmark	7.80	19	Portugal	7.31	29	Britain	6.92	39	Brazil	6.47	110	Haiti	4.09
10	Spain	7.73	20	Austria	7.27	30	South Korea	6.88	40	Argentina	6.47	111	Zimbabwe	3.89

A complete list of countries and a full explanation of the methodology are available in *The World in 2005*'s section at www.economist.com

A year of culture

Steve King

A rich feast at galleries and theatres around the world

Are you one of those people, the comedian Rodney Dangerfield used to ask in his stand-up routine, who sit down in a fancy restaurant, glance approvingly at the menu and say to the waiter: "OK, I'll take it"? Casting your eye over a list of upcoming cultural events around the world can make you feel a bit like that. What follows here is, by contrast, a sort of prix fixe blackboard: a necessarily limited choice of simple, hearty dishes, with something rich and exotic for pudding.

Rubens liked big things: big paintings, big girls, big hats, big goatee. And 2005 will be a big year for him. In Vienna, no fewer than three galleries are putting on exhibitions of his work at the same time. Together they are producing a single catalogue and running a joint marketing campaign. A bus service to shuttle sore-footed art lovers between galleries has been mentioned.

The shows at the Liechtenstein Museum, the Academy of Fine Arts and the Kunsthistorisches Museum open on December 5th 2004 and run till February 27th 2005. Shuttle bus? Nothing less than a magic carpet will be required if you want to see all three shows in one day.

And there's still more Rubens on view elsewhere in 2005. "Peter Paul Rubens (1577-1640): The Drawings" runs from January 15th to April 3rd at the Metropolitan Museum of Art in New York. It is the first major retrospective in America of his drawings, bringing together more than 100 works from collections around the world. Later in the year, from October 26th through to January 15th 2006, the National Gallery in London offers an overview of his rise from young apprentice to Old Master with "Rubens: From Italy to Antwerp, 1600-1616".

On Broadway, 2005 will be a moody, mint-julep-flavoured year, starting with two high-profile productions of classic plays by Tennessee Williams. "The Glass Menagerie", starring Jessica Lange, opens in March. "A Streetcar Named Desire" follows in April, with the impeccably pedigreed Natasha Richardson (daughter of Tony Richardson and Vanessa Redgrave, granddaughter of Michael Redgrave and Rachel Kempson) playing Blanche DuBois. Theatre-goers who enjoy the combination of eloquently scripted histrionics and a glamorous leading lady will also want to catch "Who's Afraid of Virginia Woolf?" in May, the first Broadway revival of Edward Albee's play in nearly 30 years. Kathleen Turner stars as Martha, a sexed-up, booze-swilling vamp—a nice change of pace after her recent crowd-pleasing turn as Mrs Robinson, a sexed-up, booze-swilling vamp, in "The Graduate".

Meanwhile, across the pond, an adaptation of "Mary Poppins", which blew in on an east wind in December 2004, will be settling into what is likely to be a long run. Laura-Michelle Kelly, a fetching young protégée of Andrew Lloyd Webber's, takes on the role made famous on film by Julie Andrews. With a spoonful of sugar (not to mention backing from Disney Theatrical Productions), this medicine will go down a treat with audiences. Richard Eyre, a former head of the Royal National Theatre, directs, with a script by Julian Fellowes ("Gosford Park", "Snobs").

Lord of the songs

A lavish, all-singing, all-dancing version of "The Lord of the Rings" opens in the West End in October, to coincide with the 50th anniversary of the completion of J.R.R. Tolkien's three-part epic of orcs and hobbits. With a budget of £10m ($18m), this is being touted as the most expensive musical ever staged in the West End. A.R. Rahman, who composed the music for "Bombay Dreams", collaborated on the score with a Finnish folk troupe called Värttinä. Bollyelf, anyone?

For sheer strangeness, though, the Royal Opera House's adaptation of George Orwell's "1984", which opens in May, will be hard to beat. It is composed and conducted by veteran maestro Lorin Maazel. The running time is advertised as three hours, boldly ignoring what Orwell himself nearly said: "Never use a long aria where a short one will do."

A very different kind of musical experience can, God willing, be had throughout 2005 at La Felice, a small Italian restaurant in Zanzibar's Stone Town. There Bi Kidude performs every Friday night. Ms Kidude is one of Africa's musical treasures. With her drum and a glass or two of whisky she belts out her unique version of *taarab*—the traditional, Arab-influenced music of the Swahili coast—with a near-supernatural intensity that puts today's stadium-rock acts in the shade. Not bad for a 93-year-old. □

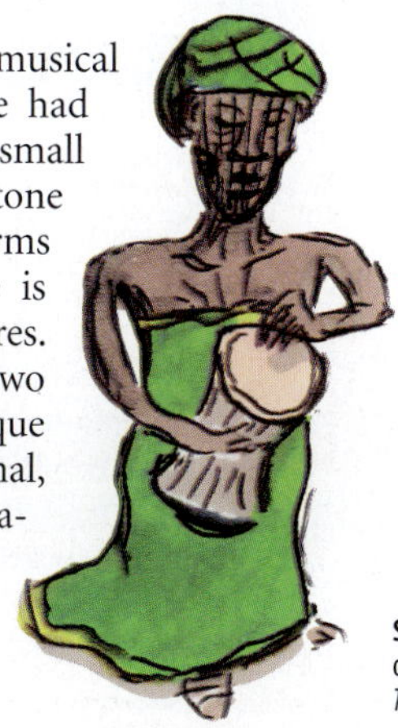

2005

Negotiations start on emissions of greenhouse gases for the next Kyoto commitment period, which begins in 2012.

Steve King: deputy editor, *The World in 2005*

How to halve world poverty

Jeffrey Sachs, director of the Earth Institute at Columbia University, sets out what needs to happen in 2005 to get the UN's Millennium Development Goals back on track

The new millennium opened with great expectations. When 147 heads of state gathered at the UN Millennium Assembly in 2000 and adopted the Millennium Development Goals (MDGs) to cut extreme poverty by half by 2015, even sceptics felt that something new might be in store. The goals were ambitious but achievable. In essence, the world leaders promised to take actions through trade policy, increased official development assistance (ODA) and technology transfer to extend the benefits of globalisation and new technologies to the world's poorest people, with quantified targets to be met by 2015. Alas, those hopes have dimmed, and with only ten years left and slow progress thus far, 2005 has become a make-or-break year to get back on course.

The immediate follow up to the Millennium Assembly was promising. Even September 11th 2001 did not seem to push the world off track. Rather, for a fleeting moment it seemed to reinforce America's commitment to shared prosperity as the way to unite the world against terror and instability. In the Doha Development Agenda agreed upon in November 2001 and the Monterrey Consensus of March 2002, America and the other rich countries confirmed their intention to reshape trade and aid in order to benefit regions which had so far been bypassed by growth, foreign investment, information and communications technology, and expanding trade.

In Monterrey, Mexico, America and other rich countries pledged to "urge developed countries that have not done so to make concrete efforts towards the target of 0.7% of gross national product (GNP) as ODA." Those of us working in the trenches for Africa, the Andes, Central Asia and other places fraught with extreme poverty knew that 0.7% of donor-country GNP could make the difference. After all, that would represent roughly an extra $125 billion in aid at today's incomes which, if well invested, could help equip Africa and other destitute regions with the roads, safe drinking water and sanitation, electrification, clinics, schools, malaria bed nets, anti-retroviral medicines, and other urgent and proven investments to get these regions on a path of sustained economic growth. Moreover, with global markets opened as promised at Doha, these impoverished countries could move from subsistence to labour-intensive exports, the reliable first step on the path to economic development.

> Can the rich world keep dragging its feet over a target it has promised for 35 years? With any serious foreign-policy thinking, the rich countries will finally make good on their commitment

These hopes have been undermined, if not dashed entirely, by American policies of the intervening years. Successive rounds of tax cuts for the rich in America gave away more than $200 billion a year in budget revenues, swamping the $60 billion a year in additional aid that America should mobilise to achieve 0.7% of GNP in development aid. Worse, the war in Iraq and related spending raised military and security outlays by at least $100 billion a year. Instead of making "concrete efforts" to reach 0.7% of GNP in aid, America gave birth to a new development initiative, the Millennium Challenge Account, funded at around 0.01% of GNP, roughly $1 billion a year, perhaps rising to $5 billion a year, or 0.05% of GNP, by 2006. This tiny increase, by no means assured, would leave America with aid equal to around 0.17% of GNP as of 2006, the lowest ratio of all donor countries in the world.

There is still hope for the MDGs, especially since the target of 0.7% of GNP is so modest. Can the rich world keep dragging its feet over a target it has promised for 35 years? With any serious foreign-policy thinking, the rich countries will finally make good on their commitment.

Indeed, two important leaders, Britain's Tony Blair and France's Jacques Chirac, building on a far-thinking plan of Gordon Brown, the British chancellor, have promised exactly that. They have pledged to make 2005 a breakthrough year, especially at the G8 summit to be hosted by Britain in Scotland in July. To lay the groundwork, Mr Blair appointed a high-level Commission for Africa, which will issue a report in the spring of 2005. It seems clear that the Commission for Africa will concur that greatly increased donor assistance, well spent, is key to helping Africa break out of its poverty trap.

Follow the road map

There is at least a path, therefore, for the world's development aspirations to be put right in 2005. In January the UN Millennium Project, which I direct, will issue an independent advisory report to the UN secretary-general, Kofi Annan, showing how the MDGs can in fact be met, through a co-ordinated programme of well-governed investments in health, education and infrastructure in poor countries; increased donor assistance from rich countries; and agreement on trade liberalisation in the Doha negotiations. In March Mr Blair's Commission for Africa will reinforce the message for the world's toughest development challenge: breaking the poverty trap of sub-Saharan Africa. That should be followed by a successful G8 summit in July, in which the rich countries commit to at least doubling ODA in 2005-15, reaching nothing less than 0.5% of GNP by 2010 on the way to 0.7% by 2015.

This would provide the backdrop for world leaders at the UN General Assembly in September 2005 to review progress on the Millennium Declaration. They would commit to a series of specific actions to lay the foundation for a decade of rapid growth and social improvements in the most impoverished places on the planet. It might sound like a long shot, but in a world desperate for hope, might it not be the time to make this a reality? □

The world in figures: Countries

TOP GROWERS

Embattled Iraq will be among the world's fastest-growing economies in 2005, helped by an 11% rise in daily oil production. Our list is awash in oil: nine of the top ten will be producing or transporting much more of the stuff in 2005, including five African countries (Equatorial Guinea, Chad, Angola, Sudan and Algeria) and three Central Asian republics (Azerbaijan, Georgia and Kazakhstan). China's economy is made of sterner stuff: it relies on manufacturing, agriculture and services.

The ranking is based on the 150 countries whose GDP is forecast in the Economist Intelligence Unit's CountryData. It excludes countries with unreliable data, notably Afghanistan, which will probably grow by 15-20% in 2005—not counting opium.

Regionally, the fastest growers will be in Asia. Greater China, which includes Hong Kong and Taiwan, will lead the way. The transition economies of eastern Europe and the former Soviet Union will grow by more than 5%, but western Europe will again lag.

The world's fastest

GDP growth %

1	Equatorial Guinea	16.0
2=	Azerbaijan	14.0
2=	Chad	14.0
4	Georgia	12.0
5	Angola	11.9
6	Iraq	10.3
7	Sudan	8.3
8	Algeria	8.2
9	China	8.1
10	Kazakhstan	7.9

2005 forecasts unless otherwise indicated. Inflation: year-on-year annual average.
Dollar GDPs calculated using 2005 forecasts for dollar exchange rates.
Source: Economist Intelligence Unit
london@eiu.com

EUROPE

Main event: Referendums in several countries on the EU's new constitution

Euro-zone growth: 2.2%

Transition economies growth: 5.2%

Austria

GDP growth: 2.4%
GDP: $320bn
Inflation: 1.7%
Population: 8.2m
GDP per head: $39,130

The right-of-centre coalition government, comprising the Austrian People's Party (ÖVP) and the Freedom Party (FPÖ), should hold together in 2005. The FPÖ is struggling to survive as a political force, but will co-operate with its coalition partner. Neither party wants an early election (the next is due before the end of 2006). Lower taxes, together with a better jobs outlook, will make for a stronger economy in 2005.

To watch: Privatisation. Concerns over job losses and an increasing reluctance to concede ownership of Austrian firms to foreign investors could lead to paralysis in the government's privatisation programme.

Belgium

GDP growth: 2.5%
GDP: $378bn
Inflation: 1.6%
Population: 10.4m
GDP per head: $36,430

The four-party coalition government, led by Guy Verhofstadt, was weakened by the European Parliament elections in 2004. It should survive 2005 but changes in regional governments in this fractious country will make co-ordination with the federal authorities difficult and could lead to a government crisis. Government debt is expected to fall below 100% of GDP for the first time in 25 years.

Bulgaria

GDP growth: 4.0%
GDP: $28bn
Inflation: 4.7%
Population: 7.7m
GDP per head: $3,590

Will the former king also become a former prime minister? Simeon Saxe-Coburg's Simeon II National Movement will lose the 2005 parliamentary election to the left-wing Bulgarian Socialist Party (BSP), which may govern in coalition with the Turkish Movement for Rights and Freedoms. A BSP-led government would retain Bulgaria's currency board and pursue the goal of EU membership, but would be less enthusiastic about economic reform.

Industrial production % change

To watch: Crime. More shootings and bombings, most linked to organised crime, will increase the focus on law and order and the weakness of the criminal-justice system.

Czech Republic

GDP growth: 4.1%
GDP: $122bn
Inflation: 2.4%
Population: 10.2m
GDP per head: $11,960

The new coalition government, led by the Czech Social Democratic Party, is weak and unpopular. Difficult budgetary, investment and labour reforms are needed, but the government will drag its feet to boost its standing ahead of the 2006 election. Disputes may bring down the government once again.

Proceeds from the long-delayed privatisation of Cesky Telecom (around $2bn) will finally reach government coffers in 2005. But the sales of other state-owned enterprises are unlikely any time soon.

To watch: The central bank, the Czech National Bank (CNB). The president, Vaclav Klaus, can appoint members without consulting government or parliament. He says the current crop bows too readily to the European Central Bank. Mr Klaus will appoint the CNB's new governor by February 2005.

Denmark

GDP growth: 2.5%
GDP: $264bn
Inflation: 2%
Population: 5.4m
GDP per head: $48,920

A general election must be held by November 2005. The governing coalition, comprising the Liberal Party and the Conservative People's Party, is not popular but will recover in time to earn a narrow victory over the three left-of-centre parties, with the support of the far-right, populist Danish People's Party. A strong economy will help. That said, any further mistakes by the prime minister, Anders Fogh Rasmussen, could tip the balance against him.

Fiscal policy will be tightened after the election, following a raft of tax cuts in 2004. But higher personal incomes, fuelled by the tax cuts, will boost the economy, as will more investment spending by businesses.

To watch: Building bridges. Denmark and Germany have agreed in principle to construct a bridge across the Fehmarn Belt that divides the two countries. Construction could start in 2005 if financing issues are resolved.

Estonia

GDP growth: 6.0%
GDP: $12bn
Inflation: 3.2%
Population: 1.3m
GDP per head: $9,310

Disagreements over economic policy could force a shake-up in the coalition government led by Juhan Parts. The economy will do better in 2005. Estonia's large subcontracting industry mainly services Scandinavian firms, and the improved outlook for the region is encouraging.

Finland

GDP growth: 3.0%
GDP: $199bn
Inflation: 1.3%
Population: 5.3m
GDP per head: $37,740

Prime minister Matti Vanhanen and his popular three-party coalition government should sail through 2005 without incident. Boosting employment—by cutting non-wage labour costs and raising skills levels—will be the main economic priority, in part to prepare the economy for the impact of an ageing population.

Inward direct investment $bn

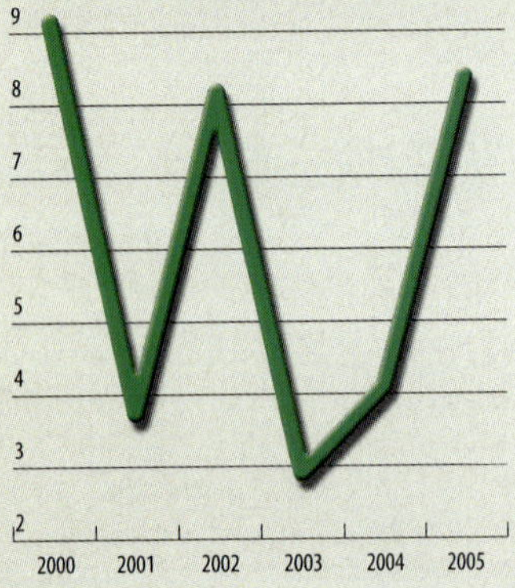

France

GDP growth: 2.4%
GDP: $2.22trn
Inflation: 1.9%
Population: 60.6m
GDP per head: $36,630

President Jacques Chirac may try to provide his government with a new sense of purpose by dispensing with Jean-Pierre Raffarin as prime minister. A leading contender to replace him could be Dominique de Villepin, the flamboyant former foreign minister.

The government will continue its slow but steady progress in selling state assets. But resistance from public-sector trade unions and huge pension liabilities could delay the part-privatisation of a leading energy utility, Gaz de France.

To watch: The EU constitution. French voters will be asked to ratify the EU's new political blueprint, probably in the second half of 2005. The credibility of European integration could hang in the balance.

Germany

GDP growth: 1.9%
GDP: $2.93trn
Inflation: 1.5%
Population: 82.7m
GDP per head: $35,450

Gerhard Schröder's government is hugely unpopular. Voters are angry about tough labour, pension and health-insurance reforms, and Mr Schröder's inability to boost the economy. But the economy will look a little better in 2005. Income-tax cuts in 2004-05 will help consumer spending, but this will be partly offset by higher health-insurance costs and tobacco taxes. The jobs outlook will improve, and the replacement and upgrading of equipment will lead to a slow recovery in investment.

Export of goods and services % change

To watch: Tax policy. Germany will push the EU hard to limit tax competition, particularly from eastern Europe, where low corporate tax rates allegedly attract investment away from high-tax Germany. Mr Schröder's efforts are bound to fail.

Greece

GDP growth: 3.4%
GDP: $216bn
Inflation: 2.9%
Population: 10.7m
GDP per head: $20,210

The government, led by the centre-right New Democracy party, looks strong after winning the 2004 parliamentary election and performing well in European balloting. George Papandreou, the new leader of the opposition Socialists, is preoccupied with ridding the party of an older generation and introducing grass-roots democracy.

To watch: Cost overruns from the Olympics—the price tag will exceed €10bn ($13bn), up from the original estimate of €5.9bn—will weigh on the economy and the budget. Government debt will surpass 110% of GDP.

Hungary

GDP growth: 4.0%
GDP: $112bn
Inflation: 4.7%
Population: 10m
GDP per head: $11,210

The new prime minister, Ferenc Gyurcsany, is a wild card who will shake up the ruling Hungarian Socialist Party and the government. None too soon, either. The Socialists have been in turmoil, their popularity is waning and their mostly elderly supporters are dying off.

The budget deficit remains distressingly high (around 5% of GDP), and the Socialists are worried about the impact of austerity on their popularity ahead of the 2006 election. A recovery in the euro zone, though, will help the economy.

Ireland

GDP growth: 4.9%
GDP: $200bn
Inflation: 2.2%
Population: 4.1m
GDP per head: $48,250

Divisions within the governing coalition will deepen in 2005. Fianna Fail fears an electoral backlash (the next vote is due by 2007) if it provokes powerful trade unions with public-sector reforms. Their partners, the Progressive Democrats, want change. The economy will grow more rapidly than any other in rich Europe as exports pick up and confidence rises at home. A vote on the EU constitution is possible late in 2005. The Irish will vote Yes.

To watch: Cork. Designated as European Capital of Culture for 2005, Ireland's fiercely proud second city will put its 800 years of history on display and do its best to outshine the booming capital, Dublin.

Italy

GDP growth: 1.8%
GDP: $1.83trn
Inflation: 2.0%
Population: 58.1m
GDP per head: $31,410

Hostility among the parties of Silvio Berlusconi's ruling coalition is rising. A change in the composition of the ruling majority or an early election is possible by mid-2005. An early election would be a close contest, with the centre-left opposition—also divided and unstable—likely to win narrowly.

Private consumption % change

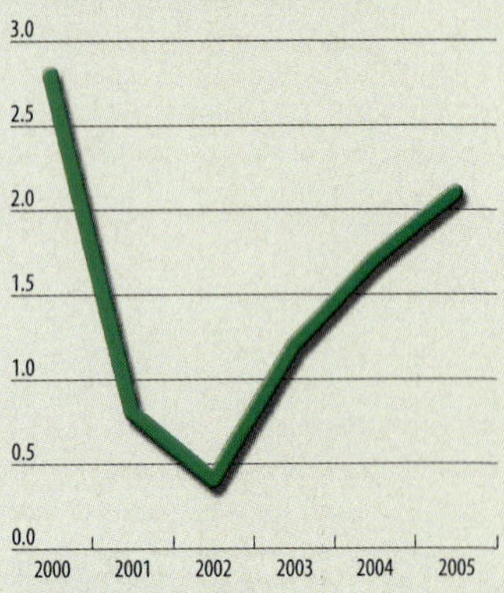

The government will probably introduce substantial tax cuts in 2005, which should boost economic growth. But if consumer confidence remains weak, the cuts could encourage savings rather than stimulate consumption.

To watch: State assets. Domenico Siniscalco, the economy minister, has made privatisation a priority, starting with the proposed sale of up to 20% of the state electricity company, Enel.

Latvia

GDP growth: 5.5%
GDP: $13bn
Inflation: 3.5%
Population: 2.3m
GDP per head: $5,800

The government comprises a centre-right coalition led by Indulis Emsis of the Union of Greens and Farmers but it lacks a majority in parliament. The support of the People's Harmony Party is crucial but the opposition will try to lure them away. The government may not last the year. Economic growth will slow in 2005 as the transit trade with Russia ebbs and weak job growth hurts consumer spending.

To watch: The lat. Currently linked to the International Monetary Fund's currency basket, Latvia's currency will be pegged to the euro from late 2004 or early 2005 as part of the government's long-term plan to join the euro zone.

Lithuania

GDP growth: 6.5%
GDP: $24bn
Inflation: 1.6%
Population: 3.4m
GDP per head: $7,110

The Labour Party triumphed in the October 2004 election, but must form a coalition to achieve a majority in parliament. The new government will not be very stable. However, economic policy will remain largely unchanged. The economy will continue to perform well but growth will slow as imports pick up.

Netherlands

GDP growth: 2.0%
GDP: $640bn
Inflation: 1.5%
Population: 16.4m
GDP per head: $38,950

Budget balance % of GDP

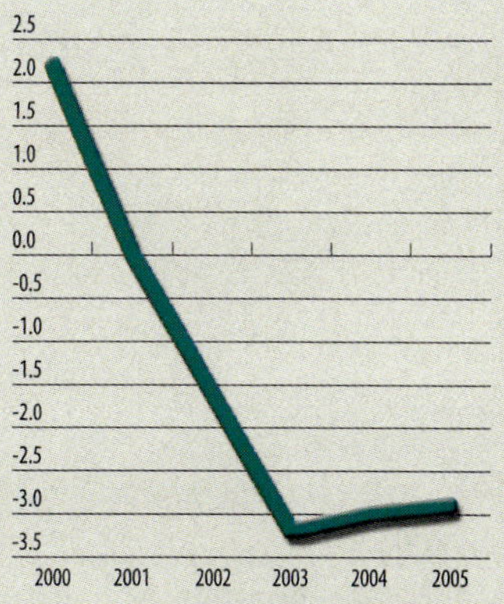

The governing coalition, in power since 2003, has much to prove. Jan Peter Balkenende, the prime minister, has failed to establish himself as a strong leader and prominent members of the Liberal Party, part of the ruling coalition, are locked in a power struggle. The government should survive, but only just.

Although the government's finances will improve, further spending cuts will be needed. This will hit civil-service jobs and welfare benefits. Dutch firms are becoming less competitive internationally because of rising labour costs. A wage freeze in 2004 and a partial freeze in 2005 will help, but only if they are adhered to.

Norway

GDP growth: 3.0%
GDP: $254bn
Inflation: 2.5%
Population: 4.6m
GDP per head: $55,290

An election is scheduled for September. The ruling centre-right minority coalition, led by the prime minister, Kjell Magne Bondevik, is facing a tough challenge from Jens Stoltenberg's Labour Party—and will probably lose. But Labour must first patch together a centre-left alliance with the Centre Party and the Socialist Left Party.

Cuts in the top marginal tax bracket are expected in 2005. Buoyant consumer spending will continue and wage growth will pick up, reflecting a tighter labour market.

Poland

GDP growth: 4.5%
GDP: $279bn
Inflation: 3.3%
Population: 38.1m
GDP per head: $7,300

Marek Belka, the caretaker prime minister, will remain in office until parliamentary elections, which are most likely to take place in May-June 2005, or at the latest in October. The governing parties, the Democratic Left Alliance and the Union of Labour, won't do well. Expect the new government to be led by the Civic Platform, in a centre-right coalition. A referendum on the European constitution will be a cliffhanger.

Whatever happens in domestic politics, improving public finances will remain the key economic policy issue. Spending cuts will have to go further if the new government is to avoid breaching the constitutional limit on public debt of 60% of GDP later in its term.

To watch: Iraq. Poland heads one of the military zones and has said that it will maintain its forces there. But some of its responsibilities have been taken over by America, and the government would like to scale down the Polish presence.

Portugal

GDP growth: 2.3%
GDP: $184bn
Inflation: 2.2%
Population: 10.4m
GDP per head: $17,680

Pedro Santana Lopes, the newly appointed prime minister, does not have a popular mandate. In a worst case, Portugal is facing two years of a lame-duck government—when it needs strong leadership to advance an economic austerity programme. The president might call an election before 2006, when the next poll is due.

The economy will pick up in 2005, led by better business investment and stronger exports, but tight fiscal policy will put a cap on growth.

Romania

GDP growth: 5.2%
GDP: $81bn
Inflation: 8.4%
Population: 21.7m
GDP per head: $3,720

The new government will have EU membership as its priority. An EU accession treaty will be signed before the end of 2005, with actual membership set for 2007. But Romania must hasten judicial and administrative reforms if it is to stick to the schedule.

Russia

GDP growth: 5.8%
GDP: $623bn
Inflation: 9.9%
Population: 143.7m
GDP per head: $4,330

Vladimir Putin will clamp down on civil liberties, increase state control over the economy (especially the energy sector), and concentrate even more power in the Kremlin. Bad news for democracy and the business environment, but so far voters don't seem to care.

The tax burden will shift to natural resources. The government may dip into its Oil Stabilisation Fund to finance increased defence and security, as well as social-welfare spending. High oil prices will make this strategy possible, at least for now.

Oil production barrels/day m

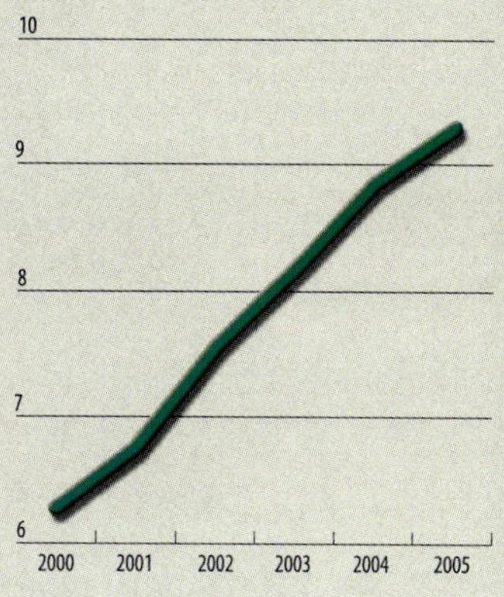

To watch: Chechnya and terrorism. Russians will not soon forget the slaughter of the innocents in Beslan. Nor should they. Mr Putin's hard line against Chechen militants will therefore get harder. A better-integrated domestic-security system will be the focus in 2005.

Slovakia

GDP growth: 5.1%
GDP: $49bn
Inflation: 5.7%
Population: 5.4m
GDP per head: $8,940

Although popular support for the ruling coalition is low, the government, led by Mikulas Dzurinda, is secure. Relations with its neighbours could be strained, however, by its plan to complete the construction of additional nuclear reactors at the Mochovce power plant.

Exports, a bellwether in recent years, will not grow as quickly in 2005, but major exporters such as German-owned Volkswagen Slovakia and US Steel's plant at Kosice will continue to support strong foreign sales.

Slovenia

GDP growth: 3.7%
GDP: $36bn
Inflation: 3.0%
Population: 2.0m
GDP per head: $17,700

The centre-right opposition Slovenian Democratic Party (SDS) won a surprise victory in the general election in October 2004. But with a narrow parliamentary majority, the government will be weak. Adopting the euro by 2007 is the central economic goal. This will mean bringing inflation down to EU levels.

To watch: Credit growth. The central bank will continue to cut interest rates to bring them into line with those in the EU. This could trigger a credit-led consumer boom, attracting imports and pushing up prices.

Spain

GDP growth: 3.0%
GDP: $1.10trn
Inflation: 2.5%
Population: 41.3m
GDP per head: $26,660

The non-violent Basque Nationalist Party is committed to holding a referendum on de facto independence for the Basque Country in 2005. The new Socialist government in Madrid is as adamant as its predecessor that such a poll is unconstitutional.

The economy will pick up in 2005 as demand for Spanish goods elsewhere in Europe increases. Consumers will feel flush as a good jobs market and earlier income-tax cuts boost disposable income. A slight easing of budget discipline will free up more money for increased spending on education and justice.

Sweden

GDP growth: 2.7%
GDP: $394bn
Inflation: 1.6%
Population: 9.1m
GDP per head: $43,480

The minority Social Democratic Party needs the support of the Left Party and the Greens to survive. It will get it, but fitfully as tensions over the budget rise. The government will cut income taxes slightly to offset higher environmental levies. Sales of the government's stakes in Nordea, the largest bank in the Nordic region, and Telia, the part-privatised telecommunications operator, may go ahead.

To watch: Employment trends. A higher percentage of Sweden's workforce is employed than in almost any other country. Impressive. But Swedes also take more sick leave than other Europeans and are more likely to draw disability pensions. The government wants to change that.

Switzerland

GDP growth: 2.0%
GDP: $379bn
Inflation: 1.1%
Population: 7.4m
GDP per head: $51,490

Most of the provisions in a new Swiss-EU economic package will be ratified in 2005. These include measures to combat tax evasion, prevent customs fraud and allow Swiss associate membership in the EU's Schengen accord, which provides for open borders in the region. A Swiss referendum is likely on Schengen membership, which some see as an infringement of its sovereignty.

The financial sector, which has suffered in recent years, will give a strong boost to the economy in 2005, but don't expect a return to the heady growth rates of the late 1990s. Reforms are planned in the utility sector and on pensions, but here again the Swiss—who love referendums—may first want a say.

Turkey

GDP growth: 4.3%
GDP: $304bn
Inflation: 19.5%
Population: 73.3m
GDP per head: $4,150

Lending interest rate %

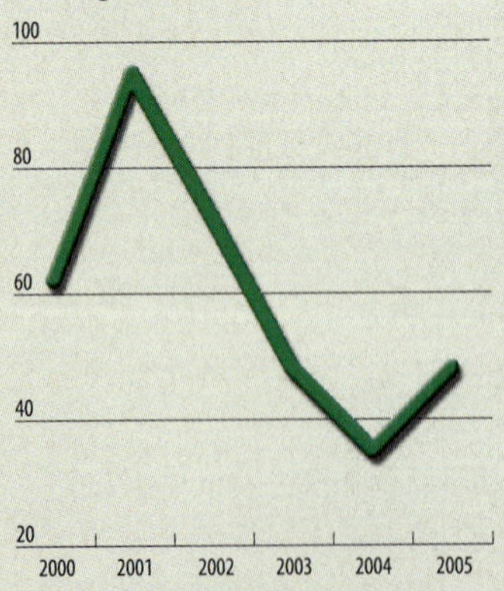

Consumer spending and business investment have been booming and will continue to do well in 2005. Exports and tourism have been especially sparkling. The economy will slow but growth will remain robust.

A new IMF funding agreement, expected before the end of 2004, will give investors confidence and improve the budget outlook. The currency, the lira, will be volatile at times—high debt is still a serious concern for Turkey.

To watch: EU membership. Turkey will begin accession negotiations with the EU in 2005, but membership will not come quickly or easily. Britain, Germany and Italy support Turkey's bid but France and Austria have real doubts. Turkey's location, size, poverty and Muslim mien are issues.

Ukraine

GDP growth: 7.0%
GDP: $77bn
Inflation: 8.0%
Population: 46.9m
GDP per head: $1,630

Leonid Kuchma is gone—no bad thing. But reforms, such as a much-needed overhaul of the coal, energy and telecoms industries, will not happen quickly. Oligarchs are still entrenched in parliament and an ongoing power struggle between political institutions will distract reforms.

Ukraine can't get a date with the EU. It would eventually like to join the European club but the signals aren't encouraging. The EU will stress instead that Ukraine work within its European Neighbourhood Policy.

United Kingdom

GDP growth: 2.3%
GDP: $2.35trn
Inflation: 1.8%
Population: 60.7m
GDP per head: $38,670

Despite a widespread belief that he misled the country over the reasons for invading Iraq, Tony Blair—chastened but still in charge—will lead the governing Labour Party to victory at the next general election, which will probably be held in May. Mr Blair will owe his victory to the resilient economy and to the failure of the bumbling Conservative Party to establish itself as a credible alternative.

It's not all good news for Labour. Voters are paying higher taxes, but have seen few improvements in Britain's decrepit public services. Trade unions aren't happy either, and some Labour voters will defect to Britain's third party, the Liberal Democrats. The consumer boom will end but Britain's economy still looks stronger than most of its big continental neighbours. Provided, of course, that house prices don't collapse.

To watch: Britain and the EU. Mr Blair, whose standing with voters has been forever damaged by the fallout from the Iraq war, will struggle to reverse the Eurosceptic tide ahead of the referendum on the proposed EU constitution likely in early 2006.

ASIA

Main event: The handling of relations between China and Taiwan
Greater China growth: 7.2%
South Asia growth: 6.8%
ASEAN growth: 5.1%

Australia

GDP growth: 3.4%
GDP: $623bn
Inflation: 2.8%
Population: 20.3m
GDP per head: $30,630

John Howard and his Liberal-National coalition won a convincing victory in the October 2004 general election, handing Mr Howard a fourth consecutive term. He will be in an enviably strong position from which to push a conservative legislative agenda. The prime minister isn't exciting and his support for the war in Iraq has hurt him. But Australia has been stable politically and successful economically. Expect more of the same.

Well-off Australians, who missed out on tax cuts in 2000, will enjoy income-tax reductions in 2005. The budget is in surplus, so the government can afford it. The economy will slow as housing construction and consumer spending ease.

To watch: Water police. A watchdog commission should be in place by the start of 2005 to curb water use. Australia has suffered from a three-year "big dry". Goodbye, green lawns.

China

GDP growth: 8.1%
GDP: $1.78trn
Inflation: 2.5%
Population: 1.3bn
GDP per head: $1,360

A demanding middle class and unrest among people in the countryside may prompt China's president, Hu Jintao, to open up the political system just a bit. "Socialist democracy", he calls it. But don't expect big changes. Mr Hu has no plans to weaken the power of the Communist Party, and will be guarding against his predecessor, Jiang Zemin.

Inflation % change

The economy, red-hot in 2004, should slow to a more sustainable pace—a soft landing seems possible. But only just. China's increasingly vast economy is hard to manage. If the authorities get it wrong, a bust could follow the boom.

To watch: The yuan. Will this be the year the currency is freed from its dollar peg? Not quite. The slowdown in foreign-capital inflows makes for a calmer environment in which to make a change, but expect a small widening of the very narrow band in which the yuan trades.

Hong Kong

GDP growth: 4.7%
GDP: $162bn
Inflation: 0.4%
Population: 7.1m
GDP per head: $22,970

Inflation % change

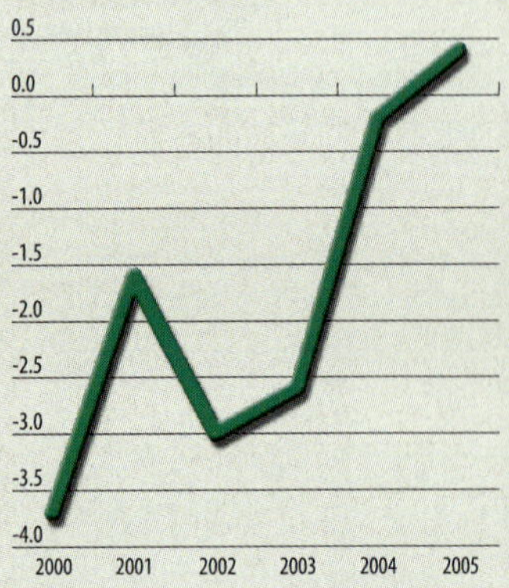

Despite a setback in legislative elections in September 2004, Hong Kong's democratic movement is deepening, and political activism will worry Beijing. Hong Kong's own government, led by Tung Chee-hwa, has promised democratic reforms, but has little room to manoeuvre: China will be pushed only so far.

The economy will do well as links with China widen and deepen. Tourism is a shining star: China accounted for more than half of all tourist arrivals in Hong Kong in 2004. As China's trade expands, so will Hong Kong's. Deflation will end in 2005 as prices rise, on average, for the first time since 1998.

To watch: A Mickey Mouse operation. Hong Kong Disneyland is set to open in late 2005 (well, maybe early 2006). Located at a land-reclamation project on the north-western tip of Lantau island, Disneyland excites the government's hopes of reclaiming the economic lustre Hong Kong lost in the late 1990s. Disney is expecting (optimistically) 5m-6m visitors in the first year.

India

GDP growth: 7.5%
GDP: $701bn
Inflation: 5.7%
Population: 1.1bn
GDP per head: $640

India's communist parties, which provide vital support to the Congress government, will become increasingly disruptive. So will the opposition Bharatiya Janata Party, which hasn't got over its 2004 election defeat. The government should survive but parliament won't achieve much.

The economy is set for another good year but 2004's sheen has dimmed. Investors are cautious about the left-leaning government. But the private sector matters as much as the government: software, back-office businesses, telecoms and motor vehicles will lead the way.

To watch: Drugs. Indian pharmaceutical companies profit by copying other people's drugs. But from 2005 drug patents will apply in India under a WTO deal. Innovative drugs will be needed. Indian companies will rise to the challenge: costs are low and scientists plentiful.

Indonesia

GDP growth: 4.8%
GDP: $281bn
Inflation: 5.6%
Population: 227.1m
GDP per head: $1,230

The new president, Susilo Bambang Yudhoyono, could face a dissonant reception in parliament: he will have the direct support of only around 10% of its members. Loose coalitions will give him some leverage.

Foreign and domestic investment should resume in 2005 to take advantage of improved access to the oil, gas and mining sectors. New legislation has cut red tape and state-asset sales will also provide opportunities.

To watch: Military links with America. Washington shunned Indonesia's military after its brutal response to East Timor's independence struggle. But America wants Jakarta's support in the war on terrorism.

Japan

GDP growth: 1.7%
GDP: $4.79trn
Inflation: 0.2%
Population: 127.4m
GDP per head: $37,550

Junichiro Koizumi, the country's lion-maned prime minister, is secure at least until the ruling party's 2006 leadership election. No one is strong enough to challenge him. Now in his final term, attention will turn to choosing a successor. The contenders? The ruling party's secretary-general (and Koizumi ally) Shinzo Abe, and the finance minister, Sadakazu Tanigaki.

Gross fixed investment % change

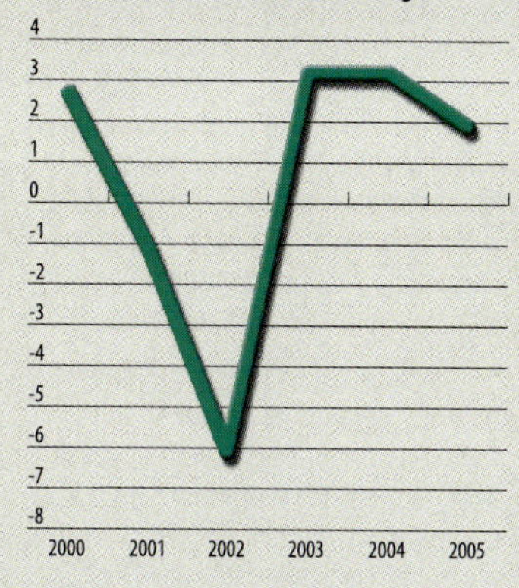

Japan's economy grew by more than 4% in 2004. But the boom won't last. Businesses will invest less in 2005, and government spending will shrink to control the budget. Stealth taxes, such as higher employee pension payments, will make consumers grumpy.

Kazakhstan

GDP growth: 7.9%
GDP: $48bn
Inflation: 6.6%
Population: 15.0m
GDP per head: $3,170

No one will threaten the president, Nursultan Nazarbayev, in 2005. Repressive and intolerant, he controls the country's media, security services and administrative machinery. Worse, he will stand for re-election in 2006. The outcome is not in doubt. Oil drives the economy, and high prices will keep the cash—and the corruption—flowing.

Malaysia

GDP growth: 4.7%
GDP: $123bn
Inflation: 1.9%
Population: 25.9m
GDP per head: $4,750

Abdullah Badawi, the prime minister, is capable and experienced, and his ruling coalition is secure after a 2004 election victory. Mr Badawi lacks the influence of his predecessor, Mahathir Mohamad, but his reputation as a moderate Muslim makes him appealing.

With Dr Mahathir gone, Mr Badawi will welcome more foreign investment in government-linked corporations. Whether this means ceding control to foreigners is another question. Stronger investment overall will keep the economy in good form.

To watch: Anwar Ibrahim. Freed from prison, Mr Anwar is seeking to clear his name. If he succeeds, the former deputy prime minister—jailed by the previous regime on dubious charges—may dip his toe into the political waters.

New Zealand

GDP growth: 3.0%
GDP: $98bn
Inflation: 2.7%
Population: 4.1m
GDP per head: $23,930

An election is due in mid-2005 and a third term for the prime minister, Helen Clark, is far from certain. The opposition centre-right National Party is enjoying a resurgence of support under its new leader, Don Brash. Fallout from the government's dispute with New Zealand's indigenous Maori over ownership of the foreshore and seabed will provide opportunities for Mr Brash.

The economy will slow, but exports—dairy products are important—will still do well. Companies will take advantage of the strong currency to import expensive capital goods.

Pakistan

GDP growth: 5.7%
GDP: $90bn
Inflation: 5.3%
Population: 156.4m
GDP per head: $580

Shakaut Aziz, a former finance minister and banker, will serve his first full year as prime minister in Pervez Musharraf's tightly controlled government. A reformer, he will push for privatisations and tax changes. But Mr Musharraf still calls the shots. The economy will enjoy another good year and the end of global textile quotas should help Pakistan's competitive industry.

To watch: Assassination attempts. To Pakistani militants, Mr Musharraf is America's lackey and Mr Aziz, formerly of Citibank, is not much better. Both have been targeted before.

Philippines

GDP growth: 4.5%
GDP: $89bn
Inflation: 5.1%
Population: 87.9m
GDP per head: $1,010

The re-elected president, Gloria Macapagal Arroyo, is proposing to change from a presidential to a parliamentary system. The reason? The Senate, which has blocked 1,000 of 1,100 bills passed by the lower house since 2001. Debate on amending the constitution will begin in January. Cutting the budget deficit is an economic priority. Total public debt, including liabilities of the state-owned power company, is around 120% of GDP.

Budget balance % of GDP

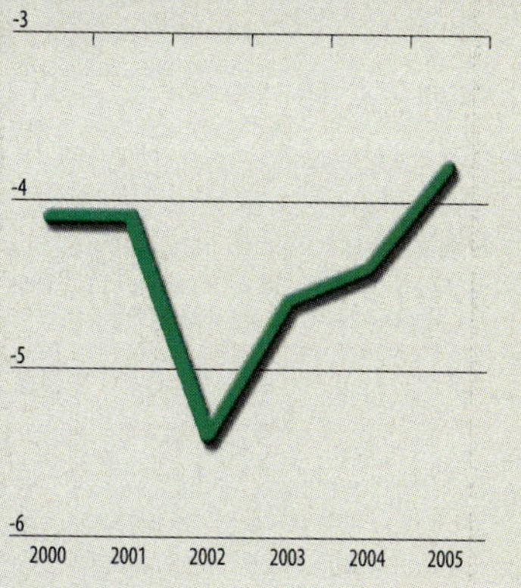

Singapore

GDP growth: 4.9%
GDP: $107
Inflation: 1.6%
Population: 4.3m
GDP per head: $25,070

Government is a closely managed affair. Lee Kuan Yew, the country's founder, handed power in 1990 to Goh Chok Tong, who in 2004 handed it to Mr Lee's son, Lee Hsien Loong. The younger Mr Lee may call an early election to secure a personal mandate.

The economy will slow as global demand for computer chips, a Singaporean staple, eases. Reducing business costs will be a priority.

South Korea

GDP growth: 4.9%
GDP: $730bn
Inflation: 2.5%
Population: 48.5m
GDP per head: $15,050

The president, Roh Moo-hyun, survived an impeachment attempt in 2004 but he remains a political neophyte: his judgment is poor and he has a taste for confrontations. Expect more turmoil.

The outlook for the domestic economy will improve. Consumers will start spending again. Relations between companies and unions, which have deteriorated in the past two years, will get worse. Expect more strikes and much feuding over the next step in the government's plan to reduce the working week from 44 hours to 40.

To watch: Closer ties with Japan. South Korea and Japan will mark the 40th anniversary of the establishment of diplomatic relations in late 2005. They may celebrate by signing a new bilateral free-trade agreement.

Taiwan

GDP growth: 4.8%
GDP: $333bn
Inflation: 1.4%
Population: 22.9m
GDP per head: $14,560

Despite ongoing investigations into Chen Shui-bian's March re-election—opponents accused him of faking an assassination attempt just hours before—he will remain in office, strengthened by his party's gains in the December 2004 legislative election.

The government has a busy agenda: restructuring the banks, controlling the budget deficit, upgrading the island's industrial base and building a social safety net. But the over-arching goal is to profit from links to mainland China's booming economy.

To watch: Relations with China. Mr Chen's plans for constitutional reform will continue to upset China, which considers this a proxy for a move towards independence.

Thailand

GDP growth: 5.3%
GDP: $170bn
Inflation: 2.5%
Population: 65.1m
GDP per head: $2,610

Thaksin Shinawatra and his Thai Rak Thai party will win the next parliamentary election, due by early 2005. But the government's mishandling of Islamist violence in southern Thailand—78 protesters died in police custody in October 2004—and the bird-flu epidemic have dimmed the lustre.

The economy will slow as interest rates rise and businesses invest less. Export demand will ease in 2005 but a healthy tourism sector will sustain growth.

To watch: Free-trade agreements. Thailand is signing these in droves. Talks have opened for the biggest one of all, with America.

Vietnam

GDP growth: 6.8%
GDP: $47bn
Inflation: 6.8%
Population: 83.7m
GDP per head: $560

Battling official corruption will remain a priority for the communist government. The Bank for Foreign Trade (known as Vietcombank) could be partly privatised. If so, this would be the first sale of a major state-owned business. The private sector will drive growth.

To watch: Cyber-dissidents. The government will work harder to prevent the spread of "poisonous" information on the internet, meting out harsh punishments to offenders.

NORTH AMERICA

Main event: Adjustment to the outcome of the election in the United States

North American (NAFTA) growth: 3.1%

Canada

GDP growth: 2.9%
GDP: $1.02trn
Inflation: 2.4%
Population: 32.2m
GDP per head: $31,780

A weakened Liberal Party oversees a minority government following the 2004 election, but no one is keen for another vote right away. The prime minister, Paul Martin, will get help from left-leaning parties on social issues and from the Conservatives on defence. The Conservative leader, Stephen Harper, will push for a more centrist platform to broaden the party's appeal.

Canadian companies are concerned about the strength of their currency against the US dollar, but Canada's exports will still grow by around 4% in 2005. Higher interest rates, though, will reduce business investment.

To watch: Mutual defence. Canada will spend more on national defence, which will please the United States. Ottawa is also poised to join the United States in a North American missile-defence system, but Mr Martin will try to defuse domestic opposition by avoiding programmes with space-based weapons.

Mexico

GDP growth: 3.1%
GDP: $669bn
Inflation: 4.1%
Population: 106.2m
GDP per head: $6,300

Politics will be dominated by the approaching 2006 presidential election. For the first time in Mexico's history the field is wide open: no clear favourite to succeed the president, Vicente Fox, has emerged from any of the three big parties. Each suffers from internal divisions, which will be deepened by pre-election jostling.

The unpopular but much-needed reforms backed by the Fox government won't advance much in the opposition-dominated legislature. Plans to liberalise the electricity and telecoms sectors, plus fiscal and labour reforms, will be watered down. Mexico's economy is particularly dependent on the United States, which buys over 90% of its exports. So Mexican growth will slow in 2005 as American demand cools, but investment will be underpinned by strong oil prices.

To watch: Burning rubber. Mexico's largest entertainment company is betting on American-style car racing. Corporación Interamericana de Entretenimiento has reached a deal with America's National Association for Stock Car Auto Racing to bring the popular Busch series races to Mexico City in 2005.

United States

GDP growth: 3.2%
GDP: $12.28trn
Inflation: 2.5%
Population: 295.7m
GDP per head: $41,530

The election resolved little. Political divisions are as deep as ever, with no real chance of reconciliation—in Washington or on Main Street. Social conservatives will redouble their efforts. Battles over gay marriage, stem-cell research and the role of religion in public life will intensify. A long list of national priorities, including tax reform and curbing health-care costs, will die on the political vine.

After a fairly robust 2004, the economy will slow. Alan Greenspan will keep raising interest rates, which have been at historic lows. Consumer spending will cool and stubbornly high oil prices will weigh on growth. The budget deficit will be an eye-popping 4.5% of GDP. Pace will be everything: if the economy slows gently, all will be well—if too quickly, a crash is likely, especially if house prices plunge.

Budget balance % of GDP

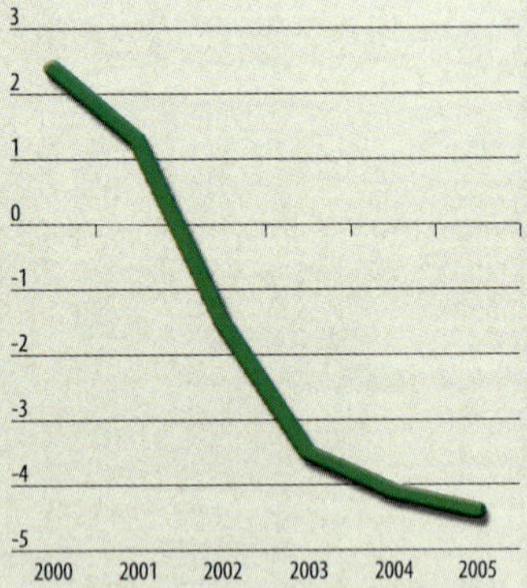

To watch: Foreign entanglements and fast exits. The number of American troops in Iraq will be reduced by the end of 2005—good news for the administration—but a quick exit is not on the cards. Iran, bent on nuclear development, will be a stern test for the president. Talks with North Korea will ebb and flow, but little will have changed by the year's end. Notable progress will be made in killing or capturing al-Qaeda leaders, but the organisation will continue to metastasise. A major terrorist strike against an American target—quite possibly in the United States itself—is likely.

SOUTH AMERICA

Main event: Free-trade agreements

Latin American growth: 3.5%

Argentina

GDP growth: 4.4%
GDP: $148bn
Inflation: 5.3%
Population: 39.1m
GDP per head: $3,800

Néstor Kirchner, the president, will continue to taunt the country's creditors, especially the IMF. This has made him popular. But he has been less effective dealing with crime and unemployment, and disruptions by *piqueteros*—well-organised groups of unemployed workers in and around Buenos Aires—will pose a test.

After very strong economic growth in 2003-04—bounce-back from the collapse of 1999-2002—the pace will slow to around 5% in 2004. But lack of investment will create bottlenecks.

Inflation % change

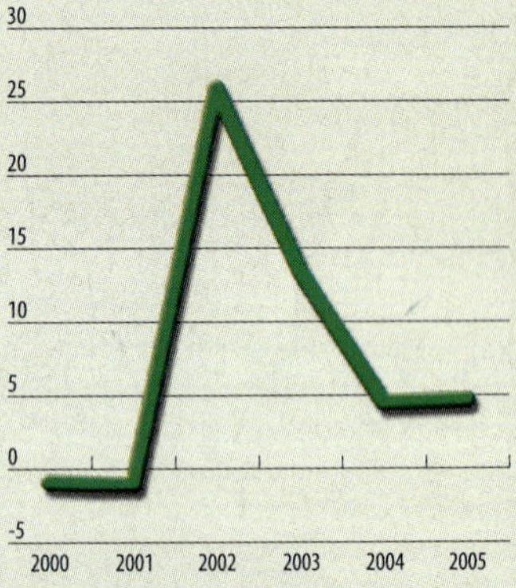

To watch: Debt negotiations. The government has yet to settle on a plan for restructuring its defaulted bonds. Until it does, Argentina will remain a pariah. Ominously, the government faces heavy repayments in 2005 on non-defaulted bonds.

Brazil

GDP growth: 3.6%
GDP: $580bn
Inflation: 5.8%
Population: 181.4m
GDP per head: $3,200

The president, Luiz Inácio Lula da Silva, is popular and the economy is doing better. But public frustration is growing over persistent poverty, crime and lack of jobs, and Congress will be less co-operative as the 2006 elections begin to loom. Look for policies more friendly towards the poor, launched with plenty of political spin, and pork-barrel favours granted in exchange for votes on structural reforms.

The government will stick to its IMF-approved goals: fiscal discipline, a floating exchange rate and inflation-targeting. Real earnings will begin to recover and there will be more jobs.

To watch: FTAA. The scheduled conclusion of the Free-Trade Area of the Americas is 2005. If approved, the pact will be weaker than expected due to disputes between Brazil and the United States. Each wants to protect sectors that should be opened.

Chile

GDP growth: 4.6%
GDP: $96bn
Inflation: 3.0%
Population: 15.5m
GDP per head: $6,180

Joaquín Lavín, the opposition mayor of Santiago, is the narrow favourite to win the presidential election in December. The ruling Concertación coalition's prospects depend on its ability to pick a candidate without too much infighting.

Tightening credit conditions in emerging markets and a likely fall in demand for Chile's exports, especially copper, will slow the economy.

Colombia

GDP growth: 3.7%
GDP: $98bn
Inflation: 5.3%
Population: 46.0m
GDP per head: $2,130

The president, Alvaro Uribe, is popular: so popular, in fact, that efforts to change the constitution to allow Mr Uribe's re-election in May 2006 could succeed. The government plans to overhaul the national tax system, reduce future pensions liabilities and introduce a fiscal plan to trim public debt. But the budget deficit, at around 6% of GDP, remains a serious concern.

Venezuela

GDP growth: 4.1%
GDP: $110bn
Inflation: 20.5%
Population: 26.5m
GDP per head: $4,140

President Hugo Chávez managed to keep his job in the August 2004 referendum, but hostility between his supporters and opponents will continue, particularly in the run-up to congressional elections in 2005. Unchastened, Mr Chávez will push his "Bolivarian revolution" and his redistributionist policies. Expect more demonstrations—and violence.

The government will have less money to fling at the economy in 2005 as oil prices ease, slowing growth. At the end of the year, real GDP will be 4% below the 1998 level. No wonder Venezuelans are angry.

To watch: South American solidarity. Mr Chávez has signed energy-development agreements with his Colombian and Argentine counterparts. Expect more of these as Mr Chávez tries to soothe testy relations among leaders in the region.

MIDDLE EAST AND AFRICA

Main event: Momentous moves: planned elections in Iraq and Israel's Gaza pull-out

Middle East & N. Africa growth: 4.6%

Sub-Saharan Africa growth: 3.6%

Algeria

GDP growth: 8.2%
GDP: $80bn
Inflation: 3.7%
Population: 33.9m
GDP per head: $2,360

Following his crushing election victory in April 2004, the president, Abdelaziz Bouteflika, will go largely unchallenged in 2005. His main goals? Ending the Islamist insurgency and reconciling with Kabylia's Berber population. No attempt, though, to curb corruption.

The spigots are wide open. Algerian crude-oil production will rise again in 2005 (by about 14%). And the In Amenas gas project will produce around 9bn cu metres/year of gas and some 60,000 barrels/day of liquids. The gas will be transported (via pipelines) to Spain and Italy.

Egypt

GDP growth: 3.0%
GDP: $77bn
Inflation: 6.5%
Population: 74.6m
GDP per head: $1,030

A presidential election is due in October 2005 and a parliamentary vote a month later. Hosni Mubarak, the all-powerful president, is a shoo-in, provided he is in good health. But the question of succession—Mr Mubarak is 76—is becoming an issue. Some believe his son, Gamal, is being groomed.

The economy is weakening. The government must restart the stalled privatisation programme and cut subsidies. But Mr Mubarak will be cautious ahead of the elections.

Exchange rate Egyptian £:$

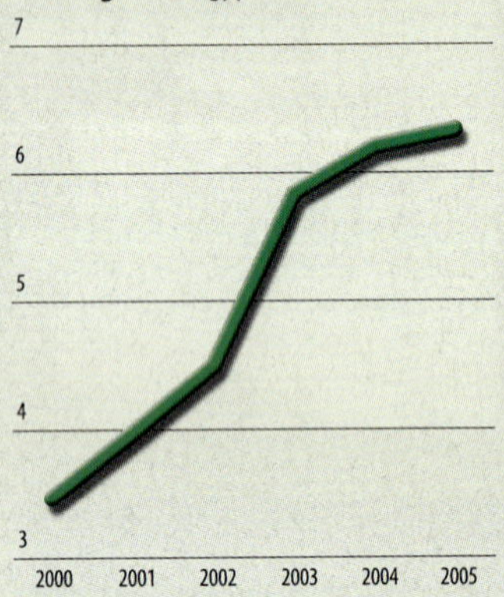

Iran

GDP growth: 4.6%
GDP: $170bn
Inflation: 14.7%
Population: 71m
GDP per head: $2,400

Iranians will elect a new president in June 2005. The embattled Mohammed Khatami cannot stand again and other reformists will be blocked. The conservative victor could, though, be a new face who takes a pragmatic view of social issues and the economy.

Apart from oil, the economy does not work well: too many subsidies, too little investment. Islamic foundations, which own swathes of the non-oil economy, and the *bazaaris* (the traditional trading class) will resist changes.

To watch: Nuclear brinkmanship. Iran says it has a right to develop nuclear power—supposedly for peaceful purposes. America sees a weapons agenda. The UN may threaten sanctions but this could drive Iran into a corner. An American—or Israeli—strike against Iran's nuclear facilities is possible, threatening a wider conflict. A deal remains feasible, though, if only because Iran's oil is essential to world markets.

Iraq

GDP growth: 10.3%
GDP: $37bn
Inflation: 20.0%
Population: 26.5m
GDP per head: $1,380

GDP % change

Elections will take place early in 2005 but not all areas will participate. No surprise there. The violence will continue, peaking as voting approaches and continuing intermittently thereafter. An elected government will be more legitimate than an appointed one but it will not quell the insurrection. A descent into chaos is a real possibility. Still, the majority of Iraqis want a viable state and will have an incentive to co-operate, if fitfully. Reconstruction will continue, but not quickly enough to provide a big boost to the economy.

To watch: Grand Ayatollah Sistani. The revered but mysterious Shia leader is the most important man in Iraq. The new government—and America—must keep his co-operation if they are to have any chance of creating a manageable political landscape. As the grand ayatollah goes, so goes Iraq.

Israel

GDP growth: 3.8%
GDP: $122bn
Inflation: 2.1%
Population: 7.0m
GDP per head: $17,540

Before the March cabinet vote on the evacuation of the Gaza settlements, Ariel Sharon will try to form a national unity government to include his own Likud party, plus Labour and Shinui. If he fails, early elections will be called in the first few months of 2005.

The economy is looking better. Steps to control government spending have helped stabilise the budget; a reduction in tax rates has boosted consumer spending. Exports will do well and tourism will continue its recovery, provided Israeli-Palestinian violence does not worsen.

To watch: Ariel Sharon. Peacemaker or ultimate hardliner? Israel's pull-out from Gaza could be the first step towards resuming peace talks, or a final Israeli move followed by tighter control of the areas it continues to occupy.

Jordan

GDP growth: 5.1%
GDP: $12bn
Inflation: 2.6%
Population: 5.8m
GDP per head: $2,010

King Abdullah will continue to walk a fine line. Many Jordanians are furious with American policy towards Iraq and the Palestinians, yet the king relies on America for strong military and financial support. The alliance brings the risk of an al-Qaeda attack, which would shatter business confidence but rally Jordanians to the king's side. Jordan's position as a gateway for duty- and quota-free exports to America and the EU—it has trade deals with both—will spur investment.

Kenya

GDP growth: 3.7%
GDP: $12bn
Inflation: 6.5%
Population: 33.3m
GDP per head: $360

The two parties in the ruling coalition, the National Alliance of Kenya and the Liberal Democratic Party (LDP), are feuding, especially over the distribution of power under a proposed new constitution. The LDP feels cheated and could pull out of the coalition, joining instead with the former governing party, the Kenya Africa National Union. This could trigger an early election.

Projected investment in telecoms, transport and electricity, combined with higher garment production (mainly for export), will boost industrial growth.

Lebanon

GDP growth: 4.0%
GDP: $19bn
Inflation: 2.4%
Population: 3.8m
GDP per head: $5,110

Syria's brazen decision to extend Emile Lahoud's term as president was a blow to his great rival, Rafiq al-Hariri, the prime minister, who resigned in October 2004. Mr Hariri will have a chance to recoup his losses when the general election is held, probably in May. He will be missed: he was beginning to play a vital role in advancing economic reforms. If Lebanon reverts to the status of a Syrian province with economic policy determined by Mr Lahoud (a former general), investors may have second thoughts.

To watch: Debt. Lebanon is among the world's most heavily indebted countries, with high annual deficits and public debt equal to 185% of GDP.

Nigeria

GDP growth: 2.6%
GDP: $53bn
Inflation: 11.5%
Population: 139.8m
GDP per head: $380

Ethnic and religious violence will persist, driven by a potent mix of communal tensions, religious intolerance and political disillusionment. The president, Olusegun Obasanjo, will use military force to put down uprisings in the country's many unruly regions. The economy will slow as oil prices ease and political unrest in the Niger Delta region constrains oil and gas production.

Saudi Arabia

GDP growth: 2.3%
GDP: $232bn
Inflation: 0.3%
Population: 25.7m
GDP per head: $9,030

The kingdom will continue to face attacks by Islamist militants, despite a heavy crackdown by security forces. Western targets and symbols of Al Saud authority—the ruling family is not popular—will be in the cross-hairs. The regime, though, is secure, at least for now. The country's first elections in 40 years—for municipal offices—are set for the early months of the year.

South Africa

GDP growth: 3.3%
GDP: $193bn
Inflation: 4.7%
Population: 47.1m
GDP per head: $4,110

A one-party state? The African National Congress's big win in the April 2004 election has strengthened its already firm grip on power. Black economic empowerment remains a priority. Over the next 5-10 years, the government wants some 25% of the banking, mining and farming industries transferred to black hands.

To watch: Zimbabwe. President Thabo Mbeki has damaged his credibility by trying—and failing—to win concessions from Zimbabwe's president, Robert Mugabe, who is rapidly wrecking his country's political and economic foundations. Mr Mbeki may now seek help from regional or international organisations.

Pasquale Pistorio, President and CEO of STMicroelectronics, says the French have a passion for business.

"This is the first time in our industry that Americans are coming to Europe to join the R&D of Europeans."

What is STMicroelectronics?

We are one of the world's largest semiconductor companies with some 50,000 people, 9 billion volume in sales, and a worldwide presence. Our market is the world, our mission is to serve the world. And France has assumed a key role in achieving this goal.

Why have you so heavily invested in France?

The microelectronics industry is driven by innovation and creativity and depends on the intellectual value added: the human capital. The quality of advanced education in engineering and mathematics is second to none. We don't work in isolation. We network with research institutes and universities, and the culture in France is very open to cooperation.

What about the cost of doing business? How do you find the tax structure?

It's a lot more favorable than you would think. France has a real passion for R&D and has passed tax laws to promote it. We are spending over $500 million a year on R&D in France. Now, we can deduct some $25 million from our tax debt. The Government is also creating competitiveness clusters where the cost of social benefits for researchers is being cut by 25 percent. A huge saving!

You talk about innovation. How can a country which values its traditions (it makes over 400 cheeses for example) be innovative?

Innovation means creating new things. But to be creative you need deep roots. People are not computers. They have a brain, a heart and a soul. And the culture is the soul. The French are rightfully proud of their culture. It's the rich soil from which new ideas can grow.

Can you really attract the best people to work in France?

This is the first time in our industry that Americans are coming to Europe to join the R&D of Europeans. At Crolles – imagine Silicon Valley with skiing - we have created the most advanced R&D center in Europe, and one of the best in the world. A colleague of mine tells the story about one of his people who was transferred to France who said: "This is paradise. We should pay you to live here. You shouldn't have to pay us."

What is your greatest achievement in France?

There's one basic acid test of success. In the last 15 years there was not one year, when we didn't keep growing employment. Even this year, when our competition is shrinking its resources to reduce overheads, we have been taking on more people.

Have you anything negative to say about France?

Yes. The food. It's a problem for me. There is such good eating. Wonderful cuisine (and not just French) everywhere. And, unfortunately, I really must watch my waistline…

STMicroelectronics in France

- Established in France since 1987 with roots dating back to 1956
- 9,500 employees in France including 3,500 engineers
- Partnership with Philips and Freescale (formerly Motorola) has produced one of the most advanced nanotechnology R&D centers in the world, at Crolles 2 France

For more information on investing in France, visit www.thenewfrance.com

THE NEW FRANCE. WHERE THE SMART MONEY GOES.

The world in figures Industries

BUSINESS ENVIRONMENT

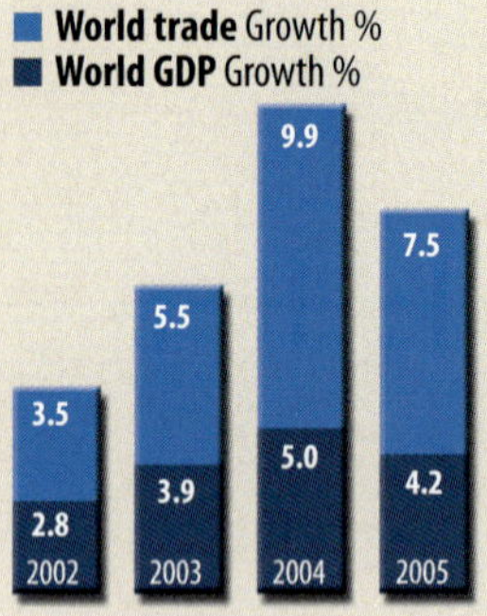

The Economist Intelligence Unit forecasts global GDP growth (on a PPP basis) of 4.2% in 2005, down slightly on 2004 but still healthy. China and America will grow fastest among the large economies. A moderate deceleration in world-trade growth is likely, to 7.5%—a pace still comparable to that set during much of the 1990s.

Risks abound. In a tight market, high oil prices pose a threat to oil importers. Global trade imbalances also loom large; much depends on the willingness of investors around the world to fund America's huge current-account deficit. After a gentle bounce at the end of 2004, the US dollar should average $1.30:€1 and ¥108:$1 in 2005. Further appreciation of the euro will make it hard for companies to capitalise on demand in America and Asia.

Many OECD countries face high private- and public-sector debt. Cautious consumers, faced with high personal debt and rising pension and health-care costs, will guard their purse-strings closely. Rising interest rates and a diminishing appetite for high-risk ventures will constrain international liquidity, which could be bad news for emerging markets. The Chinese investment bubble might burst.

Physical security is a critical issue in many markets. As well as harming tourism, any increase in terrorist attacks against foreign-owned operations will raise the cost of doing business.

2005 forecasts unless otherwise indicated. World totals based on 51 countries accounting for over 95% of world GDP.

Economist Intelligence Unit
london@eiu.com

AGRICULTURE

Eat your cereal
Global stock, % of consumption

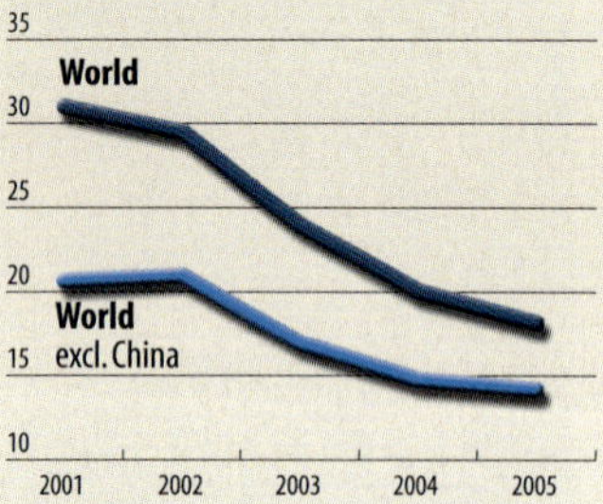

Source: FAO

● According to the UN Hunger Task Force, half the world's undernourished in 2005 will be farmers, while 20% will be urban dwellers.

Despite a broad-based increase in production, the UN's Food and Agriculture Organisation (FAO) says world cereal inventories will fall for the fifth straight year, down 9% to 363m tonnes by the end of the various 2005 marketing seasons.

Rice production will trail consumption for the fourth year in a row, sending stocks to a 20-year low. The US Department of Agriculture forecasts a global yield of 401.8m tonnes, up from 390.2m tonnes, assuming normal weather conditions in key countries. Consumption, on the other hand, will be 417.9m tonnes. As supplies tighten, prices will rise, benefiting exporters such as Thailand and Vietnam.

Efforts to streamline global farm trade will gather momentum. The WTO's member-states have finally committed, in principle, to abolishing agricultural export subsidies and slashing domestic supports. Cotton is also on the radar screen following WTO rulings which declared that cotton subsidies in America and Europe violated international trade regulations. Other segments ripe for reform include sugar and tropical fruits.

After a six-year ban, Europe's farmers will face their 2005 planting seasons with at least 17 new seed options after the European Commission granted approval for genetically modified maize developed by America's Monsanto.

Governments, particularly in Asia, will face pressure to improve animal hygiene and health. To date there have been no proven human-to-human cases of avian influenza, or "bird flu", but the World Health Organisation fears that unless efforts are intensified, the virus may acquire the ability to jump from poultry to people and lead to a pandemic.

On the high seas, illegal, unreported and unregulated trawling will continue its assault on sustainable fishing. Catches of commercially valuable fish species in some places will surpass permitted levels by 300%.

To watch: Cocoa stocks. Researchers at Cornell University in New York have found that cocoa contains nearly twice as many antioxidants as a glass of red wine and up to three times as many as a cup of tea. Confirmed status as a health food could end heavy production surpluses in the sector.

AUTOMOTIVE

Car sales by region
%

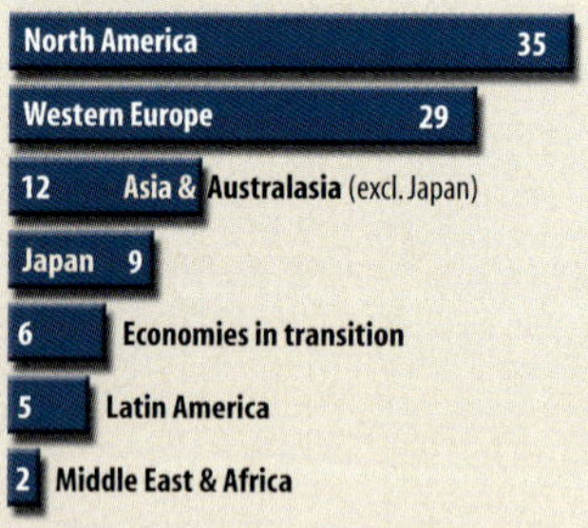

● In 2005 car registrations will go above 50m, up 2.6%.

While car sales will hold up reasonably well, global overcapacity remains stubbornly high—as much as 25-30%. This will exert enormous downward pressure on prices, making incentives the norm even in turbo-charged economies such as China's.

Oversupply in America has touched off a price war that compels makers to offer buyer incentives worth around $3,000 a car. Sales will hold steady because the producers will in effect pay customers to scrap their old cars for new ones. Meanwhile, America's Big Three will continue to lose out to Japanese and European rivals, which are more productive and benefit from investment incentives for foreign carmakers worth over $1,000 a car.

In a dash for better growth and profitability, the world's top carmakers are piling into China. Foreign carmakers will expand capacity by over 4m units by the end of 2008: Volkswagen plans to expand production by 1m to 1.6m units in 2005 and South Korea's Hyundai by over 500,000 by 2007. The increased capacity, however, is certain to fuel the price war between General Motors and Volkswagen.

High oil prices will stimulate demand for more fuel-efficient vehicles in 2005, but this slow-moving industry is not likely to be able to meet it. Toyota says it aims to sell 300,000 hybrid (petrol-electric) vehicles worldwide by the end of 2005, but capacity remains well under that figure. Purchasers of hybrids will face long waiting lists. Sales of sports utility vehicles (SUVs), meanwhile, will shrink as the popularity of the gas-guzzlers plummets.

To watch: Disappointed car thieves. Mobile tracking units for cars will become affordable. In the event of a theft, a simple e-mail or phone call will disable the vehicle starter and lock the doors.

CONSUMER GOODS

Global retail sales are forecast to rise just 1.7% to $10.36trn in 2005, a sharp decrease in growth from 2004. The slow-down will be concentrated in developed countries, where personal debt remains high. As a result, large global retailers will continue their march into emerging economies, particularly in the fast-growing markets of eastern Europe and Asia.

Discount chains will outdistance all other formats, in all markets. Wal-Mart, the world's largest retailer, plans to increase its share of overseas sales from 16% in 2003 to around 25% in 2005. It will target Japan in particular, where retail sales are growing for the first time in years, as deflation finally ends.

Another bright spot will be China, where the battle for the retail market will extend to the second-tier provinces and rural areas. The Chinese are getting richer, true, but it is also getting easier to reach them, thanks to improvements in the country's infrastructure. These have enabled companies to establish more comprehensive, nationwide distribution networks.

To watch: Chips with everything. With growth elusive in mature markets, more retailers will be investing in information technology to improve productivity. In particular, RFID (Radio Frequency ID) tagging will start to replace bar codes. These tiny chips transmit unique ID codes to readers, aiding in the management of the complete supply chain. Early users include Gillette, Home Depot, Gap, Procter & Gamble, Tesco and Wal-Mart.

DEFENCE

US military spending v the world
$bn

*Iran, North Korea, Syria
All figures 2004 except US, which is 2005
Sources: Global Issues; Economist Intelligence Unit

The United States has budgeted $420.7bn for defence for 2005, an increase of 7%. Transformational technologies, such as unmanned aerial vehicles, will be a focus, and some $9.2bn will be spent on a missile defence system. With a keen eye on North Korea and China, the Missile Defence Agency will by the end of the year deploy 20 ground-based interceptor missiles in Alaska and California, plus up to ten sea-based ones aboard Aegis cruisers.

Decisions should be complete on the closure of some American domestic bases by the end of 2005. The aim of the politically sensitive programme is to cut surplus capacity, put at 20%. That done, attention will turn to the closure of bases in Europe, especially Germany, and the opening of new ones in former Soviet-block countries.

For now, the Pentagon will continue to finance military operations in Iraq and Afghanistan with general appropriations. The 16 nations that contribute troops to the Polish-led Multinational Division Central-South have pledged to keep their forces in Iraq at least until the end of January 2005, when elections are due.

Meanwhile, the UN secretary-general, Kofi Annan, has called on member-states to provide an extra 30,000 troops to meet demand for global peacekeeping operations.

Russia's defence spending will grow by 27% in 2005, to 573bn roubles ($19.6bn). The military forces will receive almost three-quarters of that; R&D will absorb 15%. Separately, spending on "national security and law enforcement", announced just days before the Beslan school tragedy, is set at just over $13.7bn, up 25% on 2004.

Japan, officially the world's third-biggest spender on defence, has budgeted $45bn—the sharpest rise in military spending since 1997. Most of the extra money will be put towards ballistic missile defence and counter-terrorist capabilities. Since the second world war Japan has been constitutionally bound to a "defensive" role; the issue of a broader military role on the world stage will remain controversial.

To watch: Floating sea bases, designed to circumvent the reluctance of third-party nations to make their air bases, ports and other facilities available for offensive operations against their neighbours. Using platforms that can quickly be disassembled and redeployed, the new hi-tech sea base will offer everything a land base does.

E-COMMERCE

The worldwide internet population will hit 1.07bn in 2005, according to Computer Industry Almanac, up from 934m in 2004. While a boon to businesses that operate online, this kind of growth creates an ever-bigger headache for tax collectors. Expect governments to get more aggressive on this issue in 2005. Forrester Research expects e-commerce in America to grow 14% annually through 2010—three to four times faster than the economy. Growth in Europe is predicted to average 33% annually through to 2009.

Improving business-to-business (B2B) infrastructure will power Europe's online trade to €2.2trn ($2.75trn) in 2006, with France, Germany and Britain accounting for almost two-thirds of activity, Forrester says. More stunning: by 2008 China will account for half of all B2B e-commerce in the Asia-Pacific region, excluding Japan, with total revenues of $1.29trn and a cumulative growth of 81%. India's predicted growth through to 2008 is even higher, at 83%.

America's growing population of online shopping households, combined with site improvements by retailers, will see business-to-consumer (B2C) e-commerce account for 12% of total retail sales—or $316bn—in 2010 (up from 7% in 2004). Sales of home products, clothing and computer hardware and software will lead the way. Traditional catalogue-based retailers in the American market can expect to see their consumer web sales exceed catalogue sales in 2005 or 2006.

Improved attention to security should help e-marketers: Datamonitor forecasts that losses to credit-card fraud will keep falling, in Europe especially, with banks due to complete migration to the EMV (Europay, MasterCard, Visa) chip and PIN regime in 2005.

To watch: Armed with an evolving search site, A9.com, Amazon has joined the group of internet superpowers—MSN, eBay, Google and Yahoo!—that strive to be not just portals, search sites or shopping malls, but also places to get anything done online.

ENERGY

Energy consumption per head
(kg oil per head)

Few commodities are as sensitive to world events as oil—hence 2004's price spike. In 2005 things should be calmer, with average Brent blend prices around $38/barrel, provided a modest production increase and some easing of tensions in the Middle East. Over the next three years, overall crude production is expected to rise by an average of 2.8% a year.

Demand for oil and natural gas will grow in 2005—by nearly 3%—but not as fast as demand for electricity and coal. Coal is back in vogue, not least because many energy-hungry economies with coal reserves are seeking to reduce their dependence on imported oil. As coal prices lag well behind those of oil and gas, cleaner technologies for burning coal will become more viable.

Despite all the talk about alternative fuel sources, only liquefied natural gas (LNG) will make any real strides. The process of liquefying gas reduces its bulk by a factor of around 600, making transport vastly simpler than natural gas. LNG consumption will grow by a robust 10%, with most of that demand coming from Asia and Australasia.

To watch: China's first coal-liquefaction project. Located in Mongolia, it will be producing 1m tonnes of liquid fuels in 2005. The $3.3bn facility is expected to convert 15m tonnes of coal into 5m tonnes of oil products annually by 2008.

ENTERTAINMENT

The fight over the new DVD format—remember VHS v Beta?—will reach fever pitch. This time it's Blu-Ray (Sony, Panasonic, Samsung and Philips) against HD DVD (Toshiba, NEC). Both groups say their new discs will hold four to five times more digital video and audio data than the DVD currently on the market. Blu-Ray claims superior image quality; HD DVD is supposedly cheaper and more compatible with existing formats. The stance taken by the Hollywood studios will be crucial, since they create most of the content. Sony's $4.85bn acquisition of MGM, due to clear American regulators in 2005, might deliver the knockout punch. The deal gives the Japanese giant a library of some 8,000 films and 43,000 hours of TV episodes.

Either way, filmgoers will not stop marching to the multiplexes: European cinema-ticket sales are expected to pass the 1bn mark in 2005, says *Screen Digest*. Americans, meanwhile, will be given another reason to stay in when the Fox Reality Channel, dedicated to original series and re-runs of reality TV programmes, is launched in the first quarter.

Sales of traditional CDs will continue to decline—and unlicensed downloading of audio files won't be to blame. Armed with the newly acquired Musicmatch, Yahoo! will propagate digital music, in competition with Apple's iTunes Music Store. Jupiter Research predicts that soon subscriptions to streaming music will outpace ad hoc downloads.

The next generation of 128-bit games

consoles are expected in late 2005 and early 2006. But the dynamic growth will come from three sectors still in their infancy: broadband, mobile, and interactive TV. Informa Media Group predicts that such offerings will contribute 32% of worldwide games revenues by 2010, up from 12% in 2004.

To watch: Eurovision. The über-kitsch, pan-European song contest, which put the global spotlight on Swedish supergroup ABBA in the 1970s, turns the Big 5-0 in May 2005. Ukraine, winner last year with "Wild Dances" performed by Ruslana, will play host.

FINANCIAL SERVICES

The era of rock-bottom interest rates is drawing to a close in developed countries, shifting the landscape for financial services. As the global economy expands, profits from IPOs, advisory fees, commissions and lending will improve, fattening year-end bonuses once again. The good times won't be universal, however. Fixed income and emerging markets will be decidedly less fun.

Lending growth will be robust in 2005. Led primarily by corporate demand, lending worldwide will rise to $31trn from $27.8trn in 2004, with western European growth in double digits.

Insurance companies will continue to move away from demanding investment strategies and towards a greater dependence on premium income. Interest in insurance has grown across the private and corporate sectors with the perception of increased threats from terrorism, computer fraud and extreme weather patterns.

Pension funds have much less room to manoeuvre. The shift to pensions which pay out according to what is paid in (defined contributions) as opposed to paying a guaranteed amount (defined benefit) will continue. But not fast enough. As longer lifespans become the norm, the level of guaranteed pay-outs based on unrealistic forecasts of investment returns stays stubbornly high. In the United States alone pension funds will report a shortfall of more than $200bn in 2005.

To watch: Mobile credit cards. Banks are working with telecoms providers and retailers on systems which allow mobile-phone owners to purchase goods with a swipe of their phone. Prototypes have already been launched in Japan and South Korea.

FOOD AND DRINK

Consumer spending on food, beverages and tobacco
$bn

With Oreo cookies under attack, change is afoot in the food industry. But will consumers go for a thinner, low-calorie version of the famous chocolate biscuit? Apparently so, which means food manufacturers will continue shutting down plants which produce high-fat, high-calorie snacks and look for new products to please an increasingly health-conscious public.

Spending on food, drink and tobacco will continue to grow in 2005, by about 5.6% to $4.1trn. But it will be healthier products that will grab the fastest growth and highest margins. Makers of doughnuts, ice cream and pizza will need to be on their toes, as low-calorie versions will grab as much as 30% of their overall sales in richer countries.

Drinks are going the same way, with consumers buying more premium beers, low-carb beers, new-world wine and flavoured alcoholic beverages. Soft-drink makers will offer healthier, trendier drinks, such as ones with vitamins or other nutritious additives.

Functional foods—everyday food products pumped with health extras—will also gain ground. Look out for omega-3 eggs, produced by feeding hens a flax-based diet, which have less saturated fat, less cholesterol and more vitamin E. Consumers will also be swallowing less hydrogenated fat in 2005, a baddy which raises cholesterol and clogs up arteries. America's Food and Drug Administration will require the labelling of trans-fats; Denmark has already restricted the use of these fats in foods and the EU is considering a similar measure.

To watch: Ethical food. The Common Code for the Coffee Community, aimed at improving working conditions in the coffee industry and signed by Nestlé, Kraft, Sara Lee and Tchibo of Japan, will take the notion of fair trade into mainstream markets. Other industries, notably chocolate, will follow suit.

HEALTH CARE

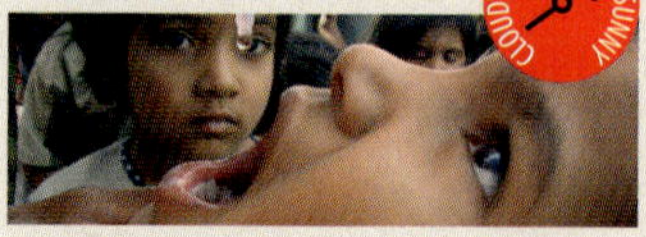

● Global health-care spending will reach $803 per person, with total sales on pharmaceuticals rising to $447bn.

The world's demand for health care shows no sign of abating. Sales of drugs, hospital services and doctors' services will outstrip world GDP growth yet again, proving that health care is one sector no one wants to skimp on. This rosy picture, however, will not make life any easier for drug companies or government health authorities, which will remain at loggerheads over costs and accountability.

Millions of people are entering the market for "western" health care for the first time, as developing countries become wealthier. While this demand helps drive growth, the main motor for the health-care industry will be the growing numbers of elderly consumers in developed countries, most of whom have good government health plans as well as disposable income to spend on everything from aromatherapy massage to yoga classes.

World pharmaceutical sales growth
% change

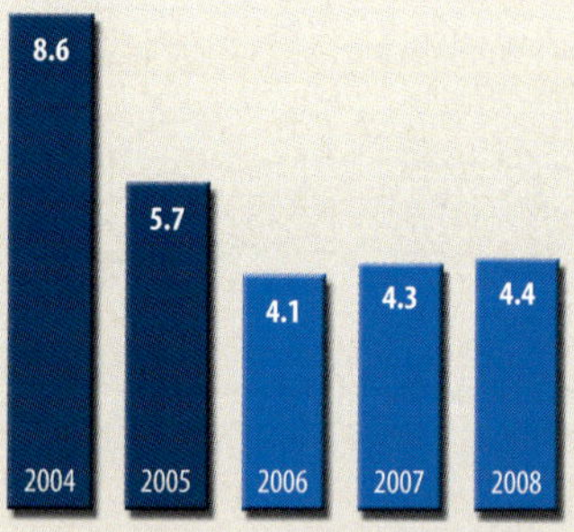

Despite its continued profitability, the drug industry will remain in the dumps over stronger pressures on pricing. With state-controlled prices in Canada around 40% less than those in the United States, American demand for Canadian drugs will surge. In Europe low-price generics will start to flow from new EU members in eastern Europe as a result of lower manufacturing costs and the ability of east European firms to develop generics before patent expiry dates.

The biotech sector, meanwhile, will flourish, accounting for more than a quarter of new drugs in active clinical trials worldwide. Expect big things from new gene-therapy drugs and DNA vaccines, which are aimed at preventing diseases such as malaria.

To watch: Robotic surgery. This will take off in 2005, following the FDA's decision to allow the use of robotic devices during coronary artery bypass surgery. Remotely manipulated by a surgeon using hand grips and foot pedals, robotic arms can perform operations with several benefits to patients, including less blood loss, fewer complications and faster recovery.

INFORMATION TECHNOLOGY

PCs
per 1,000 people

Growth in PC sales will remain strong. The demand for what is after all a 30-year-old product will be driven by replacement purchases and new users—from delivery-van drivers with tablet PCs to children demanding the second, third or fourth PC in the home. Laptop prices will continue to fall in 2005 as manufacturers, mainly in South Korea, find cheaper ways to produce LCD screens. This will allow laptops to claim an even larger share of PC-purchasing budgets worldwide.

The turnaround in the semiconductors sector will slow as global capacity lurches once more into overdrive. Growth will be a credible 18%, aided by buoyant sales of cheap consumer products such as mobile phones, PDAs, digital cameras, MP3 music players and feature-packed items such as camera-phones. But the key driver for chip sales in 2005 will be corporate IT investment, spurred by continued growth in America and Asia, followed by Europe.

To watch: Teeny-weeny hard drives. Based on the latest 0.85-inch, 2-gigabyte hard drives, ranges of micro-products will start to emerge, such as wristwatch PDAs, a digital data key and MP3 headsets. Sceptics beware—Apple's hugely successful iPod is based on a 1-inch hard drive.

MEDIA

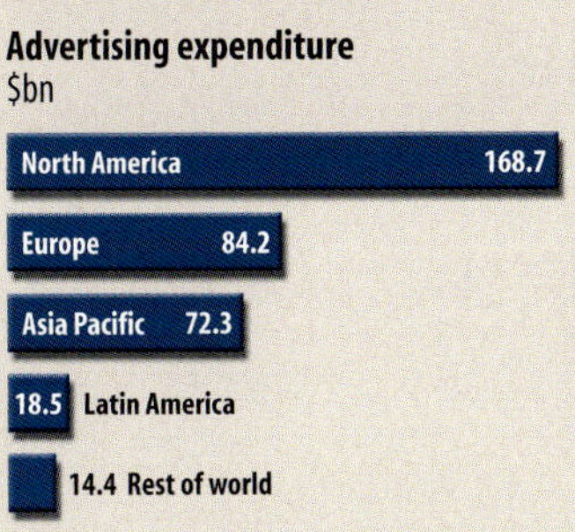

Having trailed general economic growth for years, the influential American advertising industry—representing about 45% of the world market—is set to outpace the wider economy in 2005. Universal McCann forecasts the 2005 domestic ad spend will increase by 6.5% from 2004, as pent-up corporate demand starts to play out.

The recovery should spread across the globe as wary marketers rush to match their competitors' ad spend. London-based Carat, the world's largest independent media buyer, has raised its forecast for ad-spend growth for the next two years, predicting 5.7% growth in 2005. Another market watcher, Zenith Optimedia, says that after America, the best growth rates will be in Asia. Advertising accounts for 1.4% of the American economy and a stagnating 0.8% in Europe. Asian markets should overtake the European figure in 2005.

The news will be best for online marketing. More than half (54%) of marketers who took part in a survey by US-based Millward Brown expect to increase spending for online advertising in 2005—with online allocations outperforming television, magazines, newspaper, radio, outdoor and direct mail. Greater broadband penetration and more sophisticated targeting technologies will help subscription and stream-based advertising revenue reach €715m ($900m) in 2005, up from €520m, according to AccuStream iMedia Research. Jupiter Research predicts online advertising will be a $16.1bn industry by 2009.

From July digital recording devices sold in America will have to recognise an electronic "flag" encoded in digital television broadcasts that can prevent the sharing of programmes between machines or over the internet.

To watch: FOLED. Flexible organic light-emitting diode technology will emerge as a potential replacement for paper in 2005. Made of electric-powered, light-emitting organic material, FOLED displays can be rolled up, folded or even worn on clothing. New Jersey-based Universal Display Corporation is working on a device for downloading newspapers and magazines which shrinks to the size of a pen when its FOLED screen is retracted.

RAW MATERIALS

Global consumption of finished steel is projected to rise by 4.5% in 2005, according to the International Iron and Steel Institute. China's consumption will grow by 10.4%. The country's share of global steel consumption is expected to reach 30.3% in 2005, up from 13.5% a decade ago. The outlook for the rest of the world is more subdued, with a projected rise of 2.2%.

The knock-on effect is profound, as steelmakers seize all the iron ore, coking coal, copper, nickel and zinc that mining companies can send through their mills and smelters. Miners will invest in expanding old mines and digging new ones, many of them buoyed by lucrative long-term contracts with customers keen to secure their supply chains.

But although the broad outlook for raw materials suppliers is good, fortunes will inevitably remain cyclical. According to Access Economics, government spending cuts worldwide may lead to significant price drops—lead, platinum, silver, copper and nickel may fall by more than 20% in the two years to mid-2006.

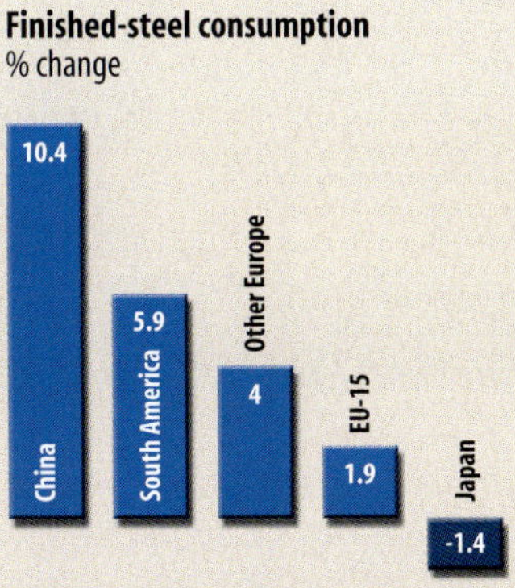

To watch: Plastics futures. After 125 years of dealing in non-ferrous metals, the London Metals Exchange will on May 27th 2005 commence trading in two plastics contracts—polypropylene (PP) and linear low density polyethylene (LLDPE). Thermoplastics constitute a $120bn market; they are increasingly replacing traditional raw materials with their strength and versatility.

TELECOMS

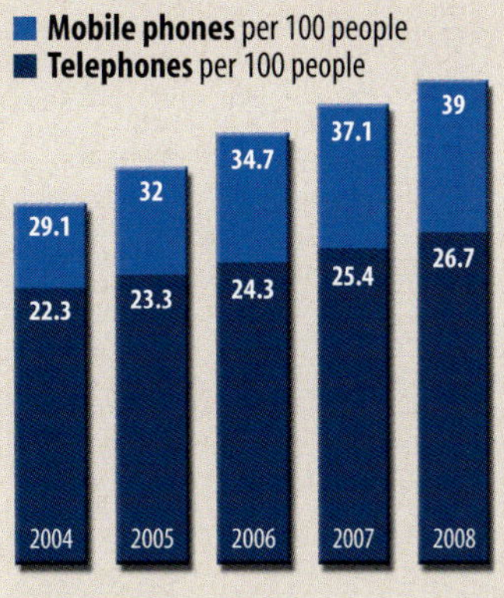

The world's favourite gadget—the mobile phone—will continue to enjoy double-digit growth in 2005. Nearly a third of people, worldwide, will own mobiles by the end of 2005, while just 23% will own a terrestrial phone.

The buzzword for telecoms will be convergence. An example is the Fixed-to-Mobile Convergence Alliance, formed by Britain's BT, France-based Cegetel, DoCoMo of Japan, Eurotel, Swisscom and Korea Telecom. The group will work to develop markets for phones that operate on both mobile and fixed-line networks. The formation of this alliance was primarily a defensive move. With internet telephony growing rapidly around the world, both fixed-line and mobile operators need to protect their customer base.

At long last, 3G mobile phones will start to take off. According to Deutsche Bank, there will be around 60 commercial 3G networks worldwide in early 2005.

To watch (not): Video telephones. Although 3G phones will be able to send and receive images in real time, consumers will nix the service. Who wants to check their hair or get dressed to make a phone call?

TRAVEL AND TOURISM

● Global spending on hotels and restaurants will hit $1.7trn in 2005.

Travel is back. After a few disastrous years, tourism returned to growth in 2004 and the trend will continue in 2005—unless new terrorist atrocities scare travellers away. The well-managed hotel groups and no-frill airlines will prosper while most full-service airlines will continue to bleed.

In America, where the budget airline was born, low-cost carriers will account for as much as a third of all airline trips in 2005 and 40% in 2006. In Europe the sector is expected to grow by between 20% and 30% a year over the next five years. Traditional carriers will need to compete on price rather than service. Europe's hospitality sector, meanwhile, will flourish as the discount carriers turn scores of previously unknown cities—from Alghero to Zaragoza—into tourist destinations by promoting new routes with rock-bottom prices.

Full-service airlines will continue to merge, like KLM/Air France; remain undead, like United Airlines and Alitalia; or start to pull the plug. The only real survivors will be those with profitable long-haul businesses, such as British Airways, Singapore Airlines and Qantas.

Hoteliers, meanwhile, would be well advised to learn Chinese. Changes in government regulations in 2004 cleared the way for Chinese tourists to visit 27 European countries without jumping through regulatory hoops. In 2005 28.5m Chinese tourists will pour out of the country, compared with just 20m in 2003. By 2007 China looks set to take over the United States as the world's biggest source of tourists.

2005 will see the first test flights of Airbus's A380, the largest passenger aircraft to take to the skies, with room for 555 passengers, 150 more than Boeing's 747 jumbos. Airbus claims the new jets will burn 12% less fuel per seat than the 747 and have 15% lower direct operating costs. This is just as well, since Airbus has spent around $11bn to develop the jet, with about a third of that money coming from European taxpayers.

To watch: Flying mobile phones. Mobile phones will be cleared for take-off in 2005, as airlines invest in the technology that will allow their passengers to keep their phones switched on during flights.

New York, USA

Business

2005

Wal-Mart, the largest retailer in the world, plans to open or extend up to 530 stores around the world, compared with some 400 in 2004.

The lure of the private firm

Matthew Bishop

Private companies stand out from the public lot

Can it really be only five years since the height of any corporate executive's ambition was to be the boss of a big stockmarket-listed company—ideally after first taking it public with all the razzmatazz of a hot IPO (initial public offering)? How times change. After the bursting of the stockmarket bubble in 2000 and the scandals that afflicted many of the market's erstwhile darlings, public companies have lost much of their allure. Instead, as will be abundantly clear in 2005, for executives and investors alike, private companies are increasingly the place to be.

Even in the late 1990s, when the appetite of investors everywhere for shares knew no bounds, private firms still accounted for the lion's share of corporate activity. But the trend for more firms to go public seemed unstoppable. In America several hundred firms a year had IPOs during the 1990s—around 500 in 1999 alone. But 2002 brought the smallest number of IPOs in any year for a decade; 2003 was little better. Nor was 2004, for all the hullabaloo about Google's listing—itself a rather half-hearted affair, with most of the internet-search firm's shares remaining in private hands.

Although the number of firms delisting their shares from stockmarkets has increased in recent years, it has hardly dwarfed even the reduced number of new listings. But these data do not tell the whole story. Delisting is a laborious, controversial process. Selling a chunk of the firm to a private buyer tends not to be—and in recent years there has been a surge in such selling.

Big companies are increasingly focused on their core businesses and looking to shed non-core subsidiaries. In the bubble years they might have been able to float a subsidiary as a separate public company, or sell it to another big public firm to which it was more suited. But few public firms are active buyers nowadays. Lacklustre stockmarkets mean that their shares are not the powerful alternative currency to cash that they once were.

At the same time there has been a dramatic growth in the purchasing power of private buyers. As well as the world's growing army of multi-billionaires, there are increasingly well-funded private-equity firms competing furiously to buy unwanted bits of public companies. Private-equity firms first achieved prominence in the 1980s. Most famously, Kohlberg Kravis Roberts (KKR) borrowed most of the money to pull off the $25 billion takeover of one of America's most venerable public ▸

Matthew Bishop: business editor, *The Economist*

companies, RJR Nabisco—which they took private. They were branded barbarians at the gate.

Now firms such as KKR and Blackstone are respectable financial institutions, flush with billions of dollars that wealthy individuals and big institutions have invested in their funds and that banks have lent them. They are spending this money globally—private-equity firms are increasingly busy in Europe and Asia (especially Japan). And the amount of money they have to spend is growing fast as investors seek higher returns than they seem likely to get from interest rates or in the public-equity market. Although private-equity returns are already coming down from the over 40% per annum delivered by some firms in the past, they seem likely to remain high enough to continue for years to attract more money away from public equity.

The top private-equity firms are already huge. Together, the firms in which Blackstone has a stake have over 300,000 employees and revenues of $55 billion—enough to rank in the top 20 of the Fortune 500. This portfolio seems likely to grow, even though the individual firms will all be sold off over time in order to return money to investors. As doing an IPO or selling to a public company are popular exit strategies for private-equity firms, there may eventually be limits to the extent to which the growth of private equity will be at the expense of the public-equity markets—although as they get larger, private-equity firms may often exit by selling their portfolio companies privately to each other.

Managers increasingly regard private companies

> Private firms need not comply in full with Sarbanes-Oxley. Nor do they have to disclose what they pay their managers

as more attractive places to work. The Sarbanes-Oxley legislation, introduced in the aftermath of the Enron scandal, has imposed on public companies much onerous corporate-governance compliance—a source of constant complaint from bosses in America and beyond. Private firms need not comply in full with Sarbanes-Oxley. Nor do they have to disclose what they pay their managers, who are thus spared the growing public outrage over allegedly excessive executive remuneration. Private-equity firms tend to focus on businesses at important transition points, which pose interesting management challenges; this may make them particularly appealing to the best executive talent.

It remains to be seen if any public firm equivalent to RJR Nabisco in the 1980s will be taken private. Unlike then, there are now huge barriers to hostile takeovers, especially in America. Banks are not willing to lend quite as generously. Yet some of the biggest private-equity firms are now prepared to combine their funds with each other to pursue ever bigger deals. It would be unwise, then, to rule out the possibility of any but the very biggest public firms (and perhaps not even them) going private. In Britain, 2004's most interesting corporate story was the failed attempt by Philip Green, a wealthy businessman, to buy the country's iconic retailer, Marks & Spencer. Judging by the continuing difficulties of the firm's new management, it will be no surprise if Mr Green returns to take it private in 2005. □

Globalcorp, 2005

Narayana Murthy *BANGALORE*

The most competitive companies will bring together the best talents around the world

2005

Foreign retailers will be allowed to take full ownership of their businesses in China.

The forces of globalisation are reshaping our world, with ever-growing economic integration as well as increasing movement of people and knowledge across borders. Global trade accounts for around 30% of world GDP—four times its share in the early 1970s. Developing countries are an important part of this story. Their stock of inward foreign direct investment (FDI) totals 30% of their GDP, compared with 13% in 1980. Globally competitive transnational corporations have begun to emerge from China, India and Latin America. Haier (China), Tata Motors (India), Acer (Taiwan), Petrobras (Brazil), Cemex (Mexico) and the IT-services companies of India are examples. Thanks to them, the outward stock of FDI from developing countries has increased from 3% of GDP in 1980 to 10% today.

Globalisation and the information revolution have raised customer expectations. To satisfy them, companies will need to source capital where it is cheapest, produce where it is most cost-effective and sell where it is most profitable, without being constrained by national boundaries. This is the essence of globalisation. It leverages each nation's competitive advantage to produce goods and services more efficiently. The development of a product or service might typically be split among countries, with experts in America defining the customer requirements; the British defining the product attributes; the Australians defining the technology architecture; the Indians doing the software development; the Germans or the Japanese doing the manufacturing; and the Taiwanese doing the packaging. This new business model will distribute high-quality jobs around the world and deepen international collaboration.

We have already seen the emergence of such a model in the IT-services industry in India, leveraging talent and infrastructure in different parts of the world. Development tasks are distributed across various locations. The work that can be done in value-for-money, talent-rich places such as India is maximised. At the same time, the effort required at the client site is minimised.

However, before this model becomes viable for all international trade, some significant challenges must be faced. Working among teams spread across various

Narayana Murthy: chairman of Infosys Technologies Limited

THE NEW GENERATION
DISCOVER LIVERPOOL
babycream
ANTONY GILFOYLE
O2
PAUL SHARMA
ALLIANCE & LEICESTER
KERRY EASTER
UNILEVER
"Liverpool has a vibrant city culture both day and night, from its museums and galleries to its busy café bar society. All around the area are excellent restaurants and wine bars.
I'm lucky enough to enjoy the best of both worlds as I'm never far away from beautiful countryside. I often take the children to watch the sailing close by at Thurstaston where there are some great sandy beaches for them to play on.
Locally I have found superb childcare facilities, which allows me to successfully balance a career in a large global company with a happy home life."
The Liverpool City Region has a sustained jobs growth rate of double the national average.*
* source: ABI
0151 237 3933
www.investmerseyside.com
the mersey PARTNERSHIP
englandsnorthwest BE WITH THE BEST
Liverpool 08
EUROPEAN CAPITAL OF CULTURE

locations requires a process-driven approach and standardisation in key areas. Cross-cultural issues have to be handled well. Robust structures are needed to ensure that risks are tracked. Speed and responsiveness to business needs are essential, to allow continuous innovation. And effective knowledge management is at the core of an efficient collaboration.

For companies, the order of the day will be to look for talent wherever it is available and create international relay teams. These virtual teams will work in unison, for faster development and delivery. Harnessing such intellectual power will accelerate growth.

> These firms will successfully blend the creativity of an Italian with the professionalism of an American and the focus of an Indian

The companies that can overcome these challenges will delight their customers with the speed of their response and the value of their product or service. These firms will successfully blend the creativity of an Italian with the professionalism of an American and the focus of an Indian—just to name a few nationalities. They can emerge from anywhere in the world, and they will be the true global contenders of 2005. □

China learns the rules

Tom Mitchell

Two can play at the trade game

Lawyers from Paul, Hastings, Janofsky & Walker, a Los Angeles-based firm, were in for a surprise when China's Ministry of Commerce asked them to defend the Chinese clothes-hanger industry from a punitive tariff petition filed by American competitors. "I had no idea there was a US hanger industry," recalls one of the firm's partners, Hamilton Loeb. "I guess I had no idea where clothes hangers came from."

There are, as some of the law firm's most expensive lawyers were soon to discover, no fewer than six major manufacturers of clothes hangers in the United States. The demand by some of them that the American government, using powers derived from Section 421 of the 1974 US Trade Act, impose punitive tariffs on Chinese-made "steel-wire garment hangers" was one of the opening salvoes in an entirely new series of Sino-American trade skirmishes stemming from China's entry into the World Trade Organisation (WTO).

Since the WTO formally welcomed its most populous member in 2001, some of the most dramatic consequences have been played out not in China but in the offices of the American International Trade Commission (ITC) in Washington. There, American manufacturers of everything from clothes hangers to cast-iron pipe fittings have described in exacting detail the onslaught they now face from Chinese competitors, and petitioned the ITC—working with the Department of Commerce—for relief.

The best form of defence

Getting on the case

That China would become a prime target of such actions was predictable. No other nation boasts so potent a combination of third-world wage rates and first-world manufacturing infrastructure and engineering talent. Even Mexico's *maquiladoras* along the Rio Grande are losing American export business to factories an ocean away in the Pearl and Yangzi river deltas.

More surprising has been the sophistication of China's response, as epitomised by the Ministry of Commerce's engagement of Paul Hastings on behalf of its clothes-hanger industry. Similarly, Shenzhen-based Huawei Technologies retained Mayer, Brown, Rowe & Maw—whose partners include a former United States trade representative, Mickey Kantor—as an adviser in its intellectual-property dispute with Cisco. Furniture-manufacturing associations in Hong Kong and Guangdong province banded together to hire Hunton & Williams, another American law firm, to represent them in yet another anti-dumping case.

From experiences such as these China's government and industries have learnt—to turn an old American football truism on its head—that the best defence is a good offence, and initiated an increasing number of their own anti-dumping cases. In 2004 China pursued cases targeting everything from newsprint to chloroprene rubber.

Even Chinese Davids are learning to use the law against foreign Goliaths. Memorably, a Chinese artist, Guan Dongsheng, won a 2003 Beijing court judgment prohibiting Dow Jones from continuing to use his calligraphy in its China logo. In 2004 a Chinese cartoonist filed a lawsuit alleging that Nike's "Stickman", used in a global advertising campaign, was copied from his own "Little Match Man". Nike rejected the charge. But a surge in trademark and patent registrations in China suggests that brand owners are gaining confidence in the ability of the Chinese legal system to protect their rights.

In 2005 America will still have the advantage in the anti-dumping and intellectual-property wars. But as in so much else, the Chinese will be catching up fast. □

Tom Mitchell: deputy business editor, *South China Morning Post*

The age of phonography

Tom Standage

Will digital cameras be overtaken by camera-phones?

When the Kodak Brownie was launched in 1900 its slogan was "you press the button and we do the rest". Photographers no longer had to be amateur scientists adept at mixing chemicals in darkened rooms, and photography quickly became a mass-market phenomenon. A little over a century later the same thing has finally happened to digital photography. Digital cameras in the 1990s were strictly for geeks: to use one, you needed to master not just that camera itself, but also the associated plethora of PC software. Not any more.

2005

Apple will release a new operating system called Tiger, capable of searching through 100,000 files in less than a second.

It is now possible to order prints from digital images at a minilab, at a pharmacy or over the internet. Even the cheapest digital cameras produce images sharp enough for a four-by-six-inch print. Some cameras plug into printers directly, so that there is no need to mess around with a PC. And digital cameras have benefited from a "digital buzz", as Chris Chute, an analyst at IDC, a market-research company, puts it. When people see their friends and relatives going digital, he says, they are more inclined to do so themselves. In 2004 digital cameras outsold conventional film-based ones for the first time; in 2005, sales of some 83m digital cameras will be more than double those of traditional film ones.

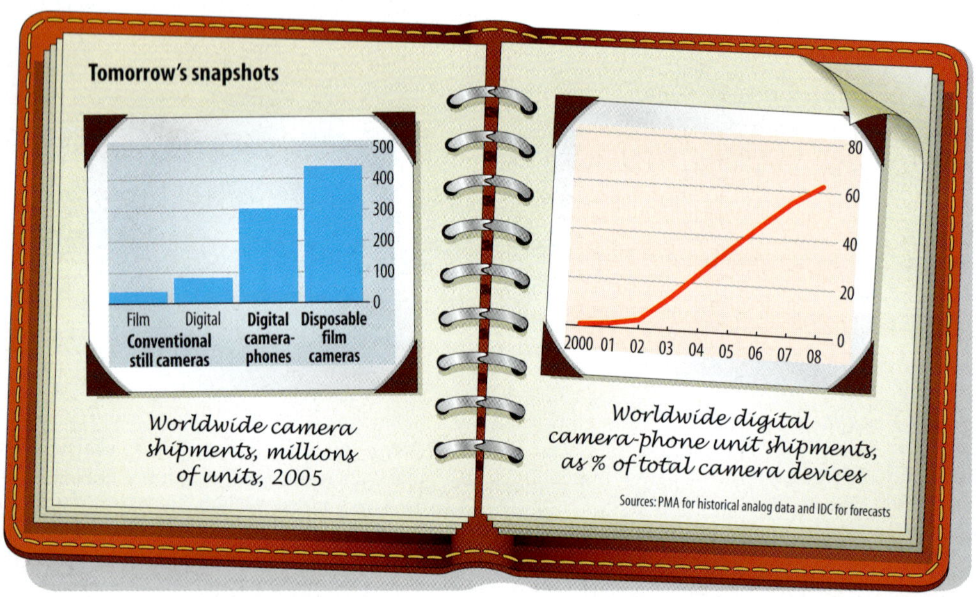

Yet this milestone in the history of photography could be overshadowed by an even more powerful trend: the rise of camera-equipped mobile phones. Of the 600m mobile phones sold in 2004, nearly a third had a built-in camera. That means that sales of camera-phones, at around 190m units, easily exceeded sales of film-based and digital cameras put together. In 2005 sales of camera-phones will soar above 300m units.

At the moment most camera-phones are hopelessly inferior to dedicated digital cameras. They produce images of much lower quality, typically containing fewer than 1m picture elements (one megapixel), compared with around four megapixels for a basic digital camera. And since the processor chip in a camera-phone has other things to worry about besides photography, there is often a long delay after pressing the shutter button before the image is taken. As a result, most people regard their phones as cameras of last resort. If no other camera is available, they will happily snap away with their phones: a grainy picture is better than no picture.

This means that camera-phones are not competing so much with digital cameras as with the existing "camera of last resort", namely single-use or disposable cameras. IDC predicts that sales of such cameras will peak in 2004 at 460m units and then decline steadily as camera-phones proliferate. By 2006 sales of digital devices (cameras and camera-phones) will exceed sales of film-based devices (cameras and disposable cameras).

> Eventually, camera-phones will probably offer good enough picture quality for most people

Might camera-phones improve in quality and start to compete with dedicated digital cameras? For the time being, this seems unlikely. As well as producing lower-quality images, camera-phones have other drawbacks. Phone-makers must please two sets of customers with competing interests: mobile-network operators and their subscribers. Most people, for example, would love to be able to plug their phones into their computers to transfer images. But network operators would rather they sent pictures wirelessly, since they can charge for that. So it is in their interests to make downloading from camera-phones difficult.

Camera-makers, for their part, will respond by moving upmarket: more megapixels, better zooms. But eventually, camera-phones will probably offer good enough picture quality for most people. At that point, will they still want a dedicated camera?

This question is part of a larger debate about whether mobile phones are poised to become the digital equivalents of Swiss Army knives, replacing multiple devices such as cameras, music players and hand-held organisers. Already, sales of hand-held computers, or PDAs, are declining as high-end "smartphones" become more powerful. Are cameras next?

Perhaps, but the fight between PDAS and smartphones did not produce a clear winner: PDA-makers added telephony features, while personal-organiser features were added to smartphones. The same seems likely to happen with cameras. Consumers will be able to choose between a camera with simple telephony features, a phone with a basic camera, or a hybrid of the two. Or they can stick with separate, dedicated devices. Prepare for a proliferation of new types of camera. □

Tom Standage: technology editor, *The Economist*

Brand new world

Rose Marie Bravo, chief executive of Burberry, foresees exciting times for consumers—and challenging ones for brands

One thing is certain: nurturing and maintaining the power of a brand will become more complex. There will be more competition and no shortage of innovation. The truism that applying one company's formula to another brand is never a guarantee of success, will take on a new resonance. In the coming years we will see breakthrough models being created from new entrants and some unexpected sources.

The competition for consumers' attention and a share of their spending will become ever fiercer as products proliferate exponentially and channels of distribution broaden. Brands nowadays think they can become all things to all people. "Sticking to your knitting" is not the order of the day as we see shoemakers moving into apparel, luggage-makers venturing into jewellery, menswear companies going into womenswear, athletic-wear companies moving into accessories, couturiers designing for mass outlets and pop stars becoming designers.

This massive blurring of boundaries, and the amount of choice available to consumers, will make it even more difficult for a company's voice to be heard. Brands will have to take more risks in product innovation and marketing methods to capture the customer's attention. The art of brand management will change radically.

More risks will be taken in selecting managers. There will be significant changes in the management of brands. The training of managers or the talent pool they come from will be different. Companies will and should think beyond the usual suspects when they look to changing management. We will see more appointments like that of Paul Pressler at Gap and Robert Polet at Gucci. A very steady hand must be in place to steer the brand ship. The whole concept of focus will take on a new meaning.

> Brands will have to take more risks in product innovation and marketing methods to capture the customer's attention. The art of brand management will change radically

Consumers have undergone a revolution in their philosophy of dressing. The concept of "masstige" (mixing mass labels with prestige) has validated shopping in high-street stores, online and in flea markets in addition to couture boutiques and speciality stores. Trends will continue to be influenced by what famous people are wearing, yet in new ways as celebrities encourage the art of individual style—where everything is personalised and customised. It is cool to mix vintage with luxury, with high-street purchases—it is all in the mix. Wearing a uniform or dressing from head to toe in one designer will become less prevalent as style becomes even more defined by the ability to create your own look.

In the coming year, I see more brands linking with other brands and flirting with new concepts. Licensing a brand has undergone its own evolution in the past three decades: from a name licensing every conceivable product, to licensing being banned from many luxury cultures. There will be a return to licensing, but in a new way—an unexpected coupling of names like Stella McCartney with Adidas, Bulgari with Marriott, Burberry with Dr Scholl's.

All of this "crossdressing" and mixing of brands will change the shopping experience. In the 1990s we prided ourselves on the exact replication and perfect execution of a concept across retail, wholesale, direct mail and other channels. Today and in the future, we are intrigued by various iterations of a concept. Brands will force change in store design and even product offering by location as we look to pre-empt customers' ennui from seeing the same thing in London, New York and Tokyo. Prada was in the forefront of this with its brave new SoHo store in New York—a total departure replete with reproduced "vintage" items.

New ways to shop

Customers will want to have different, fresh experiences when they shop. Companies must therefore work on shorter cycles: putting together more "capsule collections" of clothing and accessories and delivering them more often to create the suggestion to customers that if they don't buy it now, it may not be there later. Mixing different artistic pursuits with branding will become more common, as exemplified by the success of Louis Vuitton's collaboration with Takashi Murakami, a Japanese artist. Architecture, photography, art, sculpture and design in general will all have a growing influence on product and store design and on the customer's ultimate experience.

This "brand new world" will be a challenge for companies. When a management team can no longer rely on the application of a familiar formula but must invent a new formula every season, it becomes a much more complex task.

The challenge becomes how to embrace the spirit of risk-taking and experimentation with the financial responsibilities of a commercial enterprise. It becomes a balancing act: weighing the need to offer the customer a sense of discovery, a one-of-a-kind experience and true product innovation against this approach's inherent demands on human and capital resources, lower economies of scale and the resulting implications on profit. At the same time, this constant quest for the unique and the new must be pursued while keeping a sharp eye on the heritage, history, integrity and credibility of a brand in an ever-changing and often unexpected competitive landscape.

For brands, complacency will be fatal. "Never rest on your laurels" will take on a new urgency as we realise more than ever that we don't know what is coming round the corner. □

2005

Tobacco advertisements are due to be banned across the EU in July, court challenges permitting.

Cars and the catwalk

Iain Carson

Design is becoming critical to a car's success

Consider two new car models in North America. One is the Pontiac GTO from General Motors (GM), with a powerful engine and terrific acceleration. It's not selling well. The other is the Chrysler 300, a luxury saloon, which is shaping up to be the biggest success in the manufacturer's history. Why is one flagging and the other booming? The Pontiac GTO has a dull jelly-bean design, whereas the Chrysler 300 has an aggressive front end and a hunkered-down shape that gives it great presence. After a couple of decades when cars all looked increasingly similar, design is once more becoming a key differentiator in a crowded market.

Bold is back. This will be the year of the designer as more and more manufacturers seek to stand out from the crowd. No longer are car designers company hacks who stick with one firm for years. Today the stars move around from brand to brand and strut the stage at car launches and auto shows, like fashion designers. The Armanis and Lagerfelds of the auto world include Chris Bangle of BMW, Peter Horbury of Ford (the man who turned Volvos from fridges on wheels to sculpted cool-mobiles) and Ralph Gilles, the 34-year-old behind the Chrysler 300.

With around 25% over-capacity worldwide, price-cutting by giving cash-back deals has become as commonplace in Europe as it has been for some years in America. America has twice the number of car brands on the market that it had 30 years ago, as import brands have multiplied. In a market like this, companies are desperate for an edge that allows them to command a premium price.

Two more cars that are being talked about in design circles are the big BMW 7-series models and the Rolls-Royce. Both are striking and bold. After years of classical, straight-lined refinement, BMW has gone all curvy, with its latest 7 series and the new 6-series coupé. Bold designs walk a tightrope. The German motoring press lambasted BMW for the 7 when it first came out a couple of years ago, although it has warmed to the 6 series.

Bold is back. This will be the year of the designer as more and more manufacturers seek to stand out from the crowd

Another extremely bold design is the first new Rolls-Royce to be brought out since the company passed into the ownership of BMW in 1998. It looks like a real, proud Rolls-Royce rather than the staid, stale versions of the past 20 years. It is a huge car, yet the clever way the various proportions have been managed makes it look like a big gleaming sculpture.

The use of design is even more difficult in the volume market. Renault stands out in Europe as the manufacturer that has played the design card most vigorously. Occasionally it does not work. Its Avantime upmarket coupé never even made it into five figures before its production was stopped. In the mid-1990s Ford, in the big saloon class, came out with a Scorpio model, which looked as though the front and back had been designed by different people on each side of the Atlantic. It bombed and Ford dropped out of that segment.

But Renault is not at all deterred by failures such as the Avantime. Its mid-1990s little Twingo, with its cross-eyed headlamps, was a runaway success. So was its bold and innovative Scenic version of its Mégane saloon: the Scenic was not just good-looking, it was a whole new functional design, bringing the height and space of people-carriers down to the mid-range. Renault's boss, Louis Schweitzer, and its chief designer, Patrick Le Quément, continue to emphasise design more than any other volume manufacturer. Renault's sister company Nissan is also using the bold design of its 350z sports car as a way to boost the image of the whole Nissan brand, by associating it with something stylish.

Other manufacturers will be bringing out 2005 models designed to give a family look to their whole range. Ford will take this further with the new version of its bestselling Focus. The first version of that model defined a whole new sort of "edge" styling that can now be seen across Ford's entire range. Another example is Fiat, which ran into trouble with its new mid-sized Stilo model in 2003, because it looked like an imitation of a German car. Now the aim is to have every model with a "Made in Italy" look, trying to grab some of the glitz of Ferrari, Alfa Romeo and Maserati.

The prize for investing boldly in design is that ▸

Iain Carson: industry editor, *The Economist*

customers are prepared to pay premium prices for cars that stand out from the crowd. It is already working for Cadillac in America, where GM's vice-chairman and product-development boss, Bob Lutz, proudly points to waiting lists and above-list-price bids for a couple of the latest Cadillacs, such as the striking XLR. Attractive new designs have even enabled GM to relaunch sales of models in Europe, as design brings Cadillac in from the cold.

The pitfall is that dramatic looks can put off loyal customers and deter many potential converts who just do not like radical design. And complacency or false moves can hurt. VW's new Golf is technically very advanced, but got off to a slow start partly because it was rather dull to look at and because the company had skimped on the design of the interior. This is odd, since markedly smarter interior design is one reason VW models have been able to command premium prices compared with Fords or Opels in Europe.

All this shows how the car industry is changing. Computerised design and engineering allow companies to try out new looks and designs very quickly. The intensity of competition also means that new models have to appear more frequently and be refreshed more rapidly, without consuming vast amounts of investment. Design is a way to satisfy those needs. It does not always make a car company a winner, but you need top-class design now just to stay in the game. □

A welcome new formula

Matthew Glendinning

Vrrroom for innovation in motor sport

Formula One motor racing has a problem. Many fans are weary of watching the seven-time Grand Prix champion, Michael Schumacher, leading the pack in laps of ever-decreasing competitive interest. Others are frustrated that there is no Grand Prix-style motorsport on television in the European winter.

In 2005, however, dedicated petrolheads will have something other than the F1 circus to follow, with the launch in September of the A1 Grand Prix series. The brainchild of Sheikh Maktoum Hasher Maktoum al-Maktoum, the 27-year-old nephew of the Crown Prince of Dubai and himself a motorsports enthusiast, the project aims to create a major global racing series from scratch. Bankrolled by the entrepreneurial sheikh and two South African businessmen, A1 will distance itself from F1 by pitting identical single-seater cars against each other. The emphasis will be on driver skills rather than F1-style hi-tech gadgetry.

A1 will also appeal to national rivalries by insisting that the team franchises, drivers and sponsors are co-ordinated along national lines, with only one team per country allowed to compete. Teams from Britain, China and South Africa are among the definite starters, with between 24 and 30 likely to be on the grid for the first race in Dubai. But perhaps the biggest revolution is in the choice of venues. The championship will consist of between 10 and 14 races and take place largely in the southern hemisphere. The A1 name, says Sheikh Maktoum, is derived from Asia, Arabia, Africa and Australia, regions where many countries cannot afford F1, but which provide summer racing conditions at a time of year when F1 is in hibernation.

If this sounds not only ambitious, but expensive, it is. The 30 British-built Lola cars and V8 engines contracted by A1 represent one of the richest deals in motorsports history. But the project has been sanctioned by the powerful Fédération Internationale d'Automobile (FIA) and, perhaps surprisingly, it has found a supporter in F1's ringmaster, Bernie Ecclestone, although his endorsement does not extend to lending F1 drivers to the series. "Bernie sees what A1 can do for Formula One," says Sheikh Maktoum. "The viability of building a track in Asia has doubled, the viability of a Chinese or Indian driving for his country has doubled."

The difference is in the driver

Indeed, the A1 project reflects a broader opening of Asia and, in particular, the Middle East to the joys of world sport. Bahrain hosted its first F1 Grand Prix in 2004, and the region has recently staged international tennis, golf, athletics, cricket, rugby union and soccer events, as well as the world's richest horse race, the Dubai World Cup.

But this is the first time that an Arab-inspired event promises to reach well beyond its regional borders. "This is a gift from the Muslim and Arab world to the whole world," says Sheikh Maktoum, with an eye on the bigger picture. "There's been enough negativity. This is something positive." □

Matthew Glendinning: sports and business writer

2005

Xtreme Alternative Defense Systems expects to deliver a stun-gun designed for the United States Marine Corps which incapacitates crowds by projecting an ionised gas.

Democracy's new frontier

Charles Handy

Time for the corporate constitution

It is a paradox that in our democratic societies it is only the corporations that are resolutely undemocratic. In 2005 this will become more blatant as the front-line workers find their voice—a voice that organisations will ignore at their peril.

Charles Handy: writer on management theory

The world of work is now increasingly dominated by the service sector, where the lowest-paid workers are not hidden away in the factory or warehouse but are often the first representatives of the organisation whom the customer meets. This is true whether the worker is on the check-in desk of an airline, at the end of a telephone in a call centre, is a waiter in a restaurant, a nurse on the ward or a policeman on the beat. It is often those directly in front of the customers who are left to embody the values of the organisation; if they know what those values are, that is, and if they care.

These front-line individuals have thus become the unintended guardians of the brand, the true core workers, surely the last to be outsourced if an organisation is sensible. This gives them, however, an increasing power as well as a new responsibility, one that is often out of proportion to their pay. Organisations must expect this growing segment of their population to want more recognition of the importance of their role, better preparation for their responsibilities, more control of ▶

Ruling the roost

Tim Hindle

The business books of 2005

The bestselling business book of 2005 has almost certainly been published already. And it may well be the same as in 2004—"Good to Great" by Michael Collins, a study of 11 companies and how their managers transformed them from ordinary to extraordinary. The book has been on the *New York Times* list of bestselling non-fiction almost continually since its publication in autumn 2001, and it has overtaken the 1982 classic, "In Search of Excellence" by Tom Peters and Bob Waterman, as the bestselling business book of all time.

Perhaps the first place to look for a challenger is to Mr Collins himself. He is working on a new book which examines companies that had an IPO (initial public offering of stock) in the 1990s but somehow survived the business cyclones at the turn of the century. "The book", he says, "will appeal to anyone who has an inner unease because they don't know how their story ends." Who dares say that does not apply to them?

There is, however, at least one serious challenger to Mr Collins's dominance of the business-book market. This comes in the short but formidable form of Jack Welch. The chairman and CEO of General Electric had a global hit in 2001 with "Straight From the Gut", which he looks set to repeat with the modestly titled "Winning: The Ultimate Business How-To Book", due in May 2005.

Addressing fashionable themes helps sell books, and the subject of leadership has long been a business favourite. These books have tended to focus on what it takes to be a good leader; in 2005 the top sellers are going to be looking at what it takes to be a bad one—perhaps on the grounds that it is easier to

learn how to avoid bad habits than to learn how to adopt good ones. "The Allure of Toxic Leaders" by Jean Lipman-Blumen, a California academic, and "Bad Leadership" by Barbara Kellerman, a lecturer at Harvard, both examine flawed leaders such as Ken Lay (of Enron), Al "Chainsaw" Dunlap of Sunbeam and Leona "Only little people pay taxes" Helmsley, and ask how their thousands of followers gave them a remit to lead for so long. In 2005 "Why Most Things Fail" by Paul Omerod, a British economist, will be of interest (retrospectively, anyway) to the 83% of all CEOs whose careers, and companies, go belly-up.

One type of leadership book focuses on heroes from times past and tries to draw business lessons from his (rarely her) inspiration. Recent favourites have been Ernest Shackleton, the Antarctic explorer, and Alexander the Great. Nicholas Rankin takes a fresh approach to another perennial source of inspiration, Winston Churchill, in his study of the men who influenced the former prime minister's wartime strategies in "Churchill's Wizards".

2005 is also the bicentenary of the Battle of Trafalgar and will surely see a business book or two on the effective habits of Horatio Nelson, the battle's one-armed victor. There may be rivals in French about Napoleon, whose greatest victory (at Austerlitz) took place later that year. But publishers beware. Since Nelson died on board ship during battle, and Napoleon's final fate was scarcely more pleasant, today's leaders may not care to be reminded of how few of their endings are destined to be happy ones.

Business books sell best at airports and business-school bookshops. But a new market is arising in China, where the embrace of capitalism has brought a hunger for learning about its micro-practices. *The World in 2005* would like to suggest (for a small share of the royalties, of course) that publishers combine China's interest with another recurring feature of popular business books—the use of extended animal metaphors. For the Chinese, 2005 is the year of the rooster. So a business book entitled "Little Red Rooster" would surely be a hit. Chinese astrologers could be quoted: "The rooster enjoys being a part of the team," says one of them. Roosters work "diligently for change". But unfortunately they also "overcommit themselves" and are "unable to finish what they've started". Or, as the inimitable Mississippi bluesman Willie Dixon once put it (and Sir Michael Jagger later crooned), little red roosters are "too lazy to crow for day". □

Tim Hindle: management editor, *The Economist*

The company car park after the revolution

their personal time and more discretion over their work, unfettered by instructions on the computer screen.

Expect, therefore, increased demands for a better work-life balance and for more personal discretion in 2005. If these demands are not met there will be threats of strikes, more staff turnover and growing absenteeism—all indicators of a lack of recognition. It will be a form of negative democracy by which people vote with their feet rather than with their ballot papers. It will reflect a new malaise: the democratic deficit in today's corporations.

Organisations will not be introducing elections any day soon, nor will they be holding referendums on their strategies or allowing workers to vote their own pay packets. The challenge will be to find other ways to make democracy a positive force. Unless this challenge is faced the democratic urge will be expressed in demands for more rights with no recognition of any counterbalancing responsibilities. Just in time, organisations are beginning to understand that they are no longer humanised machines but living communities that have to be governed and led like any other community.

As so often, the words we use act as the clues to a social change. We speak today of an organisation having different constituencies, of spheres of influence, of forging alliances and partnerships, of governance and social responsibility, of individual rights, stakeholders and manifestos and mission statements, of leaders rather than managers. In this new world people want to be regarded as belonging to something, not just used by it, as members not employees, citizens not human resources. They want a voice in what concerns them, the chance and the right to make a difference. The point to note is that these are all words and concepts drawn from political theory rather than from the old language of machines and engineering.

> Expect increased demands for a better work-life balance and for more personal discretion in 2005. If these are not met there will be threats of strikes, more staff turnover and absenteeism

Federalism is one political concept that will become more useful, even if organisations avoid using the actual F-word. Federalism is a tried and trusted way of combining local responsibility with a necessary degree of central control, and organisations might usefully go back to the handbooks of political theory to find out how it works. Federalism, if properly designed, is a way to introduce a practical form of direct democracy, where more people have more influence over the decisions that directly concern them and their group.

A feature of all federal institutions and states is a written constitution, setting down the powers, rights and responsibilities of the different parties, with as much power and discretion as possible given to the local bodies. Hitherto, written constitutions have existed only in employee-owned organisations, such as the John Lewis Partnership in Britain, and in charitable organisations, where they are required by law. In 2005 we should see the first voluntary introduction of a formal constitution by a corporation. In time governments may feel it necessary to legislate for all major corporations to have such a constitution. But that is one thing that will not happen in 2005. □

Redtape.net

Kenneth Cukier

Regulators will grapple with rules for the internet

How to regulate online activities? That promises to become a contentious issue in 2005. Here are a few flashpoints.

Internet telephony. In Europe and America telecom regulators have to determine whether phone calls made over broadband internet connections should fall under traditional phone rules. The incumbent operators want a level regulatory playing field, while the nascent internet companies fret they'll be burdened with century-old rules designed for monopoly carriers. In America the Federal Communications Commission is due to issue its internet telephony policy in 2005. Meanwhile, poor countries will continue to ban internet calls to preserve the revenues of state-owned operators (though it is their citizens who bear the cost).

Internet addresses. Many governments believe that America has too much control over how the internet develops, due to its authority over the Internet Corporation for Assigned Names and Numbers, the quasi-private organisation that controls the net's addressing system (the suffixes such as ".com"). One idea is to turn the group into an international treaty organisation. This

2005

New rules ban junk faxes in America—a company or individual must have a signed permission slip before sending an ad by fax. But some analysts fear that a loophole in the legislation may mean that Americans end up getting more junk faxes than they did before.

Kenneth Cukier: technology correspondent, *The Economist*

is opposed by America and many European countries, which argue it would generate red tape and politicise the technology. A fracas is likely at the UN's World Summit on the Information Society in Tunisia in November.

Spyware. The menace of so-called "spyware"—software that stealthily installs itself on computers and monitors online activity, often to splash advertisements in browser windows—will worsen, despite attempts to prohibit it. In America, legislation to be considered in 2005 is worded so that the most prevalent form of spyware, which triggers ads, is legally permissible, albeit annoying. In Brussels the European Commission needs to interpret whether spyware contravenes its 2002 privacy directive.

Digital intellectual property. The internet has dramatically increased copyright piracy by making it easier to copy and share digital works, such as music. Meanwhile, the web has led to a radical expansion in the scope of patents, as people obtain them on software that, controversially, merely extends online ordinary methods of business. The European Commission will decide in 2005 on an EU-wide software patent policy, in the face of intense opposition from open-source software advocates. In America the strict Digital Millennium Copyright Act of 1998, which prevents users from modifying devices in basic ways, is expected to be challenged in the courts, to preserve the right to tinker with technology. As for the recording industry, expect it to start suing people in more countries who download pirated music from the internet.

The one area where everyone would welcome effective regulation—to fight spam—will remain unsolved. The most surprising issue will be a call in some countries to regulate search engines such as Google, Yahoo! and MSN. As the gateway to online information, their practices represent the power of the private sector to control what people see and do online. To some this resembles a public utility. Like so much on the internet, it ends up becoming a victim of its success: loved so much it risks choking in its regulators' embrace. □

That's all rights, mama

European copyright law is due for a revision

Whether or not a grotesquely bloated and drug-addled Elvis Presley actually died on August 16th 1977 in the upstairs bathroom of his Memphis pile remains the subject of impassioned debate. Either way, his records continue to sell faster than those of most living rockers. The King still pulls in upwards of $40m a year from beyond the grave—or beyond the public gaze, anyway.

In 2004 Elvis's debut single, "That's All Right", was re-released to mark the 50th anniversary of its recording. Music boffins now speak of "That's All Right" as the first proper rock'n'roll record—the pop-culture equivalent of Einstein's special theory of relativity. When it first came out in 1954, it was a modest success, but no chart-topper. Reissued 50 years later, it went to number one.

Terrific news for Elvis's heirs, you might think, as well as a hopeful precedent for ageing troubadours everywhere. Yes and no. Under existing European Union law, copyright in a sound recording lasts for 50 years from the end of the year in which it was released. This means that from December 31st 2004 anyone can sell "That's All Right" in the EU without paying royalties to the owner of the copyright in the original recording. (Royalties must, however, still be paid to the owner of the composition—the person who wrote the song. In this case, the estate of Arthur "Big Boy" Crudup.) But even so, would-be re-releasers should consult a lawyer. Words like "original" can take on unexpected meanings in court.

Things are different in America, where sound recordings are protected for 95 years, or, if they were made after 1976, for the duration of the artist's life plus 70 years. Music-industry types are lobbying for a revision of EU copyright law to bring it in line with America's. The European Commission will issue its recommendations in early 2005. Just in time, perhaps, to extend the copyright term on the tidal wave of classic rock'n'roll that came crashing down in the years following Elvis's humble debut. □

Totally digital

Carly Fiorina, chief executive of Hewlett-Packard, sees no end to the digital revolution, and predicts huge consequences for business and beyond

A funny thing happened on the way to 2005: the digital revolution actually became real. Walk around any city or town and what do you see? You see young people text messaging; commuters jamming to their iPods; friends snapping photos on their camera phones. Look a bit further and you see doctors' decisions aided by patient information called up on hand-held devices; teachers using wireless technology as tools; parents printing photos on cordless printers before leaving their children's football games. Look further still and you see executives going digital and cutting billions of dollars out of supply chains. And if you go to Africa or India, you may even see wireless devices providing opportunity in communities that don't even have electricity.

It's a revolution in any sense of the word. But I have another name for it: a warm-up act. We are entering an era where everything is going digital. It's going to be the main event of our lives for decades to come.

Just think about the changes taking place with photography today. Photography used to be a physical, chemical, analogue process. You took a picture and something happened in your camera; you took your film to a photo shop and something physical and chemical happened; you picked up your film, sorted your pictures and when you got around to it, you maybe put some in a photo album or mailed them. Today photography is increasingly not only digital but also mobile, virtual and personal: mobile because you can do your digital photoworks anywhere at any time; virtual in that others can enjoy it without being there with you; and it's personal in that you can edit the digital image and use it in any way you want.

> The digital shift will never fully live up to its potential if cameras still come with 250-page user guides and home theatre takes eight remotes and five miles of cable

Every process, in every industry—from banking to academia and from medicine to international security—is beginning to follow that same pattern. It's empowering, but also a bit scary, because it's a leap into the unknown. Nobody knows for sure how to equip themselves. Anybody who says they do is lying.

We've already seen glimpses of the kinds of changes this transformation will bring. For starters, it's completely changing the nature of authority. There used to be a time when access to information was the root of all power. The digital age is bringing about the democratisation of information, the removal of traditional barriers of time, distance and wealth, and the onset of total transparency. There is nothing secret about my company any more—our whole company is out there on the web for the world to see, and that's a good thing.

It's changing business models. Take television, where the traditional business model depends on earning advertising dollars by delivering a certain number of viewers at a certain time, usually of a certain age. This is giving way to a world where consumers can fast-forward through commercials, skip them altogether and watch programmes when they want, how they want and on whatever device they want. How do media companies stay profitable?

And it will change democracy. Today millions of consumers vote for "American Idol" finalists using their mobile phones. How long before they expect to cast ballots the same way? What does it do to our concept of community if the places where people traditionally come together—films, music, even grocery stores—can best be experienced individually?

Wanting it all

For those of us who are expected to deliver tangible results in this changing world—to meet quarterly expectations, to create new revenue streams, to find new ways to reach voters and consumers, to invent the markets of the future—where do we start? In particular, what does all of this mean for 2005? There are three things we can say for sure, particularly for technology companies.

First, in 2005 the demand for simplicity will grow. The digital shift will never fully live up to its potential if cameras still come with 250-page user guides and home theatre takes eight remotes and five miles of cable. For digital to become fully accepted by consumers and businesses, it must be intuitive and easier to use. Companies able to meet that demand will set themselves apart.

Second, value increasingly will be created horizontally, not vertically. Most organisations have grown up in a vertical world. We have thought about creating value through chains of command. But whether you're a CEO trying to be more efficient, a small business trying to mobilise your workforce, a government trying to deliver the best services or a consumer who wants a whole bunch of digital devices in your home to work better together, it's about horizontal connections.

Third, consumers and businesses will be less willing to compromise. As technology moves from the fringe to the core of people's lives and businesses, the need for technology to deliver more becomes important. The days of compromise are gone. Customers and consumers want it all: affordability, reliability, security, simplicity, manageability, adaptability, innovation, connection.

Getting there is going to require the right blend of realism and optimism. We need to be realistic that none of this is going to be easy. But we also need to be optimistic, because if we get this right, digital technology will make more things more possible for more people in more places than at any time in history. That alone is worth the journey. □

This is the digital networked economy. Where business is done.
SECURITY

WE DON'T JUST REACH FOR THE STARS.
WE GET THERE.

Finance

2005

Belgium will stop minting coins of one and two euro cents, joining the Netherlands and Finland in shunning small change.

Stirred but not shaken

Hamish McRae

World markets should serve up a fairly benign cocktail

Markets both react to economic events and help shape them. For the past three years they have been mostly reacting: trying to figure out how to come to terms with the fallout from the late-1990s bubble. The gradual rebuilding of confidence has a way to go. But in 2005 the markets will also have a crucial role in shaping events, for this will be the year when the big adjustments that usually happen early in the growth cycle finally start to take place.

> Pressures for a further devaluation of the dollar will grow during 2005. Some adjustment to the dollar is a precondition for greater stability in other markets

Will these happen in a benign way, reinforcing confidence, or in a rougher, more jagged way, damaging it? The balance of probability is that the markets will keep their nerve and help foster benign adjustment. But the danger is clear.

The world is awash with money, thanks to the largesse of the central banks, and that money is searching for safe homes in what will inevitably be a cooler economic climate. Economic growth may ease slowly, as more progress is made towards normal interest rates in America, and a start is made at more normal credit control in China. Those two great engines of global growth would then simply pull back a bit, allowing other economies (the euro zone in particular) to take up some of the running. Markets could then move forward. Or the world economy could slow rather more abruptly, in which case the markets will struggle.

Start with the foreign exchanges, for the key adjustment is there. Rationally, the dollar ought to experience a modest decline (though not a crash). But the movement should be mainly against the yen and the yuan, rather than, as up to now, against the euro and sterling. Timing of forex shifts are always impossible to call and in this instance these will be determined as much by Japanese and Chinese policy as by market mood. The Chinese, in particular, will not be pushed into saying when they might relax their currency's peg to the dollar. But pressures for a further devaluation of the dollar will grow during 2005.

Some adjustment to the dollar is a precondition for greater stability in other markets. Equities in particular could start to move forward again. For them, the misery of the worst bear market in equities for a generation ▶

Hamish McRae: associate editor, *The Independent*

is now just a disagreeable memory—but it is a strong enough one to colour share valuations for a long time. As a result, despite good growth and profits, equities around the world have struggled to make progress and canny investors have deserted public markets for private equity. With prospective price/earnings ratios more or less back to their long-term trend (a bit above in some markets, a bit below in others), the markets have a right to feel more confident. As for the risks, some at least are priced in already. The rational prospect for the world's main equity markets is for a year of modest advance.

In fixed-interest markets, investors will of course look for signs of inflation. But they will also look for signals as to how public-sector deficits around the world are likely to be trimmed. Most attention has been on America—ironically the country with a more manageable problem than most other large developed economies. America can fix it and eventually it will. By contrast, getting deficits back under control in slow-growing, ageing Europe and even-faster-ageing Japan will be a 20-year grind. The greater the American progress, the greater the pressure on other governments to take their debts seriously.

The question investors have to answer is whether the risks—inflation risk, currency risk and indeed solvency risk—are adequately priced. Equities do appear fairly priced to cover the likely risks, in the sense that they could cope with unexpected bad news. Bond markets, by contrast, would be less able to weather bad news, most notably from rising inflation.

The obvious pressure on inflation comes from the oil market. Supply will remain tight, as OPEC appears unable to increase output significantly, and demand is unlikely to ease quickly enough to take the pressure off. Unless Iraq and other potential suppliers can crank up production and soothe the markets' nerves, the world may have to learn to live with expensive oil.

A combination of higher energy prices, higher interest rates and slowing global growth might look like a toxic cocktail for the world's markets to swallow. It need not be. There is a host of reasons to expect a year of decent progress. The world economy is still growing well. The increasing weight of China (and also India) in the global economy helps both to add demand and to trim inflationary pressures. Global productivity is rising fast. The new EU members give a much-needed edge to Europe's competitiveness. And as long as markets can see that the huge imbalances that have grown up are at last being tackled, then they will judge that the current expansion has a lot of life in it yet. □

No longer the darlings of financial fashion

Kate Galbraith

Hedge funds' reality check

During most gold rushes, early arrivals prosper but latecomers get the dregs. It looks to be no different for the $1 trillion hedge-fund industry. Come 2005, hedge funds will no longer be the darlings of financial fashion.

Slumping returns are already causing investors to shake off their get-rich-quick delusions. They will still pile into hedge funds, but more to diversify their portfolios than to get automatic high returns. Then there are the investment banks, which not only lend generously to hedge funds but have taken to betting with abandon themselves. They too could face a reality check.

Hedge funds are mostly unregulated private-investment pools that work by placing bets that may do well even in a bear market. Investors have poured money into them, hoping for double-digit returns even as markets stayed flat. And plenty have delivered: especially in the industry's early days, returns of 15% or more were common. So everyone has wanted to share the riches. Once all of the funds' clients were wealthy individuals. Lately pension funds have piled in so as to help plug shortfalls that grew after the stockmarket collapsed.

Dizzying returns look ever harder to get. By August 2004, hedge funds' gains stood at less than 3% for the year. True, stockmarkets did worse. But the numbers were well below managers' rosy projections. Things look little better for 2005.

The trouble is that too many dollars are chasing a limited number of strategies. Take arbitrage: making a fortune this way is easy only when there is a big difference in price between securities that should behave in similar ways. The more money devoted to the same arbitrage play, the smaller the price difference and the lower the returns for each fund.

Faced with lower returns, investors may seek more diversification in managers' fees, now at 1-2% of assets, plus 20% of any gains. Funds of hedge funds, which have absorbed much of the new money, add on another hefty layer of fees. As investors wise up, running a hedge fund will lose some of its lustre in 2005. In recent years mutual-fund managers and bankers have decamped in droves to start hedge funds. More of them will fail and head back to business school or the banks.

Regulators, conversely, will just be joining the game. They are concerned by the hedge funds' rapidly expanding client base and want to know more about them. In the year ahead, more hedge-fund managers can be expected to register with America's Securities and Exchange Commission, ahead of a requirement to do so in 2006. This will come just in time for the industry's natural slowdown. □

Kate Galbraith: finance correspondent, *The Economist*

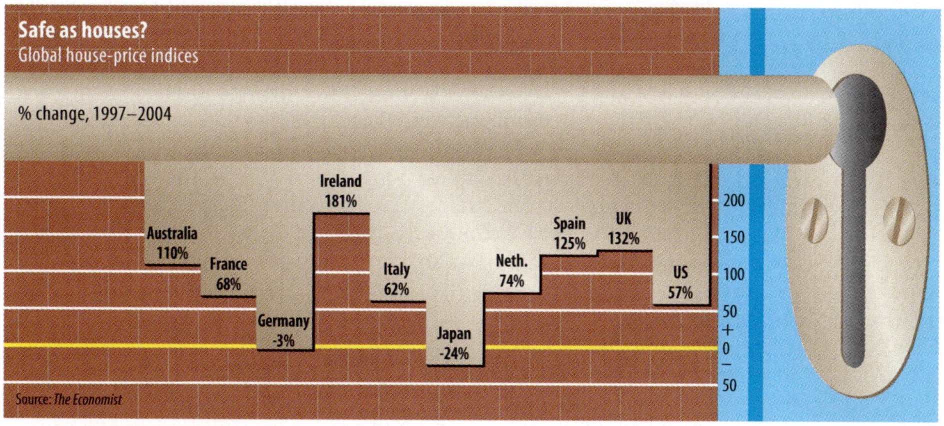

Home truths

Pam Woodall

House prices have lost touch with reality. In 2005 they will come back down to earth

From London to Los Angeles and from Melbourne to Madrid, everybody is obsessed with the value of their home. The recent boom in house prices is one of the main reasons why many economies held up better than expected after the stockmarket bubble burst. Rising prices made home-owners feel wealthier and by taking out bigger mortgages they could spend their capital gains. Unfortunately, in 2005 the housing bubble will start to deflate.

Never before have house prices risen so fast in real (inflation-adjusted) terms in so many countries. Over the past year they have increased at double-digit rates in 11 of the 20 countries covered by *The Economist*'s global house-price indices. Since 1997 house prices have more than doubled in Australia, Britain and Spain, and almost tripled in Ireland. In comparison, the near-60% rise in average American home prices may seem modest, yet in real terms this is by far the biggest gain in recorded history and more than twice as big a rise as in the previous two house-price booms in the 1970s and 1980s. The big exceptions to the boom are Japan and Germany, where house prices have fallen.

> Home prices have begun to fall in London and Sydney. In 2005 the rot in the housing market will spread wider

The combination of record-low interest rates and a loss of faith in equities has encouraged more people to view homes not just as a place to live, but also as an easy way to make money—either through buy-to-let or by buying a bigger home than they need and then trading down when they retire. But buy-to-let has become less profitable, as rents in many countries now barely cover interest payments. No problem, say investors, we will make our profits from capital gains. That sounds ominously like an echo of the dotcom era, when analysts and investors argued that the link between share prices and profits no longer mattered. Home-owners are making a similar mistake today by ignoring the link between house prices and rents and buying on the expectation of capital gains. That is the very essence of a bubble.

Home prices now look significantly overvalued in America, Australia, Britain, France, Ireland, the Netherlands, New Zealand and Spain. In America the ratio of average house prices to rents or incomes is around 25% above its long-term average. In Britain, Australia and Spain homes are between 40% and 60% overvalued by this gauge. That makes them more overvalued than at previous peaks from which prices fell sharply in real terms. Add in China, Russia and South Africa, where markets also look dangerously frothy, and two-thirds (weighted by GDP) of the world tracked by *The Economist*'s indices have a potential housing bubble.

Many housing experts deny that home prices are overvalued, but their logic is flawed. Low interest rates, they argue, justify higher home prices. But interest rates are low largely because inflation is low. It is certainly true that initial interest payments are smaller, but because inflation is low it will not erode the real burden of debt so swiftly; in later years mortgage payments will absorb a much bigger slice of a borrowers' income than when inflation was higher, so buying a home is not really cheaper over the whole life of a mortgage. Another popular claim is that home prices must continue to rise because there is a limited supply of land and the number of households is growing. The flaw in this argument is that if population growth is pushing up house prices, one would also expect rents to rise; instead they have been flat or falling in many countries.

A third argument of the optimists is that even if house prices are overvalued, prices will not fall but simply level off for a few years. House prices tend to be sticky downwards, because sellers prefer to stay put rather than accept a lower price. It is true that in most countries house prices have rarely fallen, but today two factors make a drop in prices more likely.

In the past, high general inflation helped to reduce real house prices back to fair value without the need for a fall in prices. But in a world of low inflation, house prices might need to stagnate for as long as a decade to allow incomes and rents to catch up. A second factor is that, unlike in previous booms, buy-to-let investors have played a big role in pushing up prices in many countries. If the market starts to wobble, investors are more likely to sell than owner-occupiers. That could put further downward pressure on prices.

The cracks have already started to appear: home prices have begun to fall in London and Sydney. In 2005 the rot in the housing market will spread wider. Prices will not suddenly crash like in the stockmarket; more likely they will slide gradually over several years, with a total drop of 10-20% in America, and 20-30% in Britain, Australia and Spain. Some markets will continue to inflate a bit longer than others, but eventually all housing booms end. This is the first global house-price bubble in history and its bursting could be painful. □

2005

A £3.3 billion ($5.9 billion) lawsuit brought by Equitable Life, a troubled insurance society, against 15 of its former directors, begins in London.

Pam Woodall: economics editor, *The Economist*

2005

Personal disposable income worldwide will exceed $25 trillion, up by more than a third in the past five years. Around $1 trillion of that will be in China.

Over a barrel

Vijay Vaitheeswaran

The OPEC cartel faces crucial tests in 2005

Consumers smarting from high petrol prices could be forgiven for thinking that the Organisation of Petroleum Exporting Countries (OPEC) is now very much in charge of oil markets. In fact, though oil prices did soar above $50 a barrel in the second half of 2004, that is far from the truth. And several developments worth watching closely in 2005 will reveal how tenuous the cartel's grip on oil markets really is.

Oil prices rocketed in 2004 not because OPEC rigged them that way, but because it lacked the market power to control a wild surge in speculation. Saudi Arabia, the king of the cartel, usually keeps spare capacity, which it taps whenever oil prices overheat. Years of underinvestment, however, meant that global spare capacity was close to a 30-year low. So Saudi Arabia was as powerless to stop the price surge in 2004 as it was to halt a price collapse six years earlier (when OPEC foolishly expanded its output just as the South-East Asian financial crisis hit, and oil prices plunged to $10 a barrel).

Fuel for thought

World oil price (annual ave)

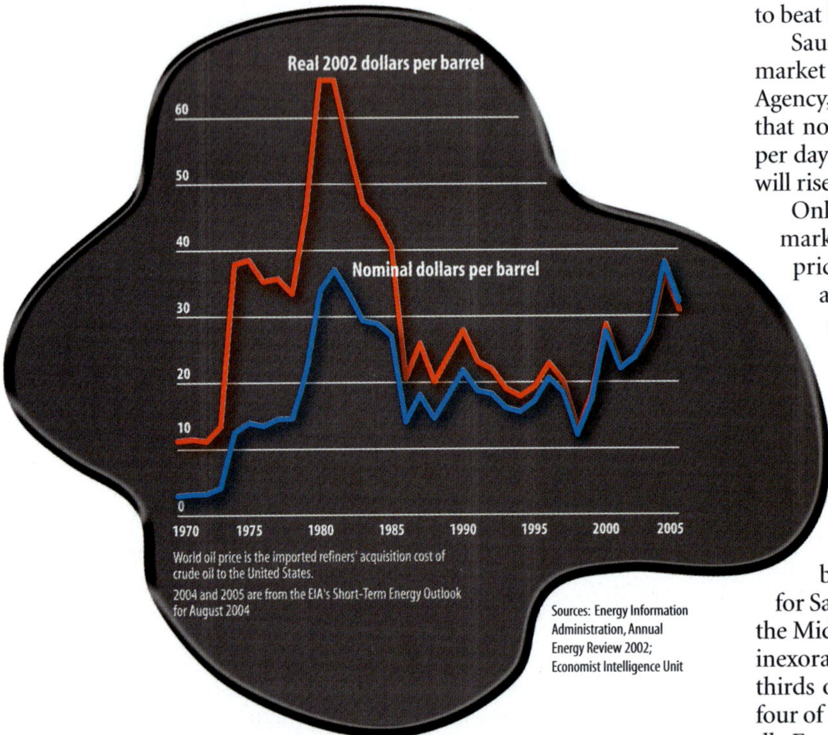

World oil price is the imported refiners' acquisition cost of crude oil to the United States.

2004 and 2005 are from the EIA's Short-Term Energy Outlook for August 2004

Sources: Energy Information Administration, Annual Energy Review 2002; Economist Intelligence Unit

If OPEC's grip on oil markets is precarious now, several factors could undermine that grip further in coming years. For a start, OPEC faces market pressure from countries outside the cartel. The chief threat comes from Russia. The temptation posed by high oil prices, combined with concern about slowing growth, will mean that free-riding Russia is unlikely to abide by any informal export-restraint promises it might make to OPEC. If so, OPEC could find itself with a powerful rival. Whether Vladimir Putin intends to take on the cartel should become clear in 2005.

Meanwhile, Iraq might leave the cartel. At least, that is the fantasy long expressed by neo-conservatives in America. Iraq has the second-largest reserves of proven oil in the world, after Saudi Arabia. In gratitude to its American liberators and in keeping with its new free-market ethos, goes the argument, surely Iraq will dump OPEC and start cranking out the oil?

> If attacks on oil infrastructure wind down, 2005 will reveal whether the Iraqi government intends to bolster OPEC—or try to beat it

Maybe, but do not bet on it. For one thing, the security situation in Iraq will limit the country's ability to grow production. For another, Iraqis are fiercely nationalistic, and see state control of oil as a national priority. Besides, it makes little economic sense for Iraq to flood the market and prompt a price collapse. If attacks on oil infrastructure wind down, 2005 will reveal whether the Iraqi government intends to bolster OPEC—or try to beat it.

Saudi Arabia faces its own challenge: yielding market share. Experts at the International Energy Agency, a quasi-governmental agency in Paris, estimate that non-OPEC production will surge by 8.3m barrels per day from now to 2010; OPEC's output, they reckon, will rise over the same period by only 5.5m bpd.

Only by enforcing cartel discipline and cutting market share will Saudi Arabia be able to prop up prices over the next few years. The alternative is a free-for-all that would lead sooner or later to a price collapse, maybe all the way back down to $10 a barrel. That would be great news for consumers, but devastating for the world's petro-economies (which typically need an oil price of $20 a barrel to balance their current accounts).

A price collapse in 2005 looks unlikely (given the constraints on oil supplies and the prospect of consumption rising by some 3%), but even if it happens, do not shed too many tears for Saudi Arabia. After 2010, and especially after 2020, the Middle East's share of the world oil market will rise inexorably. Most of the world's remaining oil—two-thirds of the proven reserves—is in Saudi Arabia and four of its neighbouring countries. That is why the Middle East is expected to account for two-thirds of all the growth in oil supply from now to 2030.

In sum, OPEC's grip on the oil market is precarious for the moment. Developments in 2005 should determine whether the cartel can keep a handle on prices over the next five years or so. But even another price collapse will be merely a temporary blip on the path to Saudi Arabia's eventual stranglehold of oil markets. If the recent unnerving volatility in oil prices was not enough, surely that frightening spectre should prompt western governments to end their addiction to oil sooner rather than later. □

Vijay Vaitheeswaran: environment and energy correspondent, *The Economist;* author of "Power to the People" (Earthscan)

As flexible as the needs of your natural investing instinct: index funds.
INDEXCHANGE allows you to react to markets immediately. Our index funds can be traded via Xetra® as flexibly as shares during normal trading hours. In addition to continuously up-dated trading, you also benefit from low charges. No up-front fee; only a management fee of between 0.15% and 0.50% per annum.
Contact INDEXCHANGE +49 (0) 89 92694 - 8888 for further information or www.indexchange.com.
INDEXCHANGE – Specialist in EXCHANGE TRADED FUNDS.
Berger Baader Hermes
The natural force of the market.
INDEXCHANGE
Exchange Traded Funds.

Doha-ha

Clive Crook

Can America get serious on trade liberalisation?

The prospects for a breakthrough in global trade reform in 2005 are poor. To be sure, it is something that those prospects are better than zero. The Doha round of trade talks was rescued from outright collapse this past summer. As a result, a meaningful round of trade liberalisation, which could be a win-win game for all concerned, is within the bounds of possibility. John Kerry's defeat in the presidential election helps too. He had aligned himself with his party's protectionists: a Kerry presidency would have been bad for trade. Even so, success will require something that can no longer be taken for granted: committed American leadership in the cause of liberal trade.

The Bush administration—above all, its energetic chief of trade policy, Robert Zoellick—has worked hard to keep the Doha round alive. Mr Zoellick was instrumental in brokering a tentative agreement to bring developing countries back to the table after the earlier fiasco at Cancún, which some had seen as heralding the demise of the whole multilateral trade-reform effort. At his urging, the rich countries made admittedly vague promises to curb and eventually eliminate farm subsidies, a matter of pressing concern to many poor nations. Also, the rich countries moderated their demands for talks in new areas (such as investment rules) and for market-opening measures that many poor countries mistakenly believed were pushing them too far and too fast. So the talks do still have a pulse.

This hesitant revival showed, however, just how necessary American purpose is in all this. If America chooses not to make Doha a priority in 2005, the exercise will fail. It is that simple. The forceful Mr Zoellick may soon be replaced. Meanwhile, at Mr Zoellick's direction, the Bush administration has been busy developing what it sees as a complement to the multilateral process overseen by the World Trade Organisation (WTO), in a policy it calls "competitive liberalisation". The idea, appealing on the face of it, is to reach bilateral agreements wherever possible with compliant like-minded countries, circumventing the complex global bargains that need to be struck at the WTO.

Whether these proliferating one-on-one deals, with countries such as Australia, Morocco, Chile and Jordan, are desirable in their own right is in doubt. They certainly distort trade in some ways, while at the same time promoting it in others. Whether, in the jargon, "trade creation" exceeds "trade diversion" as a result of such agreements, thus yielding a net benefit, is something that needs to be looked at case by case.

These pacts entrench constituencies opposed to further reform (because the existing beneficiaries would rather keep their special privileges to themselves). Also, they tend to include illiberal undertakings on matters such as labour and environmental standards. When America negotiates with small countries one at a time, it has enormous bargaining power: it can extract large concessions in these controversial areas, because the benefit of access to its market is so great for the trading partner concerned. Nonetheless, those concessions may not in themselves serve the smaller country's interests: the cost may be more than poor countries can sensibly bear and they may hamper the growth of exports to other countries. A further danger is that such concessions embolden anti-trade interests in America to demand the same trade-restricting conditions in all such agreements. The unequal bargain struck when America negotiates with Jordan, say, then sets the floor for all such agreements.

The main thing, though, is simply that the bilateral-agreement alternative saps momentum from the WTO process. This is especially disturbing because the Bush administration's basic commitment to freer trade, with or without Mr Zoellick, is anyway in doubt. The imposition of tariffs on steel was a surprising reversal. The policy is reckoned to have destroyed more American jobs (owing to the increase in costs faced by industrial users of steel) than were at stake in the entire American steel industry. But this subtracted little from its political appeal and is an ominous sign for the future. The administration's vastly expensive farm bill was another measure that no free-trader would care to defend.

Despite Mr Zoellick, and the Bush administration's avowed devotion to the principles of liberal commerce, the record in practice is mixed. As long as America's labour market remains weak—as it may for some time—the pressure for greater protection will increase. The administration's ambitions on trade may well be confined to avoiding an outright collapse of the WTO process. That is not the strong leadership that the system demands. The result would be a far cry from the bold "development round" that once seemed possible. □

If America chooses not to make Doha a priority in 2005, the exercise will fail. It is that simple

2005

Japan and Mexico are due to reduce or eliminate tariffs on the vast majority of each other's exports by April 1st, including agriculture, car and steel products.

Clive Crook: deputy editor, *The Economist*

Waiting for America

2005

By the end of the year OECD members and over 40 tax havens must cease "harmful tax practices" such as providing financial tax shelter without durable investment benefits.

Bean-counting goes global

Joanne Ramos

International accounting standards are finally becoming international

The new year is a time to break old habits and form new, better ones. For European companies, this ritual takes on a heightened level of seriousness in 2005. Starting on January 1st, the 7,000 quoted companies in Europe will be required by law to ditch the mishmash of national accounting rules used in the past for International Financial Reporting Standards (IFRS).

The idea is that such "convergence" will boost the efficiency of Europe's markets. Investors will make better decisions because comparing firms across borders will be simpler; companies will save time and money by reporting under one accounting standard (with an exception for derivatives) rather than a multiplicity of them.

The new rules emphasise market values and economic substance rather than smooth earnings, as did the old ones. For example, they require companies to record pension deficits at their current (ever-fluctuating) value rather than letting firms hide these shortfalls off the balance sheet and "smooth" their impact on profits little by little over many years. Inevitably, rules like this will mean more volatility and, for many investors, more confusion—at least at first.

All the more so because, although most firms have been hard at work for months training staff and installing the systems needed for the new accounting framework, some smaller outfits are unprepared. Moreover, applying the new accounting framework will involve subjective judgments by company accountants and auditors. These interpretations will no doubt vary in the early stages, leading to more inconsistency in financial reporting during the first few years.

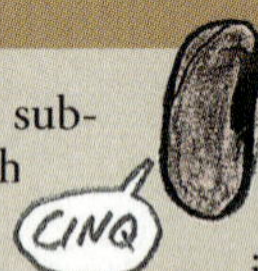

Europe is not alone in facing these challenges. In total, almost 100 countries in six continents will be using international standards by 2005, either directly or through national accounting rules aligned to them. Even some American companies—which are governed by American rules and not international ones—will feel the sting, including American subsidiaries of European firms or those with big, foreign investors that require international accounting.

The ultimate goal? A single set of accounting rules worldwide. Since 2002 American and international standard-setters have slowly but steadily worked to narrow the gap between American rules and IFRS. Next on the agenda is Japan. Stay tuned. □

Joanne Ramos: banking correspondent, *The Economist*

Street cred

Lionel Barber *NEW YORK*

The new leaders on Wall Street

After three years of dirt-cheap money, courtesy of Alan Greenspan, Wall Street will have to dig a lot deeper to generate revenue and profits in 2005. But the tougher environment will offer opportunities for a new generation of leaders, several of whom will move centre-stage. These men—Wall Street's finest are still largely male, with one or two exceptions—are a different breed from the cocksure investment bankers and dealmakers who held sway during the bubble years.

Jamie Dimon, chief operating officer and president of J.P. Morgan Chase, is the most illustrious leader-in-waiting. A native New Yorker raised in a family of stockbrokers, the rough-edged Mr Dimon was once tipped to take the top job at Citigroup, only to be ousted by his one-time mentor, Sandy Weill. Now, after the $58 billion marriage of J.P. Morgan and his own Bank One, he has a second chance to become King of the Street.

Mr Dimon is on a fast track to take over from William Harrison, the courtly southerner whose Chase Manhattan swallowed J.P. Morgan in 2000. Insiders insist that Mr Harrison will not be rushed out of his job as chairman and CEO until a two-year interregnum expires in 2006. Mr Dimon will be counting the days in 2005. Like Chuck Prince, the newish boss at Citigroup, Mr Dimon must demonstrate the virtues of scale. Unlike Citigroup, J.P. Morgan Chase is not obviously number one in any business, except derivatives. It lacks a brokerage to compete with the likes of Merrill Lynch. Its investment-banking business is battling with Goldman Sachs, Morgan Stanley and up-and-coming UBS. And it must compete with the retail powerhouse being assembled by Bank of America. Another merger in 2005 looks unlikely from Mr Dimon. Expect more grinding out of efficiency and stripping away of layers of management.

Over at Citigroup, Mr Prince, a low-key lawyer, must show whether he can produce organic growth. One worry is that Citigroup's size may be a recipe for increased reputational risk as well as higher profits. Citigroup's blockbuster profits in 2003/04 were dented by provisions to settle lawsuits relating to WorldCom and other corporate scandals. Mr Prince will step forward in 2005 and show he is big enough to fill Mr Weill's shoes.

Another newcomer to watch is Lloyd Blankfein, the favourite to succeed Hank Paulson at Goldman Sachs. Mr Paulson says he's staying put. But Mr Blankfein is a popular manager whose star soared in 2004, thanks both to his successful integration of the debt and equities business and Goldman's formidable trading record.

Also making their mark will be Warren Spector, Bear Stearns's chief operating officer; Joe Gregory, the new chief operating officer at Lehman Brothers; and Vikram Pandit, the brilliant strategist at Morgan Stanley. These and other leaders-in-waiting will compete to shine in answering the biggest question of all in 2005: where is the growth going to come from? □

Lionel Barber: United States managing editor, *Financial Times*

No half measures

Rodrigo de Rato, managing director of the International Monetary Fund, wants more concerted action to prevent crises and reduce poverty

The rapid expansion of trade and cross-border capital flows in the 1990s created unparalleled opportunities for growth and financing. But capital flows to emerging markets introduced vulnerabilities that produced crises and contagion, in some cases taking the world by surprise. Some important lessons have been learnt. The global rebound since 2001 is a tribute to the resilience of the world economy—and a demonstration that the policies and reforms implemented since the 1990s have made a difference. That success should only strengthen our resolve to do more.

One lesson of the past decade is that there is no alternative to strong defences against crisis. This is true for industrial countries facing unprecedented demographic change, emerging markets seeking a secure place in the global economy and developing countries struggling to reduce poverty. Crisis prevention must be built on commitments to policy discipline and actions to address a rapidly changing world.

The IMF has a crucial role to play. It must enhance countries' understanding of the policy issues and it must be a catalyst for vigilance and reform—built on true international co-operation. Many of the Fund's 184 members have addressed their immediate vulnerabilities by strengthening financial sectors, enhancing the transparency of economic policymaking, building up foreign reserves and increasing exchange-rate flexibility. The IMF has made an important contribution to this effort with its policy advice and work on standards and codes.

But many long-term vulnerabilities remain. America must address its excessive budget deficit and some European countries still need to energise their economies, especially by freeing labour markets. Japan needs to build on its progress with financial and corporate reforms. These actions would help reduce global payments imbalances, including America's large external deficit.

> Imbalances and vulnerabilities must be corrected before they become problems—for the country itself, its neighbours and the global system

Although emerging-market countries have strengthened their defences, much more remains to be done in governance and transparency. A number of countries, including many in Latin America, must strengthen their fiscal positions over the medium term and bring debt-to-GDP ratios back to tolerable levels.

The recent surge in oil prices has brought energy issues back to centre stage. Once again we are confronted with the need to expand production capacity, diversify energy sources and enhance conservation. Countries cannot overlook the need for comprehensive energy strategies. Furthermore, many oil-producing countries need to use their windfall revenues wisely—with debt reduction a priority. And they need to become more transparent with the money they earn, among other things by participating in the Extractive Industries Transparency Initiative, launched by Tony Blair at the Johannesburg summit on sustainable development in 2002.

Another key issue is ageing populations. Most industrial countries are facing the burden of rapidly ageing workforces and falling tax revenues. Although some countries are trying to address the looming fiscal issues, many others are putting off the costly and difficult issues of health-care and pension reform. This problem is acute in some industrialised countries, but many developing countries will also have to face it, in many cases without the cushion of affluence.

In the course of its dialogues with member countries, the IMF is paying increasing attention to the policy implications of demographic change. It also monitors capital-market developments and analyses financial sectors and assesses debt sustainability. These efforts can enhance early warning—but can be effective only if they prompt timely action. Imbalances and vulnerabilities must be corrected before they become problems—for the country itself, its neighbours and the global system. International co-operation through the IMF aims to deal with problems before they erupt into crises.

As with crisis prevention, so with poverty reduction

This same international co-operation—through the IMF and the World Bank—also plays a major role in the fight against poverty in low-income countries. Hundreds of millions of people live on less than $1 a day. Child mortality remains unacceptably high in these countries, and HIV/AIDS and other diseases hold sway. Real progress has been made in China and India, thanks to their rapid growth, but sub-Saharan Africa has been left behind.

The 2002 Monterrey conference agreed on a way forward: the rich countries will provide aid and trade opportunities; the multilateral institutions will offer policy advice, technical help and financing; and the poor countries themselves are committed to improving their governance and focusing on more effective poverty-reduction programmes. Now is the time for rich countries to fulfil their commitments on aid and trade. But both issues are unresolved because of a lack of political leadership. Recent proposals at the UN and at our own annual meetings in October have been encouraging, but decisions must be made. And the trade negotiations in Geneva must build on the July 2004 breakthrough on reducing agricultural subsidies and enhancing trade on a multilateral basis.

It is possible to reduce poverty. Now the challenge is to achieve success worldwide. Five years ago the IMF made poverty reduction the central objective of its involvement with low-income countries. As with crisis prevention, it is an effort that doesn't allow for half measures. □

Science

Return of the robots

Alun Anderson

Coming soon to a surgeon's screen near you

It will be the 50th anniversary of the construction of the sci-fi world's first real robot hero in 2005. Robby the Robot was the lumbering giant who starred in the cult film "Forbidden Planet". Standing seven and a half feet (2.3 metres) tall with a transparent domed head and spinning antennae, he provided inspiration for the robot heroes of "Star Trek" and other movies to come. And like all good robots he was there to ensure humans came to no harm. Posters of Robby, cradling the film's heroine in his bulging steel arms, still adorn student rooms around the world.

Fifty years on, real robots that can save human lives are at long last beginning to appear. But what exactly do the new robots of 2005 look like? Can you expect help from an intelligent humanoid that walks on two legs and is always there to protect its master (or mistress)? Should you instead be waiting for rescue by a comic-strip giant robot that can rip the doors off cars with giant claws? Perhaps your imagination runs to something stranger: a robot that looks more like a giant spider but with arms tipped with super-sharp steel blades and metal pincers? Or even a long, flexible robot that crawls along the ground like a snake?

If you bet on having help from an intelligent humanoid, you are going to be disappointed. Even getting a two-legged robot to walk effortlessly in a straight line on a smooth laboratory floor is proving much harder than scientists thought. But if you backed any of the other three robots, you are on to a winner. All will be out there in 2005.

First, the clear leader: that's the spider-like robot equipped with knives and pincers. It is a surgical robot that is now spreading rapidly to hospitals around the world. The robot is called da Vinci and is built by Intuitive Surgical of Sunnyvale, California. In 2005 we can expect more surgical robots to be working harder and to be licensed to carry out more types of operation.

A robot does not operate like a conventional surgeon. It has no need to open up your chest or abdomen to let in big human hands. Instead, the robot's long, spidery arms roam deep into your body through a set of tiny incisions, called "ports". Inside your body it can wield instruments to repair heart valves or remove diseased prostate glands. Its tiny robot hands don't tremble as they work and can twist and turn with a dexterity that beats the limitations of a human wrist. When it's finished, it can withdraw leaving just some small holes needing a few stitches.

A robot-equipped operating room is a strange sight. The robot sits alongside the operating table with its long arms bent down over the patient. One arm carries a miniature stereoscopic camera. Others carry blades, pincers and surgical instruments needed to cut, clamp and suture. An anaesthetist and nurses will be present as usual. But the surgeon is not towering over the patient, calling for forceps and scalpels. He or she will be sitting at a distance, at a console that looks like a sophisticated computer-games machine. The surgeon's eyes will be locked on a colour display providing a three-dimensional view from within the patient. The machine gives a remarkable feeling, almost as if the surgeon has been miniaturised and stepped inside the patient's body.

Patients often recover much faster than after surgery requiring the body to be opened up. After a conventional heart-valve repair, for example, a patient may need to spend weeks recovering in hospital, not because of the work performed on the heart itself but because their chest had to be cracked open and a large incision made in order to give access to the heart.

The da Vinci is descended from robots that the US Department of Defence began working on in the 1980s to enable surgeons to operate on soldiers at a safe distance from the battlefield. At a little over $1m, it is still too expensive for many hospitals. But so-called "minimally invasive surgery", which includes conventional ▶

2005

Builders' labourers will come to resent specially designed robots that can read instructions direct from architects' drawings and squirt layers of concrete to build walls and roofs.

Alun Anderson: editor-in-chief, *New Scientist*

Science of the small

Natasha Loder

Nanotechnology takes off

In 2005 nanotechnology, the "science of the small", will pass a milestone. It will be the first year when corporations outspend governments on it, predicts Lux Capital, a New York-based venture-capital firm. As activity shifts from basic research to the development of applications, we will start to see the arrival of many more products.

Nanotechnology has already contributed to a better suncream (making it clearer), tennis racquet (stronger and lighter) and window glass (self-cleaning). Nanostructures and particles are making car parts stronger, creating completely novel materials such as Metal Rubber (an elastic conductive material), as well as making fabric that is stain- and wrinkle-resistant—using fibres engineered to repel oil and liquids.

This is only the beginning. If NEC Corporation of Tokyo can put a fuel-cell notebook PC on the market in 2005, as it hopes to do, then nanotechnology could start to sizzle. NEC's fuel cells use carbon nanotubes (tiny tubes of carbon), and the company is working towards the commercial production of a notebook PC equipped with an internal fuel cell offering 40 hours of continuous operation.

Natasha Loder: science and technology correspondent, *The Economist*

Basking on a nanobubble

Ever since the dotcom bust investors have been searching for the Next Big Thing. Many are intrigued by nanotechnology's promise. In some cases this interest appears entirely unrelated to whether a company is likely to create products in the near future. Some companies have little more than intellectual property. And there are a number claiming to be nanotechnology companies (with "nano" in their name) that are nothing of the sort. Buyer beware.

Fear will also drive interest in technology. Worries over self-replicating nanorobots—"grey goo"—may have been consigned to the dustbin. But people will still fret over the safety of nanoparticles. Very fine particles are already produced when traditional combustion occurs. Many new products seek to take advantage of the novel, and sometimes unusual, properties of tiny particles. The weird effects of quantum-scale physics mean that a particle of titanium dioxide, for example, can behave radically differently if it is in the nanometre (billionths of a metre) scale. This unpredictability led one British group to recommend recently that new nanoparticles be regulated as if they were new chemicals—a wise suggestion. There will also be broader concerns over the power and control of the corporations that deploy nanotechnology.

But the chances are that the public will accept nanotechnology more readily than GM food. The improvements it offers will be widely seen as valuable, and people are more tolerant of new technologies if they don't have to eat them. Will people really want a cotton shirt that never smells, however much you sweat, and that releases its odours only during a wash? Of course. And it may be a social gaffe not to wear one in 2005. □

keyhole surgery where the surgeon peers into the body through a small incision, is taking off. New research and training centres around the world will drive demand for the more sophisticated view and capabilities that a robot can provide. Robot-assisted surgeons have already taken on heart-valve repairs, coronary artery bypass operations, prostate removal and oesophageal surgery. Expect other machines to appear in other specialities, such as neurosurgery, where a robot has the potential to provide absolute precision, as well as in relatively standard operations, such as the removal of kidney stones.

> Enryu did indeed behave like a comic-strip hero, ripping a door from a car, waving an iron girder and tossing heavy objects out of its way

Robots don't always need precision and delicacy to be helpful. You might also encounter the giant super-strong clawed robot in 2005. It is called Enryu (meaning "rescue dragon") and stands 3.5 metres tall. During recent trials in Kitakyushu in Japan, Enryu did indeed behave like a comic-strip hero, ripping a door from a car, waving an iron girder and tossing heavy objects out of its way. The caterpillar-tracked monster can lift 500 kilos (1,100 pounds) in each of its claws and comes from a company called Tmsuk that has already created home-guard robots and robot receptionists. Enryu was developed with co-operation from Japan's National Research Institute of Fire and Disaster and is planned to go on the market in 2005, ready to roll in the event of a major disaster, such as an earthquake or nuclear accident, when it can enter a danger zone and clear rubble from collapsed buildings.

In the hunt for survivors it might want to call on the last of the robot menagerie. Snake robots are now gliding around laboratories, and tethered versions that look more like elephants' trunks are also under test. Several are being designed to worm their way into confined spaces, such as collapsed buildings, and search out survivors. Others will do more conventional tasks, including cleaning out pipes.

None of these robots is terribly intelligent. All require human guidance. An autonomous robot like Robby won't escape from the sci-fi movies for many years yet. □

Medicines for millions

Shereen El Feki *ADDIS ABABA*

Treatment is on the way for AIDS sufferers worldwide

2005

According to a government study, obesity will become the leading cause of death in 2005 in the United States, overtaking tobacco as the country's top killer.

Forget the feeding of the 5,000. A modern miracle is in the making: getting, and keeping, 3m AIDS sufferers on anti-retroviral drugs by the end of 2005.

Mahari is a 34-year-old living in one of Addis Ababa's teeming slums. What he most wants is to play the *krar*, a traditional musical instrument, with his band at a local nightclub. All he can do, however, is lie in the tiny tin shack he shares with half a dozen relatives, and waste away. Mahari is in the final stages of AIDS. While various NGOs provide him with food, vitamins and other basic care, they lack what he needs most: anti-retroviral drugs to fight HIV, the virus that is killing him. A month's treatment costs $30-85, which patients currently have to pay themselves. But the total monthly income of Mahari's family is less than $12.

Mahari is not alone. There are an estimated 38m people in the world infected with HIV, almost 95% living in low- and middle-income countries. The World Health Organisation (WHO) reckons that 6m of them will die within the next two years without anti-HIV therapy. Today, 440,000 such patients are actually receiving treatment—almost a third of them in one country alone, Brazil. But in parts of Africa hardest-hit by HIV, less than 4% of those in desperate need of drugs are currently thrown a pharmaceutical lifeline.

This could change in 2005. A broad coalition of national governments, international health agencies and NGOs is working to scale up treatment to millions of AIDS sufferers in the developing world. The WHO calls the initiative "3 by 5"—putting 3m people on anti-retroviral therapy by the end of 2005. It is by far the most ambitious international health project since the drive to eradicate smallpox three decades ago.

Shereen El Feki: health-care correspondent, *The Economist*

Help

Estimated anti-retroviral therapy coverage and needs

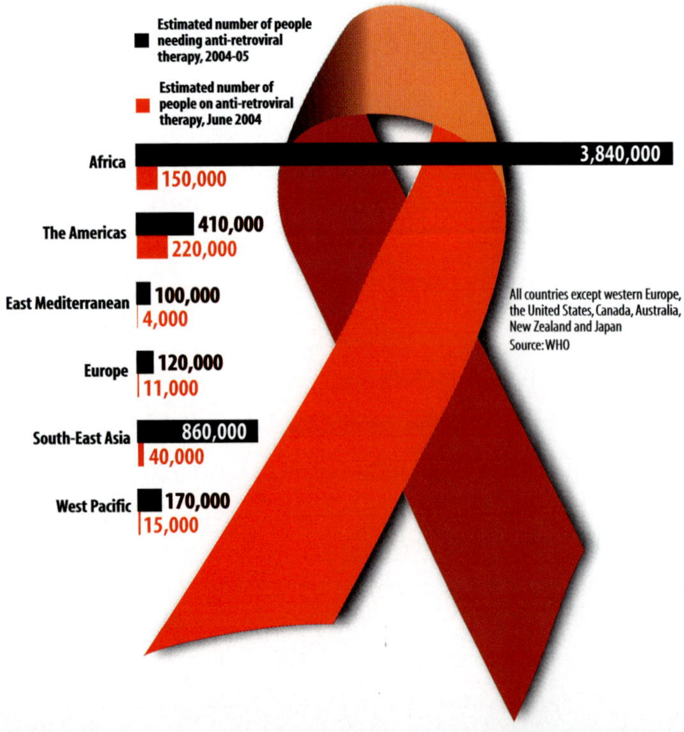

What makes this massive campaign conceivable is a sharp drop in the price of drugs. Four years ago, a basic cocktail of anti-retroviral medicines cost $10,000 a year; today that price has fallen to as little as $140 in some countries. The dramatic decline is largely thanks to the introduction of cheaper generic medicines from Indian, Brazilian and Thai manufacturers, as well as discounting by multinational drug giants.

The other essential ingredient is money to buy medicines for the world's poorest. In 2003 global spending on HIV reached a new high of $5 billion. Further funds are on the way, for example from the Global Fund to Fight AIDS, Tuberculosis and Malaria and from the American President's Emergency Plan for AIDS Relief. But this is still a far cry from the $12 billion that UNAIDS reckons the world needs to spend in 2005 alone.

There are other obstacles on the road to 3m. Most daunting is the lack of doctors, nurses, community health workers and medical administrators to work on these projects. Many of the new initiatives offer money for training, but producing medical workers takes time. Moreover, many developing countries are worried that donor-financed projects, with their relatively high salaries, will lure medical talent into competing AIDS-specific programmes, leaving the rest of the public-health service struggling for manpower. Done right, however, AIDS could be a catalyst for rebuilding ramshackle national health-care systems across the developing world.

> The World Health Organisation calls the initiative "3 by 5"—putting 3m people on anti-retroviral therapy by the end of 2005

Then there are cultural hurdles. There is enormous stigma associated with HIV; Mahari's family refuses to acknowledge he has AIDS. The hope is that when anti-retroviral therapy is more widely available, more people will turn up for testing and there will be greater openness—which, in turn, will help with prevention.

It is not enough for the rich world to talk about starting poor people on anti-retroviral drugs; it must be prepared to continue their treatment, and monitor their progress, for as long as they live. The arguments for sustaining treatment are medical as well as moral; breaks in therapy can speed the emergence of drug-resistant strains of HIV, which is trouble for everyone. And until there is an effective, affordable AIDS vaccine, there will be ever more people requiring treatment. All this means that 2005 is just the beginning of a very long and expensive process; few countries have yet to talk seriously about how to meet such lengthy obligations.

These and other concerns should shape, not stop, the current drive to treatment. As Jim Kim, head of the 3 by 5 programme at the WHO, puts it, "Backing off would be back to the same old stuff we've had in HIV for the past 20 years: it's too complicated, there's no infrastructure and so on. Just sitting around contemplating it is the worst thing we can do." In 2005 the relief effort will scale up dramatically, but it may well take a miracle to reach 3m by the end of the year. □

Let there be bacteria

Geoffrey Carr

Artificial life may arrive on the planet in 2005

Craig Venter, the man who led the privately financed version of the Human Genome Project, which deconstructed the genetic recipe for making an organism, has since been busy doing the reverse. He and his colleague Hamilton Smith have been trying to construct the entire genomes of living creatures, starting with off-the-shelf chemicals that can be bought from any reliable supplier. In November 2003 the team announced that they had made a synthetic replica of a virus (they picked one that infects bacteria, rather than people). But whether viruses are truly alive has been a matter of philosophical debate since they were discovered. Now they have embarked on making a bacterial genome. And bacteria are definitely living things.

Making a fully synthetic bacterial chromosome would partly be about showing off. But proving principles is important, and as Mr Venter observes, you cannot say you really understand something until you can make a version of it that works. The reason he wants this understanding is that he is one of a group of visionaries who believe that this sort of "synthetic biology" will form the basis of an important—and possibly revolutionary—technology.

The efforts of these people are being co-ordinated by America's Department of Energy, in the person of Ari Patrinos. Mr Patrinos is famed in the world of genomics for his diplomatic skills—he brokered the truce between the public and private human genome efforts which allowed President Clinton to proclaim a tied finish in the race in 2000. Now he is running the department's "Genomes to Life" programme, which aims to put this sort of bacterial engineering to practical use.

Humanity has a rather biased view of what the biological landscape looks like. Most people, when asked to pick typical examples of living things, would choose large animals or, possibly, plants. But, actually, most living things are bacteria. And bacteria, besides being simple (simple at least for living organisms), have a biochemical diversity that far exceeds that of plants or animals. It is this combination of simplicity and diversity that makes them attractive to those who want to incorporate living things into the industrial economy.

Mr Patrinos is particularly interested in two sorts of application: energy generation and cleaning up pollution. Some organisms generate hydrogen as a by-product of their activities. Others generate methane. Both are useful fuels; hydrogen, in particular, is seen by some as the likely "currency" of a future energy economy that would be far less dependent on oil. As far as cleaning up pollution is concerned, many bacteria are able to chew on heavy metals that are poisonous to higher organisms and one, at least, is incredibly resilient to radiation. The energy department is particularly interested in these properties in the context of detoxifying the sites of nuclear work carried out in earlier, more careless days.

Where synthetic biology fits into all this is to provide "bespoke" bugs designed to do exactly the task in hand and no other. Mr Venter, as usual, is bullish. At a recent conference also attended by Steve Jobs, Mr Venter suggested that biology is at the point Mr Jobs found computing to be in 1976, when he and Steve Wozniak created the first Apple computer. The Apple I, though

> Now they have embarked on making a bacterial genome. And bacteria are definitely living things

a formidable piece of design, was put together from pre-existing parts. In Mr Venter's analogy, these parts correspond to the biochemical pathways of organisms, which have been designed and built by evolution, and which he thinks can be taken, off the shelf as it were, and assembled in novel ways to do humanity's bidding.

Researchers such as George Church, at Harvard Medical School, are going a step further in their thinking. Mr Church proposes creating something akin to biological Lego. This would employ a set of standardised connectors that would allow genes to be "snapped together" in various combinations, to produce the desired organisms.

Building bacteria from scratch like this would also allow them to be tailored in ways that would make it hard for them to escape into the wild—a not entirely unreasonable fear held by many of those opposed to genetic engineering. Mr Venter is alive to the ethical issues involved—he has involved a bioethicist, Arthur Caplan, in the project from the beginning. □

2005

Human trials will begin for a diagnostic tool, designed by a company called Kereos, that uses nanotechnology to detect tumours as small as 1mm in diameter.

Geoffrey Carr: science editor, *The Economist*

Ecotecture to the rescue

Architects will help to save the planet, argues **Norman Foster**, a leading practitioner

Two trends that are affecting global practice in architecture will strengthen in 2005: the need to pursue sustainable patterns of development, and the opportunities presented by the developing economies in Asia and the former Soviet block. These two trends are, of course, interconnected.

The need to address man's impact on the environment has never been more urgent. As I write, environmental disasters make the headlines: from flooding in Bangladesh to drought in the Yellow River valley; from the destruction of the Greenland ice sheet to the loss of an entire ecosystem in the North Sea and hurricanes in the Caribbean. Scientists predict that the Earth will warm by 1.4-5.8°C by 2100—more than temperatures are thought to have changed since the dawn of humanity. It is now widely accepted that this is largely due to rising concentrations of greenhouse gases, most significantly CO_2. But how many people are aware that in the developed world buildings consume half the energy we generate and are responsible for half the CO_2 emissions, the remainder being divided almost equally between transport and industry?

That is alarming enough. But what will happen as the developing world catches up? Recently I have been to China, Kazakhstan, Russia, Libya and Cuba: countries that only a short time ago were out of bounds to western interests. The pace of change in many areas is breathtaking. China predicts a doubling of GDP in 2010 compared with 2000. Its building boom is unprecedented, fast and furious.

> Virtually every new building can be designed to run on a fraction of current energy levels. But even if the buildings were zero-energy and carbon-free, we would still have problems

Our new terminal under construction in Beijing offers a sharp contrast with experience in Europe. Over 1m square metres, it is larger than all four terminals at Heathrow plus the future Terminal 5. But the entire process from commissioning to completion will be faster than the public inquiry for Terminal 5—and was the outcome of that ever in doubt? Cities such as Beijing and Shanghai change by the day. China is home to half the world's construction cranes. Yet the environmental implications are sobering. For example, China currently consumes half the world's cement, and manufacturing one tonne of cement produces one tonne of CO_2.

To avoid global environmental catastrophe, every country has to adopt sustainable development strategies. Sustainability requires us to think holistically. The location and function of a building; its flexibility and lifespan; its orientation, its form and structure; its heating and ventilation systems, and the materials used—all affect the amount of energy used to build, run and maintain it. Virtually every new building can be designed to run on a fraction of current energy levels. But even if the buildings were zero-energy and carbon-free, we would still have problems.

Densely does it in Monaco and Kensington

There are two further crucial issues: population growth and the shift towards living in cities. The world's population stands at 6.4 billion; in ten years it is expected to reach 7.5 billion. By 2015 there will be 23 "megacities", with populations over 10m each. Nineteen of them will be in developing countries, where up to half the population will be urbanised. What will those cities look like?

Cities that sprawl are far less energy-efficient than densely planned communities. Car travel is a crucial factor. Imagine somebody driving 20km (13 miles) to work each day. His or her housing will consume 720 litres of oil a year, the workplace 285 litres and transport 900 litres. Alarmingly, in most countries car usage is still increasing. China is the most extreme example. Car sales are predicted to grow by up to 30% annually from 2005.

To reduce car travel we have to encourage compact cities and high-density new development. Critics argue that higher densities lead to poorer environments. But that does not follow. Monaco and Macao, the world's densest urban communities, are at opposite ends of the economic spectrum. In London some of the most densely populated areas offer the most desirable lifestyle: Kensington and Chelsea have population densities up to three times those of London's poorest boroughs.

Holistic thinking must equally be applied to infrastructure, transport systems, streets and public spaces—the "urban glue" that holds cities together. The quality of infrastructure directly influences the quality of urban life. The clean nature of much post-industrial work means that workplaces can be combined with housing and localised communities can be sustained when transport connections, businesses, schools and shops are all within walking or cycling distance of home.

Architects will have a vital role as advocates in 2005, encouraging sustainable solutions around the world. But we also need more progressive developers and politicians with the courage to set goals and incentives for society to follow. Some countries have taken a lead: Germany has long understood the need to reduce consumption and adopt renewable energy sources, and that is reflected in building codes. Others, to varying degrees, lag behind. There are no technological barriers to sustainable development, only those of political will. If we are to avoid the environmental damage wrought by the unsustainable patterns of the past, then the rich and emerging economies must act in unison and with urgency: 2006 could be too late. □

SKIING AND OTHER WINTER SPORTS

Marit Claridge and Cheryl Evans

Designed by Nerissa Davies

Illustrated by:
Mick Posen, Kathy James, Chris Lyon and Guy Smith

Special location photography by Mark Junak

Ski demonstrators:
Eric Mermod, Micheline Morerod, Jean-François Morerod, Julia Snell, Mike Whealey, Leonie Coppard, Nigel Winter and Ben Rix

Consultant editors:
Mike Nemesvary, Nick Fickling, David Goldsmith and John Shedden.

Contents